SMALL COUNTRY HOUSES OF TO-DAY

A DISTANT VIEW OF MR. GIMSON'S HOUSE AT SAPPERTON

SMALL COUNTRY HOUSES OF TO-DAY.

EDITED BY LAWRENCE WEAVER

"The classic work of the Edwardian period"

ANTIQUE COLLECTORS' CLUB

© 1983 Antique Collectors' Club
World copyright reserved

ISBN 0 907462 34 0

First published by Country Life in 1911. This edition published for the
Antique Collectors' Club by the Antique Collectors' Club Ltd.

British Library CIP Data
Weaver, Lawrence
    Small country houses of today.
    1. Country homes — England — History
    2. Architecture, Domestic — England — History
    I. Title
    728.8'3'0942   NA7620

Printed in England by Baron Publishing, Woodbridge, Suffolk.

CONTENTS.

128504

PUBLISHER'S INTRODUCTION
TO 1983 EDITION

WRITING in 1911 Sir Lawrence Weaver surveyed nearly fifty houses which he considered representative of the better class of small house which had recently been built. His avowed purpose was to demonstrate that there was a real alternative to the product of the speculative builders. "Building needs in fact to be brought back into the normal current of intelligent thought", and with this in mind his selection of houses is successful, though perhaps he was unduly optimistic about the originality of all the designs. But his own introduction follows and needs no interpretation or apology for his is a marvellously fresh style of writing, his comments and stories are compulsive reading and give the keen sharp flavour of the period.

The Red House, Upton, Kent (page 180), is the exception to the "today" of the title and provides the key to the author's selection. The design was discussed during a "three men in a boat" trip down the Seine in 1858. The men were William Morris, the key figure in the arts and crafts movement, who had just got engaged and needed a home, the Red House architect Philip Webb, who, with Nesfield and Norman Shaw, revolted against the constant regurgitation of historical styles and turned back to the vernacular and gothic for inspiration. The third man, Faulkner, became Morris's partner in the firm which carried their names and which changed the direction of interior decoration throughout much of the civilised world.

Morris and his friends despised what he termed "square stucco boxes with slate lids" and turned back to honest red brick designed in an "artistic" manner. They saw the virtues of asymmetric arrangement, careful siting, hanging tiles, tall chimneys and hipped roofs. Interestingly, the simple use of red brick was refined still further when the Queen Anne style was revived in the 1870s. The Red House, however, was not altogether a success. Morris himself describes it as in the style of the thirteenth century and no doubt Pugin would have approved, even though the internal plan was sunless and looks to us like a fussy Victorian parsonage.

This book consists mainly of houses designed by men steeped in the arts and crafts movement, who had studied the vernacular in detail and understood the materials in which they worked. Like the great Lutyens, who naturally features in the selection, they were as familiar with the workings of the builder's yard and the abilities of the specialist craftsman as they were with their own discipline. In revolt against the strident polychrome and excess decoration of the Victorian house, they employed muted colours, sand faced bricks, and reused old timbers, bricks and peg tiles. Morley Horder, for example, building at Minehead, disliked the local chocolate colour stone and found in the ruins of Cleeve Abbey an oatmeal coloured freestone which appealed. He searched and found the original quarry and had it reopened, following a similar procedure with the slates. But that was for a big house. Most of those featured in this selection were built to a strict budget and their virtues lie in their pleasing shapes and forms. Some of the houses have a timeless quality, and one is not immediately sure of the date. Gilhams Burch,

Rotherfield (page 103), snuggles into the Sussex countryside with a broken roof line that could have been derived from centuries of gradual expansion. Similarly, some of the simple Cotswold stone houses by Guy Danber melt into the landscape. Seventy years on, how many of us would guess the age of Oswald Milne's cottage on page 107?

The local vernacular house is only one type Weaver selected. Others, imitations of earlier periods, are simple to categorise, but many have a quite persistent individuality which demands attention. Of the former are the late seventeenth century 'H' types like Bengeo House, Hertford, viewed from the south-west (page 29), or The Hurst, Moseley, in a happily multi-gabled Jacobean style, seen from the garden front (page 15). There are plenty of examples of tall chimneys, half timbered ''Elizabethanish'' houses, which in down-market speculative form became Osbert Lancaster's ''by-pass variegated'', while the traditional tile hanging of the south-east is liberally employed.

But it is the second, more individualistic type, which breaks new ground. There is Voysey's characteristic The Homestead, Frinton (page 171), stone dressed, leaded light windows, white walls, chimneys with tiled projections and the accent on the horizontal. There is also the older-than-old thatched house at Sapperton (page 50) by Ernest Gimson, its tortured roof line and great chimneys typifying the boldness and confidence of those at the heart of the arts and crafts movement.

The interiors of the houses are interesting too; here there is a high degree of uniformity. Eighteenth century chairs from Queen Anne to Sheraton, pad foot tables of varying quality in mahogany and oak, together with dressers or court cupboards and Windsor chairs. Only in the main reception rooms might Frenchified furniture be found, but the abiding impression is one of sparse furnishing based on the eighteenth century. The exception, of course, is the strongly 'art conscious' house with custom-made furniture. Interestingly too the loggia is almost a universal feature. Were summers warmer or the inhabitants tougher?

But perhaps it is the doctor's house at Belcoombe, Saxlingham (page 160), built by F.W. Troup, for 5½d. per cubic foot — a low price even then, which looks both comfortable to live in as well as having a distinct character of its own, that makes us realise that house building before the First World War reached a high level of quality, not just among the great names but among a generation of architects unshackled from historical style and with a strong consciousness of the needs of their clients.

INTRODUCTION

WHILE there is no lack of books which illustrate various types of small modern country houses, both by photographs and plans, they are, as a class, singularly devoid of critical explanation, whether from the practical or the æsthetic point of view. House-building is, moreover, a primitive instinct, and the story of its development takes an important part in the larger history of social growth. Monographs on representative Small Country Houses of To-day designed by architects of established reputation serve, therefore, a double purpose. They explain the buildings themselves, setting out the conditions which determined their plan and treatment, and they estimate their place in relation to English culture and habits.

Since the end of the eighteenth century, architecture has been struggling with many vicious influences, and not least, with the lack of tradition, both in design and construction. The battle of the styles has been fought, not without fierceness, but with no good result. Now, after the lapse of a century devoted to groping experiments and detached eclecticisms, there are definite signs of the renewing of sleeping traditions, not on merely imitative lines, but in the spirit of the old work. This happy renaissance cannot march to success, unless the public at large concerns itself with architecture and becomes informed as to the problems to be faced and the ends to be attained. Building needs, in fact, to be brought back into the normal current of intelligent thought, instead of being relegated to the limbo of technical mysteries. That is not to say that the layman is wise to fill his mind with the details of construction, or attempt to master what is the absorbing study of an architect's lifetime. There are, however, certain qualities of architecture which lie open to the cultivated eye : mass, proportion, scale, and texture, and these become visible with observation to anyone with artistic perceptions. The time has come when educated people should shake off the shackles of the speculative builder and turn their backs finally on the desirable villa residence. Fifty years ago the architects who were doing honourable service in house-building were a small but brilliant band. One need name only the giants : Philip Webb, Eden Nesfield, George Devey, and Norman Shaw. To-day there are scores of young and brilliant men who have carried the pioneer work of their elders to its natural conclusion, and gone far to re-establish English architecture on a logical and national basis. Much remains to be done, especially in the larger field of town-planning and civic architecture, where this country lags behind the Continent ; but the driving power must come from an enlightened public opinion. The present need seems therefore to spread, as widely as may be, the knowledge of what is being done to-day. In the long last, every movement which has a claim to endure must have a sound economic basis. It is idle to ignore the fact that there still prevails in some minds the idea that " an architect's house " is necessarily a more costly matter than " a builder's house." In every case therefore where the information was available, not only the total cost of the house has been given in the following pages, but also the price per cubic foot. The latter method of calculation has not been adopted with any idea of instituting comparisons between the work of one architect and another, and, indeed, any such comparison would be futile and mischievous. It may be well to set out here how a cubic-foot price is calculated. The usual way is to take the height from the top of the foundations to halfway up the roof slope where there are no rooms in the roof, and to two-thirds the way up where the attic is utilised. This dimension multiplied by the length and breadth of the building gives its cubic content. Assuming, say, fifty thousand cubic feet, and a total expenditure of one thousand two hundred and fifty pounds, the cube-foot price of sixpence is the result. So far, so good, and it sounds simple and accurate enough ; but there are causes that tend to make it misleading.

In this imaginary house the foundations are assumed to be normal in quantity and cost, but if the ground be treacherous and need specially deep or solid foundations, what then ? An extra cost of over two hundred pounds may easily be incurred without the addition of a single extra cubic foot of useful space in the house. This would bring the cubic-foot price from sixpence up to sevenpence, and there would be nothing to show for the extra expenditure. Then, again, local conditions of building vary greatly. If a house is three miles from a station, instead of near by, every ton of brick and timber carted will cost about half-a crown more. Some districts are rich in materials, as, for example, Peterborough, where bricks cost little more than half their price delivered in London. Moreover, wages vary markedly, and those ruling in Greater London are on a higher scale than in the country. All these conflicting factors tend to vitiate the accuracy of comparison between the cubic-foot price of one house and another, even where the materials used in each are of the same intrinsic value, and no comparison is reasonable at all when one is built, say, of stone, with oak-panelled rooms, and the other of brick, with walls plainly plastered. So much for the danger of laying too great stress on such a rough-and-ready method of calculating costs.

Its real value is in the proof it gives that houses can be built in solid fashion and with definite artistic quality at such low costs as sixpence or sevenpence a cubic foot. When that is made clear there disappears much of the objection to embarking on building a house that will suit its owner's tastes and habits to a nicety.

To the readers of this book who are about to build it may not be impertinent to offer a few words of advice. Let it be said at once that the momentous question of success or failure rests wholly upon the wise choice of an architect. The builder who works to his designs is an important factor, and unless he is an honest and experienced man, the architect will have trouble in getting sound work. The powers conferred on him by the terms of the ordinary contract and specification enable him, however, to insist on good materials and workmanship even in the unhappy event of a shirking and incompetent builder securing the work in competition by submitting a very low estimate. In this, as in all else, the client will be wise to accept the advice of his architect and reject a very low tender in favour of a higher one if the lowest offer does not come from a builder of repute. Clients subject themselves to no small embarrassment and loss if they fail to summon to their counsels the architect of their choice immediately they have decided to build. His experience is of the greatest value, not only in the design of the house itself, but in the choice of a site. . Many factors have to be taken into consideration which it is unlikely that the layman will remember. It is impossible to set them all down, but here are nine points of the law of site-choosing :

Soil.—Questions of health are involved in the choice of clay, chalk or gravel. People who have gouty or other unpleasant tendencies discover by rude experience that one or other of them is to be avoided. A site which is poor in top soil will involve considerable expenditure before a productive garden can be made there.

View.—If a distant prospect can be secured, so much the better ; but a site which at first seems unsatisfactory may yet have considerable possibilities if the architect treats it skilfully. Some unpleasant outlooks may be avoided by thoughtful disposition of windows, and others masked by walls and by the planting of quick-growing hedges and trees.

Altitude.—Popular favour leans markedly to-day towards building on hill-tops, and in the main this seems wise ; but people who hate the cold or suffer from weak hearts or insomnia and other troubles derived from overstrung nerves should consider the benefits of milder and less stimulating airs. Though it is an artistic, rather than a practical, point, the importance of securing a good sky-line must not be overlooked in the case of a hill-top house. A caveat may be entered against sites where the level of the subsoil water is not far below the ground, and against all places liable even to a remote risk of flooding. The modern man should not be misled by the analogy of old houses, which were often placed with reference to considerations not now operative—of defence, carriage and water supply.

Protection.—A place which is swept by north or east winds is an unhappy choice for a house, and the ideal site is certainly that which is protected on these two quarters either by rising ground or trees.

Slope and Contour of Ground.—If a site slopes upwards to the south, not only is it more likely that it will be unprotected from the north winds, but the devising of a pleasant garden is made more difficult. Very uneven or sharply sloping ground may suggest to the architect very delightful possibilities or put in his way obstacles almost insuperable. In any event sharp slopes are likely to involve considerable extra cost in foundations and approaches.

Neighbourhood to Road.—Nothing at once costs so much and gives so little to show for it as road-making. If the chosen site of the house itself is not close to a good road, and a long drive is needed in consequence, a sum for road-making must be set aside which will probably distress the client not a little. In this connection the liability to motor dust must be considered, a factor governed largely by the prevailing wind.

Accessibility.—Neighbourhood to a railway station is not only a question of the personal convenience of those who live in the house, but affects the cost of building. Thoughtful folk will also consider how near the site will be to post and telegraph office, church and shops.

Public Services—Drainage, Water and Light.—Connection with municipal sewerage is a factor in cost. If there is no system near enough, when the house is built, it should be ascertained whether any extensions are likely in the future, as the design of house drainage somewhat varies according to whether it discharges into a public sewer or into a private cesspool or septic tank. If it is contemplated that the house drainage shall discharge at a point beyond the site, by arrangement with an adjoining owner, care must be taken to ensure that such right is secured in perpetuity. A pure and plentiful water supply is infinitely important, both for drinking purposes and for garden use, and if no public mains are available, the possibility of getting a permanent supply from a private artesian well needs to be carefully explored. For lighting, in default of public gas or electricity, the respective merits of a private installation of electric light, acetylene or petrol gas need careful consideration.

Setting of House on Site.—The aspects possible for the chief rooms with respect to view, prevailing winds, contour of site, etc., need careful thought. As to what are the best aspects for various rooms, he is a bold man who will lay down dogmatic rules, and I certainly lack the needful courage. It is generally held that south-east is the best outlook for the garden front, on which will be the principal living-rooms. A recent encounter with an architect of large experience in domestic work, however, is worthy of record. He habitually designs houses for his clients with a view to securing the maximum of sunshine in the living-rooms, but does so in obedience to what he regards as a popular delusion. For himself he prefers a north aspect, and will design his own home on these lines. He is likely, however, to find himself with few supporters.

So much for the general points which need to be considered before even a site is purchased. They are set out here with the express purpose of showing that expert advice is essential to the layman from the very inception of the idea of building. I know many cases where a client, captivated by the natural beauties of a site, has incontinently bought it, allured perhaps by a pleasant slope on which trees make a sunlit tracery. An examination of it in the cold light of the nine points of the law discussed above has then proved that its practical disadvantages so far outweighed its native charms as to involve its abandonment, with consequent disappointment and loss of time and money.

I come now to the all-important question of the house, its planning, its architectural treatment and its setting. Mr. Rudyard Kipling has said " there are nine-and-sixty ways of constructing tribal lays, and every single one of them is right." The same is exactly true of the making of houses, and it would be wholly futile to discuss the question on vague and general lines. The old Metaphysical Society had one rule—that there should be no rules—and domestic architecture needs a like freedom from fetters. Every site, every difference in personal need, every vagary of individual fancy, sets up new conditions. These have to be examined in the light of architectural traditions and possibilities and translated into the substance of brick and stone by the skill which the architect is able to bring to his work. There are, of course, some outstanding differences in principle and practice which distinguish various schools of design. There are plans, rambling or symmetrical. Some façades rely on eighteenth century motives, and others take their inspiration from the purely vernacular building traditions of an earlier day. About these divergencies it is useless to dispute. My motive has been to exclude no types of house which have intrinsic merit and are free from affectations, but rather to exhibit to the public eye the immense variety which lies open to the straying choice. In an introductory chapter it is impossible, save at inordinate length, to discuss the broad stylistic divisions of treatment or the individual characteristics which thoughtful architects stamp upon their work. In any case, it seems better to deal in a separate monograph with each house, which thus has its chief qualities explained and emphasised. The problems which arise for solution when an old house is repaired and enlarged form a subject by themselves. They are discussed generally in a separate chapter (page 191), and six houses so treated are described in the pages that follow it.

I would add that I am responsible for all the monographs but ten, which are by other hands, and that I have endeavoured to treat the subject clearly and without technicalities, and to criticise the work illustrated sympathetically yet frankly. The character of the houses taken as a whole, not only shows the admirable work which is being done to-day, but gives infinite hope for the future. It enables us, in our architectural outlook, to hold with firmness the cheery general creed of Robert Louis Stevenson: "I believe in the ultimate decency of things."

LAWRENCE WEAVER.

UPPER DORVEL HOUSE, SAPPERTON.

DESIGNED BY MR. A. ERNEST BARNSLEY.

Additions to an Old Cottage—The Idea of Growth in Building—Cotswold Traditions—The Art of the Plasterer.

THE house which Mr. Ernest Barnsley has built for himself at Sapperton calls to mind two others in its neighbourhood. It stands not far from Mr. Gimson's house, which is included in this volume, but keeps closely to old Cotswold traditions, forms and materials, while Mr. Gimson's house, always avoiding anything which would strike the most sensitive Cotswoldian as intrusive and foreign to the locality, does, both by certain features of its disposition and by its roof material, assert a measure of independence of strict local law and of affiliation to more distant custom. Mr. Barnsley's house is a type of what may be done by those who want to build anew and simply in the Cotswold district and have the very proper wish to maintain the individuality of one of the very best local architectural manners which we possess.

It was Mr. William Morris who " discovered " the Cotswolds. The founder and prophet of the school that has sought to restore right principles to the handicrafts and simple habits to life found in these hill-lands abundant object-lessons to aid his teaching, and, since he led the way, many artists and designers have gone thither for environment and for inspiration. The larger Northern villages, such as Camden and Broadway, have, as a result, become well known—almost too well known perhaps. But most of the

I.—THE HOUSE FROM ENTRANCE TERRACE.

Cotswold parishes retain their old-world air, and Mr. Barnsley has settled in one where that air is quite uncorrupted. Nor will it be his fault if inroads are made upon its purity. For though the members of the little coterie to which he belongs have built themselves new houses, and, by their introduction of local industries, have added to the life and importance of Sapperton, all has been done with a full appreciation of the past and a desire to infuse its spirit into the present.

Mr. Barnsley's house is not built from an abstract design set on paper as the unrestricted fulfilment of his ideal of form and arrangement. It is an adaptation to circumstances of an assertive kind. It is included in this volume, which has been made as varied as possible, not only as a type of appropriateness to its surroundings, but as an able solution of the problem of how to build a house that shall fully satisfy the requirements— æsthetic, ethical and domestic—of its occupants, on a site that imposes definite restrictions and already has a building which is to be retained and incorporated. There are men in all avocations who, when all lies easy before them to carry out what they please, produce but a commonplace and ineffectual result, and only reach success when they meet difficulty in the path and work under conditions of compromise. Without for one moment suggest-

2.—' THE BUILDING TOWERS UP FROM THE STEEP LANE."

ng that Mr. Barnsley's powers are restricted to this field, it is beyond question true to say that he is thoroughly at home in it. He had to deal with a site awkward in shape, access, aspect and gradient and

3.—FROM BELOW THE ENTRANCE TERRACE.

4

4.—THE HALL

having a plain and featureless cottage standing in its midst. None of these difficulties has he encountered in a spirit of hostility or destruction. He has met them in a friendly way, has entered into partnership with them, has disciplined them into line with his leading purpose. The house may be less complete, balanced and co-ordinated than it would have been, had there been no conditions of situation to fulfil. But it has gained rather than lost thereby, for it presents an unforced originality of outline and grouping, an unpurposed individuality of disposition and arrangement, and an appearance of extent and spread. The long, narrow existing cottage was so placed that it naturally and conveniently formed the centre, with the new buildings as wings at each end, but wings of greater size, height and presence than the centre. The house, therefore, covers more ground, and possesses more skyline, than is normal to its size, and yet it does this not of conceit, but of necessity. It conveys the idea that it had to be so. It has the good fortune of avoiding, without any affectation, the close-knitted squareness which, owing to right or wrong views of convenience and inexpensiveness, is the characteristic of most small modern houses. Mr. Barnsley, without any departure from architectural honesty, has been able to give himself ample space for the eye to roam from feature to feature, and for the foot to pass from room to room. Yet the house is of the simplest in design and in accommodation. The main approach is off the main road through Sapperton and beyond the church. A little private way runs along the highest level of the ground, and widens out into a terrace as it reaches the south-east or office wing. The whole building lies below this terrace, and there is a homely, modest look about the sunk gable-end of the kitchen and the diminutive yard and outbuildings reached down a flight of steps. Another flight of steps to the left gives on to the formal garden and to the paved way which leads to the porch. Though curiosity may attract us within, the charm of the little garden makes us pause without. It at once gives the impression that it is right; that it fulfils the particular requirements; that it is of the shape, size, material and construction needed at this special spot. This enclosure, dominated at one corner by the entrance terrace, bounded where the ground rises by the house and where the ground falls by a dry wall of local stone of such height that the exquisite view of the narrow winding dale and the steep wooded hills is thoroughly enjoyed, is the requisite semi-formal link between the straight lines of the building and the tumbled Cotswold landscape. The building is not one of Palladian symmetry, therefore the garden is not rigidly geometrical. The house, though with its outbuildings it covers some ground, is of cottage-like simplicity, therefore the garden is very small and of no architectural pretension. The walls enclose but the twentieth part of an acre.

They are not perfectly rectangular and have curved corners, obeying in some measure the lie of the land. But the surface is levelled as a plat whose horizontal lines are in sympathy with the vertical ones of the house, for its straight paths surround square and oblong flower-beds and borders, to which clipped box shrubs and hedges give point and variety. Here is very little expense of initial making or future upkeep. That is worth attention in these days, when the measure of the purse is in so many cases not the measure of the love for the garden. But that love may be indulged in without great outlay. It is a question of taste, of a true sense of the fitness of things, rather than of money, of the paying for large and often inappropriate works. This mechanical age, giving man command over natural forces, and therefore power of emulating Nature's large way of doing things, has unduly developed our taste for bigness and costliness. To have a thing larger and dearer than our neighbour has become too common an ambition and is a very stupid one. It is so much better to leave our neighbour alone, and think out for ourselves what is just the right life to live, house to inhabit and garden to create according to the special circumstances of their plan and position and of our powers and possibilities, mental and material. That surely is what Mr. Barnsley has done, and that is why his house and garden fit into their little corner of the Cotswolds and at the same time represent his own ideas and habits.

Of the exterior of the house one illustration is taken from the entrance terrace and another from the lawn which lies beyond the little formal garden. The original cottage was featureless and uninteresting, but, owing to Cotswold tradition, both in material and construction was entirely unobjectionable. The new kitchen wing has been made of the same height, so as to continue the ridge-line, but it is turned at right angles, the roof is brought down much lower, and two high-pitched gables are introduced. At the other end, where the view is best enjoyed, and several rooms are needed taking up as little ground as possible, height is given which affords the needed bedroom accommodation and adds much character to the group. The full value of this arrangement is seen on the north-east side, where the building towers up from the

5.—THE SITTING-ROOM.

steep lane. Daneway cannot have been wholly absent from the designer's mind when he decided on this feature. Here are the same proportions and line of roofage as in the high part of that old house, but they are carried out with more reticence and severity to suit a smaller and simpler dwelling. The walling is of the local stone, to hand in abundance on Sapperton Common, needing only to be dug out from the quarry and carted to the site. It is therefore an inexpensive material, and permits of both extent and thickness of walls without great outlay. On the other hand, the dressed stone used for the windows and coigns of the house, and for the steps and copings in the garden, comes from Minchinhampton, and its large use is to be counted rather as a luxury. Stone tiling, *facile princeps* of all forms of our native roofing, is of the essence of all Cotswold building. In using it Mr. Barnsley continued what he already found on the cottage. It is into the old cottage that we step from the porch—that is, into the space contained by its walls, for all else has been changed. The ground floor has been cleared of partitions and made into a long hall whose chief feature is its ceiling. Mr. Barnsley belongs to the same school of thought as his friend Mr. Gimson. To them beauty consists in line, proportion, texture, workmanship and most of all in appropriateness;

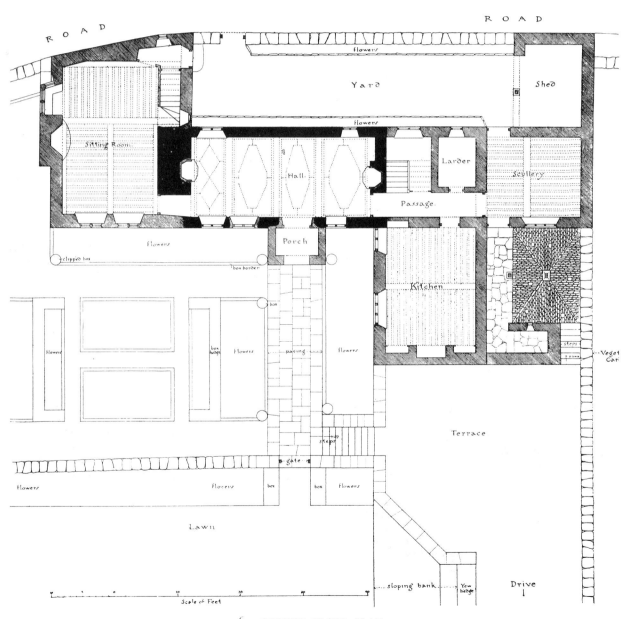

6.—GROUND FLOOR PLAN.

indulgence in ornament for ornament's sake, in patent decorative mediums and in mechanical patternings, is among the deadly sins. In Mr. Gimson's quite cottage-like house ornament finds no place. Mr. Barnsley, working on a slightly larger and more elaborate scale, rightly decided that it ought not to be wholly absent from the composition. The hall, nearly thirty feet long and leading to the sitting-room, might be accused of self-advertising puritanism, if it sternly excluded all the higher imaginings of skilful craftsmanship. The plasterer, at his best, has therefore been given the ceiling as a field for his art. With what excellent purpose the craftsmen of the days of Elizabeth and James wrought upon ceilings, even in lesser folks' houses, may be seen near by at Daneway ; and the Daneway ceilings, quite rich though quite modest, rather rough but very virile, commended themselves to those who wished, on no sumptuous or extravagant scale, to take advantage of this reviving art. That it is a reviving art, and that it can be used with excellent effect in simple manner, is shown by the accompanying illustration of the hall. The old school of plasterers were apt to reserve this form of ornament to rooms that had no ceiling beams, their designs being, as a rule, of elaborate ribbing and panelling, everywhere heavily enriched and suitable to large and lofty rooms only. But Daneway is one among several small houses where a beamed ceiling in a low room has been sufficiently enriched to give it distinction without any sense that it has been overdone or belongs to a room of another calibre. In exactly the same spirit has Mr. Barnsley worked. Heavy cross-beams were necessarily present in his hall to support the floor above. To carry the ceiling below them was to make the room too low. Moreover, the height and character of the room suggested the need of beams. As they were the salient feature of the construction, so should they be the chief field for the ornament, and they have been enriched by running scrolls of vine, oak and rose leaves of simple drawing and in low relief. The cornice round the wall carries out the scheme, but in its own manner. It is a little deeper than the beams, and has a narrow running pattern at top and bottom between which are detached sprigs of such flowers as flourish in the garden borders. The ceiling proper is very simply treated. It is in correspondence with the plain walls, and with them forms the background and foil to the decorated beams and cornice. The simple outline of ribbing is best seen in the plan, but it also just shows in the illustration with the small insets of ornament at corners and centre. The furniture both here and in the sitting-room consists partly of old examples and partly of new pieces designed by Mr. Barnsley and produced in Sapperton. One and the other equally enter into the picture, and are exactly what we expect and wish to see there. In the same manner the sitting-room, in the honesty of its construction, the sufficiency of its forms, the disposition of its adjuncts, declares itself one in which thinking and working can be done at their best.

Of this house Mr. Barnsley was not only the designer and the occupier, but builder and paymaster too. He therefore knows precisely how it has been done and what it has cost. It is done well, and therefore it is not done cheaply—not, at least, in the unpleasant sense in which circumstance now forces us generally to use that good old word. In a right sense the work has been done cheaply, for there is real and adequate value for the outlay. Mr. Barnsley has kindly supplied a schedule of the cost under the headings of the different forms of labour and material, and it is as follows :

			£	s.	d.				£	s.	d.
Mason—labour on house ..	..	..	580	0	0	Plumbing on house..	.. ..	..	91	0	0
,, ,, stable, etc.	..	..	98	7	10	Plaster floors ,, ..	.. ..	..	45	6	3
,, ,, hauling	..	..	32	0	0	Dressed stone ,, ..	.. ..	..	110	0	0
Carpenter ,, house ..	..	..	350	0	0	Timber ,, ..	.. ..	..	80	0	0
,, ,, stable, etc.	..	..	50	0	0	Cement ,, ..	.. ..	..	20	0	0
Tiler and plasterer—labour on house	..		199	0	0						
,, ,, ,, stable, etc.			45	0	0				£1,700	14	1

Deducting the sum for which the stable, garden and other adjuncts are responsible, the cost of the house was about one thousand four hundred and fifty pounds, and though the centre part was there already, there can have been little saving in retaining it. It is generally as dear to alter, convert and incorporate such a portion as it is to sweep it away and begin afresh. It was probably retained in this case in order to stamp a character of growth and adaptation upon the completed work and not as an economy. Few, then, will doubt that the sum paid was not by any means too large for the result attained. If all who have need to build anew in the Cotswolds will build in this manner, that district will earn as high praise for its present as for its past architecture.

REDLANDS, FOUR OAKS

DESIGNED BY MR. CHARLES E. BATEMAN.

The Conditions of House Planning—Aspects—The Lighting of Kitchens—Porches—Red and Yellow Brickwork.

IT comes to some architects to specialise in one type or another of public building, such as schools or churches, and to others to range freely over the whole field, but nearly all take their turn at domestic work. In such buildings as schools there is a code of rules laid down by the Government department concerned, which leaves the architect comparatively small scope for invention ; but in domestic building the problem is never twice the same and the variety of plan and treatment endless. There is, too, a human quality about the making of homes which is absent from the design of buildings of a public sort (churches always excepted), and with churches the very aloofness of their aim lifts their conception on to another plane. One remembers Ibsen's Master-builder :

"I build no more church-towers now. Nor churches either."

"What do you build then ? "

"Homes for human beings."

Though there is an inherent falseness in this contrasting of home-building and church-building, as Hilda Wangel shrewdly indicated when she countered Solnes with "Wouldn't you build a little—a little bit of a church tower over these homes as well," one sees the Master-builder's point. There is an intimacy between domestic architecture and the common life which it serves, that demands of the designer infinite

7.—THE ENTRANCE PORCH FROM THE STABLES.

patience and sympathy with people's habits and tastes. Because life is an endless succession of seeming trivialities, successful house-building is based not so much on the gift of large conceptions, as on the observation of ordinary needs and skill in ministering to them. In such work Mr. Charles Bateman has built success on large experience, and the arrangement of Redlands is a good example of convenient and economical planning. To take first the question of aspect : the whole range of reception-rooms faces the south-east. The contour of the site suggested it, and, though one hesitates to dogmatise on so thorny a question, it is probably the best possible, for it gives sunshine in the dining-room both for breakfast and luncheon. The drawing-room has a big bay also on the south-west front, so that it catches the late afternoon sun. The cleverest feature in the planning of this front is in the lighting of the kitchen. A main window facing the

8.—THE SOUTH-EAST FRONT.

9.—THE DRAWING-ROOM BAY.

south-east which let the sun stream in on the cooking range would have been a blunder ; but the range has been most ingeniously set in an ingle-nook, which has windows in the east and west walls, and so secures cross-lighting and cross-ventilation. There are also air outlets above the range, and the kitchen is thus kept admirably cool. Some architects have laid it down that a kitchen should always project from the main body of the house, and have windows at either side. This demand would often affect so materially the rest of the planning (besides confusing the roof), and would create the risk of such serious draughts, that Mr. Bateman's solution seems infinitely better and, indeed, ideal, for it gets the best of both worlds. The covered yard between the kitchen and the forecourt is used for the rougher scullery work. As it has a sparred gate it is always cool and hygienic and serves for the hanging of game, while the larder proper opens from it. The kitchen is used for cooking only, and the servants take their meals in the adjoining

room. The china pantry is between the kitchen and the dining-room, and is, therefore, convenient for serving. Special attention may be drawn to the admirable access to the verandah. Usually this is possible only from one room, but here doors open both from the dining and drawing rooms into a little lobby, which in turn gives on to the verandah. As the best aspect is secured for the three reception-rooms, Mr. Bateman wisely abstained from making a feature of the hall. It is adequate in size, and forms a convenient waiting-room ; but the staircase rises from it, and it is therefore not used for sitting. In many houses illustrated in these pages, the hall is the principal living-room. In such cases it is obviously desirable to shut off the staircase, and this can only be done structurally, if it is to be satisfactory, for curtains are insufficient to prevent draughts. At Redlands, however, the hall takes a subordinate place, but is cheerful withal by reason of its good south-west window. The porch is a fairly but not wholly successful solution of a difficult problem. As Mr. Bateman (giving hostages to criticism) once wrote himself in a valuable paper on small houses : " Porches are not easy to treat, as, when small and of the usual type, they seem to be stuck on, and to have the character of a dog kennel or of a furniture van." He is doubtless right in thinking more kindly of recessed porches, but at Redlands recessing would have meant an abstraction from the hall of space, which could have been ill spared.

10.—THE TERRACE.

The grouping of the stables with the house on the north-east side of the forecourt is very successful. Between the loose boxes and the carriage-house is a washing space shut off from the forecourt and from the stable court by big gates, and, as the first illustration shows, the archways make an agreeable feature. So much by way of describing the plan of the house, which has many points of marked interest. The exterior is treated in a simple and satisfactory fashion. Mr. Bateman has eschewed anything like a conscious feature, which is all to the good. He has relied on the dignity which is always secured by a long level roof-line. The chimneys seen from the garden are bold, and their positions, two issuing at the apex of the roof and one, that of the kitchen, projecting on the south-east front, reveal another point of good planning. The sitting-room fires are all in inside walls, an arrangement which conserves the heat where it is wanted, whereas the kitchen is the cooler for having its range built into an outside wall. The mass of the kitchen chimney, moreover, joins with the two-storey gabled bay in adding a touch of reasonable variety to the garden front.

Though the garden wall which runs from the east corner of the house is high enough to provide good shelter for wall fruit, it does not hide the charming little group formed by the dovecote which serves to crown the stable wing. It is not a mere constructed feature, but a reasonable and useful way of finishing off the staircase from the harness-room, while the slightly projecting parapet to its left marks the presence of a capacious soft-water tank. The only conscious ornaments to be espied are the pleasant lines of the gable of the main bay and the quiet patterning with projecting bricks on its front, treatments very proper to the material. It is a house like this, of red brick and tiles, with foreground of gay flowers and bright-leaved creepers invading the red, and background of dark-leaved forest trees, that makes one wish that the keen eye of Heinrich Heine had not formed his judgment of English brickwork from the dour dirtiness of London.

It was in 18₰8 that he published the brilliant impressions of his visit to that " forest of houses," where he anticipated, but did not see, great palaces. " These houses of brick, owing to the damp atmosphere of coal smoke, become uniform in colour, that is to say, of a brown olive green; they are all of the same style of building, generally two or three windows wide, three storeys high, and adorned above with small, red tiles, which remind one of newly-extracted bleeding teeth; so that the broad and accurately-squared streets seem to be bordered by endlessly long barracks." This is all in the spirit of Ruskin, who said that everything in the world came to an end, even Gower Street. Like most swift generalisations based on imperfect knowledge, it is as untrue of England at large as it is convincingly true of the

II —THE DOVECOTE.

core of London. The yellow stock brick of Kent, which was the chief material of London's building before red bricks were brought within reach by cheap transit, can be and is a beautiful material, if rightly used.

No one can see the interior of Westminster Cathedral without delight at the dull gold of its huge expanses of wall. For exteriors, however, it must be confessed that red or purple brick is more attractive. The architectural taste of the late eighteenth and early nineteenth

12.—THE GARDEN FRONT FROM THE EAST.

centuries took a gloomy view about red bricks and tiles, as is clear from Heine's rather savage reference to "bleeding teeth"; but fifty years of revived interest in traditional ways has given back to the clay-worker an æsthetic place he is not likely again to lose.

Fine effects in brickwork are secured rather by the thought and care exercised by architects than by any costliness in the method of building. Although Redlands is solidly equipped indoors with stone mantelpieces, substantial panelling and the like, Mr. Bateman's judgment has achieved its very admirable effects at a cost per cubic foot of only sevenpence farthing, or, putting it another way, at sixteen shillings and sixpence per superficial foot of ground floor area. The latter basis of cost for a typical lesser country house, well constructed and well equipped, is likely to be of service to those who are dreaming dreams about building; but it will hold good only where the architect can be relied on for good planning and sound judgment in avoiding costly features, and, of the two, the cubic foot price is the safer guide.   W.

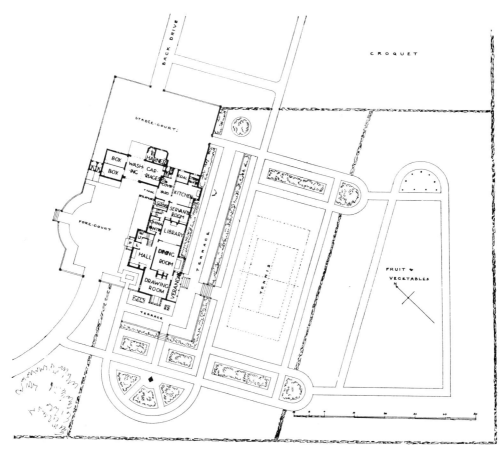

13.—PLAN OF REDLANDS

THE HURST, MOSELEY, BIRMINGHAM.

DESIGNED BY MR. W. H. BIDLAKE.

Birmingham Architecture—Houses and Habits—The Placing of Organs—Leigh Hunt on Brickwork.

BIRMINGHAM is hardly an architectural paradise ; indeed, it has grown up from its small Georgian beginnings in a very haphazard fashion. It is poor in public buildings. St. Philip's Church, now the cathedral, was the work of William Archer, and the tower and dome are a brilliant *tour de force*. The nave is not notable, save for the windows designed by Burne-Jones and made by William Morris. They are ablaze with brilliant colours, and give beauty to an interior otherwise uninteresting. The exterior was refaced some time ago, and in the process lost whatever character the talent of William Archer had impressed upon it. St. Edward's School was the work of Sir Charles Barry, a fine, masculine building, but a little lacking in imagination. Pugin is represented by the Roman Catholic cathedral, interesting, too, but rather thin. Of the more modern public buildings little can be said in praise. The

Law Courts, built in the eighties, are a wild whirl of moulded brick and terra-cotta, ornamented with a lack of reserve which arises from their employment by thoughtless hands. It must be confessed that the Courts have had a very unhappy influence on recent architecture in Birmingham. If so grave a business as Justice is to be housed in a place where the decoration rollicks unheeded and unrestrained, can one wonder if other buildings have yielded to an orgy of machine-made ornament and a profusion of harsh colours ?

There are some among the more modern offices, such as those by Professor Lethaby and Mr. Leonard Stokes, which help by their quiet character to redress the balance ; but any general survey of the architecture of the city is bound to result in gloom. When one comes to the suburbs and the outlying villages which are rapidly linking themselves with the city, there is, happily, a different story. Nowhere, perhaps, does the professional and business man of moderate means more readily accept the idea that a house built for himself, and not for some nameless abstraction, is his proper habitation. For this reason a vigorous school of domestic architecture has arisen, which is a great credit to the Midlands. It is inevitable, of course, that the majority of folk should still prefer the ready-made house of the speculative builder. The alternative is the more troublesome, but in the end less costly, process of employing an architect to design a dwelling that

14.—GATE AND PORCH.

fits its owner's tastes and habits. The Hurst, Moseley, is a good example of how such an individual taste can find its proper setting. To Mr. A. J. Bowen, its owner, an organ is the most desired feature of a home, but in an ordinary house its placing presents problems almost insoluble. The height required makes it impossible to set it in a room of any usual dimensions. If the difficulty be evaded by separating the pipes from the keyboard and making the connection electrically, the breaking up of the instrument has an unhappy effect decoratively, even though it may have no disadvantage musically. People are generally driven to add to an existing house a music-room lofty enough to take the instrument, but such a room tends to remain separate, and useless for ordinary purposes. In the case of The Hurst, Mr. W H. Bidlake was able to provide for the organ from the beginning, and very wisely put it in the sitting hall, which he carried up two storeys, and so allowed it ample room. The result is eminently satisfactory. The instrument has been treated as an integral part of the design of the hall, and, indeed, of the house, the arrangements of which are greatly modified by it, but in no way to their disadvantage. An organ which has been added to a room

stands out with oppressive insistence and overwhelms all other decorative impressions. In this case its own chamber has been built, so that the case projects into the hall only so far as is needful to give right emphasis to what is the main feature of the house. The panelling of the room is carried up to the same height as the case of the organ, and a rich plaster frieze appears above. The hall, as becomes so fine an apartment, is the key to the planning of the whole house. A vestibule separates it from the porch and communicates also with the servants' quarters, so that it need not be crossed save for access to the drawing-room. The gallery at the east end of it is the main passage of the first floor, and the risk of draughts in winter can be obviated by heavy curtains. It is not in the nature of things that so lofty a room with great windows and open gallery can ever be quite comfortable in cold weather, but in summer it is delightfully cool and airy. On the first floor there are five bedrooms, and above them four bedrooms and a recreation-room, which will presently be devoted to billiards.

It may be wondered why the aspects of the house are somewhat unusual. The main rooms face the west instead of the south and so get only the declining rays. The explanation is that, though the house looks as though it should stand on a large and

15.—THE HALL FIREPLACE.

free site, it is, in fact, in a suburban road, and the ground on which it stands has a frontage but slightly in excess of the width of the house. It was, therefore, impossible to place it otherwise. The feeling may arise that it is a pity to build a house of so much character and quality on a site which so narrowly limits its possibilities; but that seems hardly the right point of view. Rather may the owner be congratulated that even for so small a site he allowed Mr. Bidlake to design so interesting a building the cost of which was three thousand seven hundred and fifty pounds. Were all owners (and in this case the owner is builder also) so wise-hearted, the sting would be taken out of the usual gibes about suburban architecture. As it is, good use has been made of the ground, and room found not only for a motor-house, but for stable and harness-room for a saddle-horse. The exterior is conceived on typically English lines with the Tudor feeling that is not unnatural from a hand which, like Mr. Bidlake's, has achieved so much that is distinguished in ecclesiastical work. It is all very quiet and scholarly, but some criticisms suggest themselves.

The rather heavy horizontal moulding over the entrance doorway would have been better dropped to just above the arch, as it would have divided the height in happier proportion. On the garden front the

16.—THE GARDEN FRONT.

17.—THE EAST FRONT.

scheme of the hall reveals itself in the great window with its mullions and transoms. This generous fenestration has its dangers, for the big gable above it seems to sit rather heavily on its seemingly slender supports. The little projection built out to the north side of the garden front, which serves the necessary purposes of boots and knives, looks like an after-thought, and seems to disturb the gravity of the long front. This is said in the full knowledge of the cramped nature of the site, and the arrangement may have been inevitable. Perhaps the boots annexe might have been incorporated with the harness-room building by extending the latter a few feet to the east. These, however, are only slight blemishes on a design marked by great dignity. Not the least of its merits is in the long, unbroken ridge of the roof. It is worth noting that gables, however varied in spread and height, do not impart a sense of restlessness if they are backed by the serious lines of a large and simple roof.

The house is fortunate in its materials, for the bricks are good both in colour and texture. And what an atmosphere of enchantment there is about this age-long trade, we have the pleasant gossiping pen of Leigh Hunt to put us in mind. "Why, the very manufacture is illustrious with antiquity —with the morning beams that touched

18.—THE HALL: ORGAN AND GALLERY.

the house-tops of Shinaar;—there is a clatter of brickmaking in the fields of Accad; . . ." and so we may be transported "into old Babylon with its tower and its gardens; and there we drove our chariot on the walls, and conversed with Herodotus . . . and returning home what do we descry? The street itself alone! No! Ben Jonson, the most illustrious of bricklayers, handling his trowel on the walls of Chancery Lane, and the obstinate remnants of Roman brick and mortar lurking still about London, and Spenser's celebration of

Those bricky towers
The which on Themmes brode aged backe doe ride."

But what has all this got to do with Mr. Bidlake and a house in a Birmingham suburb? Only this, but it is enough—that buildings, in suburbs and elsewhere, will fail of their appeal as homes, unless the imagination can relate them credibly with the houses of past days.   W.

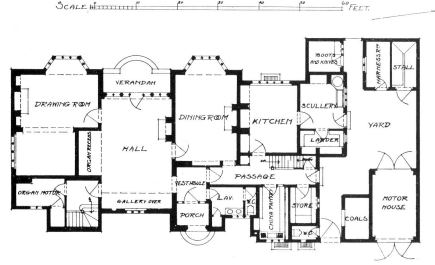

19.—GROUND PLAN.

LARKSCLIFF, BIRCHINGTON, KENT.

DESIGNED BY MR. ARTHUR T. BOLTON.

A Seaside Family Home—The Right Use of Rough-cast—An Outdoor Dining-room—Ali Baba's Cave—Greenhouse—Attic.

TO many who dwell in crowded cities, the call of the sea is insistent. In contrast with their hurried lives is the quiet of wide spaces, the breezy conflict of wind and water and the merging of the horizon in an indeterminate haze of distance and colour. When to these natural elements is added the human interest that belongs to the relics of the great name of Rome, we have unveiled the secret of the prestige of the Kentish Coast. Nowhere is this greater than in the famous Island of Thanet. So much one reflects naturally when contemplating the unbroken vistas from the windows of the seaside home illustrated in this chapter.

The village of Birchington is about a mile from the sea; but a colony of bungalows (and among them that in which Dante Gabriel Rossetti died) has sprung up between the station and the cliffs. West of the bungalows a building estate was schemed some years ago and a parade begun; but, for reasons which are not very clear, building has been small in quantity and unpleasant in quality. The air of Birchington, like

20.—LARKSCLIFF FROM THE SANDS.

that of its bigger neighbours, Westgate, Margate and Broadstairs, is extremely bracing and of peculiar value for young children. On the edge of the chalk cliffs Mr. Arthur T. Bolton has built a house that is, above all, a family home. The site has been admirably chosen and the house so devised that, in its main outlook seawards, the view is untroubled by buildings. Looking westwards, for five miles the open sea skirts the ancient marshlands of Sarre, beyond the curving reach of Minnis Bay, until it meets the venerable ruin of Reculvers. The twin towers of the ruined church stand within the still more ancient walls of the Roman fortress of Regulbium, that guarded the inlet of the sea which once made Thanet an island in fact as it is now only in name. The house stands on the chalk cliff which, reaching round from the Dover headlands, is here about to disappear before the Thames estuary is reached. Eastwards, beyond the bungalows, is the reddish mass of Westgate, and, some six miles away, the grey chequered outline of the older Margate. Beside the house wild flowers and chalk weed grow in profusion. Larkscliff, as the house-name, has

18

21.—A WALL IN FLINT AND TILE.

22.—THE GARDEN FRONT.

its plain meaning. The larks, their song and their secret architecture, have not yet been driven away by man's obtrusive building. It is obvious that such a situation as is here described demands an architectural treatment altogether different, both structurally and æsthetically, from that of an inland house. The designer had to bear in mind that his building would be searched by every wind that blows. Just as the cliffs are being slowly eroded, so the sea salt would affect his walling, while the maximum allowance of brilliant sunshine, of which Thanet is so proud, calls for special provisions. Raging winds and driving rains are no respecters of the picturesque conventions that may rightly find their place in the seclusion of a tree-embowered site. Whether seen in a hot sunlight across a shimmering sea, or in the pearl grey tones of its haze, ingenious combinations of polychrome architecture will be neither restful nor agreeable. In order to obtain the tone and texture that befit such conditions and yet resist the penetrating force of angry gales, without recourse to the doubtful merits of hollow walls, the house was sheathed in a rough-cast of granite and cement. There is, perhaps, no treatment more apt to be misapplied than rough-casting. Mr. Bolton has adopted the logical idea of it, and treated it as a protective cloak for the whole house. It is a too common practice to rough-cast isolated surfaces, leaving the brickwork of other parts uncovered. Sometimes also a brick

23.—THE ENTRANCE.

or stone arch is left untreated to emphasise the decorative value of such constructional features. It would be unwise to dogmatise on such a question as this, for it is closely connected with the architectural needs and intention of the particular house so treated. It is safe to affirm, however, that the uniform use of rough-cast at Larkscliff is altogether wise. The speculative builder is much addicted to what has been profanely, but not unhappily, called the blouse-and-skirt style. This method leaves the lower part of the brickwork plain to a height of from four feet to ten feet all round the house, the upper parts of the walls being rough-cast. It has been whispered that this is due to a passion to utilise, for a large proportion of the building, bricks so common, that they will not bear the light of day. Not the least of the disadvantages of rough-cast is the question of colour. The mixture of sand or fine gravel with Portland cement produces a cold, dull, bluish grey tone, most unattractive in itself, which is often veiled by distemper of cream or other pleasant colour. This, however, means a recurring cost, galling to the economic mind of the householder. Mr. Bolton has solved the difficulty by having his rough-cast made of red Leicestershire granite. This is not so strong as to overcome the cement and produce a pink effect, but modifies it to a warm and kindly grey. The roofing is of Kentish tiles employed in the traditional way. The eaves are restricted by remembrance of the lifting power of the

24.—THE UPPER CORRIDOR.

25.— THE ATTIC PLAYROOM.

gales that search the house on all sides. The main outline of the building is emphasised by the gathering of the chimneys into two masses, which rise boldly above the roof. The broadly designed main gable is a good feature, for it tells from a distance as well as close at hand. The bay windows of drawing and dining rooms are subdued and embodied in the general composition of this gable. It is by the merging of lesser features in the main elements of a composition that a reasonable variety is achieved without any frittering away of the mass.

An essential element in the design is the outdoor dining-room, which is afforded by the verandah and terrace adjoining the dining-room. Above it, the enclosed connecting balcony is not only a very practical feature, but gives a strong defining mass of shadow, which adds value to the design of the front. Except for a sundial, the owner's initials and a date in bronze, there is an entire absence of carved ornaments. The qualities of architecture have been sought—and found—elsewhere, but there has been no insistence on them. The house has grown round its plan, on the traditional lines which governed the development of the farm-houses of the county. The simple character of the exterior is helped and emphasised by the white-painted weather-boarding, which has been so judiciously used. Any sort of elaboration would have been out of place, for the intention was simple. A family seaside home was wanted at an outlay so moderate that the interest would mean an ordinary rental. Such a rental usually gives the inferior accommodation of a builder's ready-made house, and it was to escape this that Mr. Bolton designed Larkscliff for himself. The actual cost, exclusive of the garden walls, but including more than the usual allowance of sanitary fittings, e.g., two bathrooms, was one thousand three hundred pounds, which works out at sevenpence halfpenny a cubic foot. The site included an old chalk-pit, and this presented obvious advantages for flower culture, as a sunk garden escapes the gales that come so

25.—FROM DRAWING-ROOM TO DINING-ROOM.

vigorously from the sea. In this valley, too, one may have tea comfortably without the wind taking too violent liberties. For the formation of paths chalk was wanted, and was obtained by tunnelling. The inside of the cave so formed has been concreted and palisade gates put at one of its two entrances, the other being a rubble archway with a porch of stout poles brilliant in July with rambler blossoms. We have said that Larkscliff is a family house. The uses of the cave may be divined. It is the home of Robinson Crusoe, the cave of Ali Baba's brigands, the scene of high smuggling exploits, and even on occasion a Bond Street shop. In one of the illustrations can be seen three of the *dramatis personæ* near the entrance of this novel playroom. An admirable feature of the garden, and one that adds greatly to the privacy of the house, is the enclosing wall of rough flint and quarry tiles that looms large in one of the illustrations. As befits a wall in Thanet, it is built in the Roman manner. Tiles in flint walls have a great decorative value, but like all good ornament they have a strong structural significance. They serve, in fact, as reinforcement, and notably increase the strength of the wall. The handling of the flint shows that Mr. Bolton's early studies of mosaic art have not been in vain.

At Larkscliff the greenhouse difficulty has been cleverly overcome. There is no question that green-houses are the bane of an architect's life, and on no other question is the garden-loving client so likely to come into conflict with the architect. In big houses they can be exiled to a walled garden, but in the case of a site of a quarter acre the difficulty is insistent. At the right-hand end of the garden front are two large, round-headed windows. These light the little conservatory, which also has windows at the two ends. The space thus afforded is enough in proportion to the small garden, and though it lacks a top light, it is an admirable compromise between a conservatory, which would be a blot on the house, and none at all. The windows in its back wall give added light to the kitchen, which is, however, adequately lit otherwise. This brings us inside the house and at the domestic end. The kitchen arrangements are much more ample than is usual in a house of this size. The inner kitchen is, in fact, a servants' hall, and the domestics thus enjoy an uncommon degree of comfort. The reception-rooms are two only, the place of the third being taken by the open-air dining-room. They can, however, be turned into one for children's parties, as they are connected by folding panelling.

Other practical features of this well-thought-out plan are the children's lavatory on the ground floor and the small room by the front door that takes the wheeled transport of the family. It is a great advantage to get this accommodation at the front rather than the back of the house, and at Larkscliff there are many wheels of all sizes to be considered. The plan of the bedroom floor provides a complete suite of bedroom, dressing-room and bathroom, either for guests or for isolation in case of illness—a thoughtful provision. Once more, on the principle of *juniores priores*, the nursery has the central position on the garden front.

The covered balcony is available for the little ones, either for play or as an open-air bedroom, while it also gives access to their mother's room. It is, however, on the top floor of this children's home that they find their paradise. The attic is given up as a playroom, and lined throughout with fireproof slabs. The arching over the flues forms a natural proscenium for dramas more stately and ordered than belong to the robbers' cave in the garden. Despite the fact that space has been everywhere economised, and chiefly in hall and corridors, the stairs and passage on the bedroom floor have a pleasant character. Growing plants are a happy feature in a house; but the casual flower-pot is apt to suffer from the sudden movements of the young. A little opening to the left of the stairs has been given over to the uses of greenery, and leads an agreeable freshness to the house.

The plan should be carefully studied, for it is the outcome of much thought directed to producing a thoroughly comfortable and workable house. Its construction even recognises the age of the majority of its inhabitants. The floors and partitions are specially packed with sound-proof material to deaden the noise of the young folk, who can enjoy their holidays unchecked and without undue reference to the nerves of their elders. For the housewife, let us add that the cupboards are legion. She will probably reply that in this richness are comprised both the law and the prophets of domestic architecture. W.

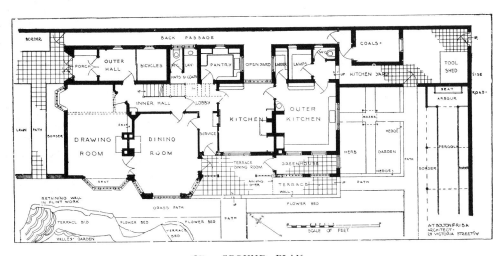

27.—GROUND PLAN.

BISHOPSBARNS, YORK.

DESIGNED BY MR. WALTER H. BRIERLEY.

A Pebbled Forecourt—Ingenious and Practical Planning—The Traditions of Yorkshire Building—The Right Use of Materials

BISHOPSBARNS derives its delightful name not from any barn-like quality in itself, but from the fact that its site belonged to the See of York, and that barns were on the spot where the house now is. If the truth is to be told entire, the house is not by situation a country home, for it stands in a suburb of York ; but Mr. Brierley has so ingeniously placed it on its site that it lacks no country quality either in plan or treatment. For this very reason it is the more fruitful subject for study, and shows that in some sort the defects of suburban houses are due not so much to the inherent difficulties as to an usual lack of skill in their solution. As the site is not deep from north to south, no attempt was made to secure a front garden, but the house is set back from the road just so much as was needful to provide an open forecourt before the entrance door. This has been paved with black and white pebbles from the beach at Flamborough in a design of plain chequers, which have this large advantage, that they give an air of coolness to a colour scheme which is dominated by the rich red brick of the house itself. Such paving has the practical advantage that it gives a firm foothold to horses in all weathers, and needs no upkeep as does a gravel drive. The illustration of the entrance front unfortunately fails in one way to give a fair idea of its proportions, because, in the photographer's effort to avoid an ugly street lamp by a side-long view, the left-hand gable, with its massive chimney, seems unduly large compared with its right-hand fellow. The two are, in fact, of the same size, and the projections, which they mark, stand out

28.—THE SOUTH FRONT.

solidly at either end of the long line of concave roofing on the north side. The entrance door has a fine hood n massive oak, with its supports admirably but unobtrusively carved. We pass through a lobby into the staircase hall, separated from the sitting hall by a screen of stout square-wrought balusters. Here and elsewhere throughout the house, panelling and doors have the look of satinwood, but they are made of Kauri pine untouched save for elbow and wax polishing. This is an admirable treatment and inexpensive for the charming effect it gives, but it is possible only if done in picked pine, free from defects and perfectly seasoned. The sitting hall is a good room to sit in and looks out through a long range of casements on to the brick parlour or loggia which faces due south. The fireplace, which appears in an illustration, is of unpolished

29.—FROM THE SOUTH-EAST.

30.—THE STREET FRONT.

Hopton Wood stone, a material of so quiet a colour that one marvels it is not more generally used for such purposes. Separated from the sitting hall by wide folding doors is the drawing-room. Its ceiling is struck to a flat and pleasant curve, and is decorated with plaster-work by Mr. Bankart. On the other side of the sitting hall is the dining-room, with doors both from the entrance hall and from the kitchen quarters. Rarely does one see pictures looking so well as here, but the background explains it ; the walls are distempered a French grey. The brick parlour is so spacious that in summer many meals are taken there. As it is set under the main roof and thus protected fully from east and west, it is thoroughly practical in every way. In this word " practical " one reads the reason for success at Bishopsbarns. The arrangement of the house is a compendium of domestic comfort, and makes for a perfect organisation of household affairs. The kitchen is a business kitchen, with a capacious sink, and the larder and pots-room open from it. There is no scullery, and none is needed, for all work is done in the kitchen, and the servants' sitting-room is the place for their meals. This plan need not absorb more space than the provision of a scullery involves, and it adds vastly to the servants' comfort. The tradesmen's entrance is well away from the kitchen, which is placed so that there is no traffic through it, and the art and mystery of cooking can thus be pursued without interruption. In the housemaid's pantry there are three sets of cupboards, for glass, silver and china respectively. The lower range is kept for the things in daily use, fixed a gas stove, a thoughtful arrangement which

31.—THE SOUTH GABLE.

the upper series is consecrated to spare sets. Here is prevents the kitchen being disturbed by so light a matter as the preparation of afternoon tea, and leaves the field clear for the later solemnities of dinner. Next to this pantry is the storeroom, a sanctuary of capacious cupboards, where also flowers may be arranged. Altogether it would be difficult to devise a plan for the working quarters of a house more convenient for their purposes. We go upstairs by a simple, spacious stairway, to find a scheme of floors which has many merits. The corridor runs east and west, and, with the outer hall below, divides the house in an ingenious fashion which gives a first floor only on the south side, where are the principal bedrooms, and first and second floors on the north side. The first of the latter is taken up chiefly by storerooms, housemaid's room, etc., and the second by the servants' bedrooms. This enables the ground floor and first floor rooms on the south side to be lofty (a necessary condition where, as in the drawing-room, the ceiling is arched). At the same time, it gives plenty of light and pleasant rooms on the north, for the extra space on that side is gained by keeping the ground floor offices low, height being there needless and, indeed, wasteful. The exterior of the house is characterised by that breadth of treatment and sedulous care for sound building which belong to the architectural traditions of Yorkshire, and find no more successful exponent than Mr. Walter Brierley. The outside woodwork is everywhere of oak, and the rain-water pipes are of lead. There is, consequently, no repainting to be considered, with its inevitable destruction of the creepers, which already begin to clothe the house. The use of the best materials for outside work

32.—THE LOGGIA.

26

involves, of course, some increase in initial cost, but cheapness in such a connection is merely a will-o'-the-wisp. A great architect of the last century, who lacked a reputation for designing cheap buildings, used to say, " People forget about the expense of building. They never forget bad work, for it is always there to remind them." There is a massive common-sense about this observation, which one wishes could make it more widely accepted by those who build. It has obviously been in this spirit that Mr. Brierley has designed for himself, and, indeed, always designs for others.

The view of the

33.—THE SITTING HALL.

house from the south-east gives a good idea of the dignity with which gables, dormers and chimneys have been massed. Anthony Trollope made a jesting reference to an architectural truth when he commented

34.—THE DRAWING-ROOM.

on the taste in dress of one of his characters, " She well knew the great architectural secret of decorating her constructions, and never descended to construct a decoration." At Bishopsbarns there is no line and no decoration that does not arise out of the nature of the materials and their workmanlike use. The projecting courses of brickwork in the gables help to throw the water clear of the wall. The tiling is " swept " to soft curves (a technical word may be pardoned, as it seems expressive) to avoid mitres. The lead flashings are nicked at the edges into a gay little line. The window-sills are of ordinary roofing tiles, but the nibs are turned outwards to serve as drips, and they give little spots of shadow. On the gable ends the cement verges are finished in a simple pattern with the point of the trowel. It is to the wise choice of the chief materials that much is due. Both bricks and tiles are hand-made; the former are only two inches thick and of a rich red, while the latter are a full inch thick and have weathered to a dark brown. It is an odd thing that the ignorance in the right use of materials which was universal during the first half of last century and prevails to-day in ninety per cent. of our building, drove people to make bricks thick when they should be thin, and tiles thin when they should be thick. It is in a reversion to the elder traditions that Mr. Brierley has established a fine technique of building, which shows his work informed with thought.

An architect may, however, be defeated by a careless builder. At Bishopsbarns the work is particularly good, for the builder took a pride in it. Mr. Brierley adopted the satisfactory method of paying a

35.—THE STAIRCASE.

percentage on the net cost, instead of entering into the usual form of contract, and the cost of the house per cubic foot did not exceed ten-pence. This is unquestionably the way to get things well done, for the competitive system breeds scamped work and inferior workmen.

For the garden at Bishopsbarns there can be nothing but praise, for though it is small the best use has been made of the available space, and its planting was devised by Miss Jekyll. It is superfluous to say more than that the colour schemes are worthy of her, and that for summer and winter alike they have been worked out in consummate detail. They make one wonder once more how such elusive contrasts can be conceived and set out in all certainty without the practical aids of trial and error. Sitting in the loggia, one sees across the warm brick paving of the path the grey of stachys receding through the light turquoise of Japanese iris and the powerful blues of delphinium to the backing of deep green in the trim yew hedge. The illustrations show what fine play is made with lupins. They do not reveal (for the time was not ripe for photography) the treasure of ramblers on the big oak pergola. Enough, however, can be seen to establish for Bishopsbarns the charm of its setting and to win for the house itself a generous appreciation.

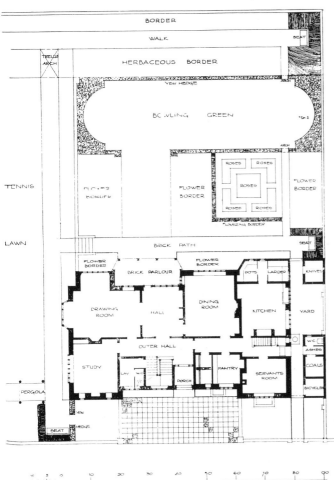

36.—GROUND PLAN.

BENGEO HOUSE, HERTFORD.

DESIGNED BY MR. WALTER CAVE.

Sanity in Architecture—Thoreau on Furnishing—The Importance of Escaping the Inessential.

BENGEO HOUSE takes the place of an old building which was burnt to the ground not long since. The north front does not lend itself kindly to photography, for it stands scarcely twenty feet from the road and a rather high wall shuts out the lowest storey from view. Mr. Walter Cave, however, elected to treat it on pleasant Georgian lines, and as both north and south fronts follow the same motive, the garden elevations explain the whole. Fire happily spares gardens,

It is difficult to say whether one is more satisfied with the house within or without, for it is in every way delightful, with sanity written all over it. The Luton brick walls, of a colour in which grey, purple and brown mingle, have an air of ripeness which is enlivened by the bright red of the quoins, while tiles which came from a demolished malting at Ware make a rich crown above the boldly treated cornice. and southwards the outlook is across the level lawn flanked by fine old trees to the Ware Road and Ware Park House—a characteristic Hertfordshire prospect, quiet and smiling.

37.—THE GARDEN FRONT

We reach the vestibule from the street door by a covered passage, and through it enter a charming spacious hall, with the staircase rising from its corner. From the hall open the three chief sitting-rooms. The kitchen is separated from the dining-room only by a passage and by the admirably contrived serving lobby, from which also open the pantry and plate cupboard. In the drawing-room, as the accompanying picture shows, is a fireplace of considerable merit, with a hob-grate of an old pattern which always looks well. We go up the staircase, very well lit by a tall window in three tiers, to the first floor, where there are eight bedrooms, and so to the attic floor, which boasts nine. Though the latter are partly in the roof, and though, moreover, Mr. Cave has kept the dormers within reasonable dimensions, so that from without they are in scale, the rooms are bright and charming. Everywhere there are cupboards and household dodges of various sorts to make easy the working of the house. The simple fact is that it is soundly planned and thought out in every detail, and there are no architectural fads. It is a monument to Mr. Cave's common-sense, and no less to his economic skill, for, despite its five-and-twenty spacious rooms, Bengeo House was completed for less than four thousand pounds, which represents eightpence three farthings a cubic foot.

Too often an architect's intent is defeated by his client's unhappy activities in furnishing; but here is a house where moderation and taste have directed it. It is hardly possible to be too insistent against the overcrowding of rooms with furniture. The Early Victorian passion for what-nots cannot, however, be dismissed as incredible. It would be pleasant to think that those egregious tiers of shelves were so called because they were receptacles for *what not* to exhibit to the public eye. Unfortunately, one cannot escape the belief that they and the litter that covered them represented a decorative policy very dear to people. Though the what-not is dead, and people talk of Art furniture instead, the spirit that created it is very much alive. Few of us have the courage to abolish the inessential, whether in furniture or ornaments. Thoreau was brave. "I had three pieces of limestone on my desk," he wrote at Walden, "but I was terrified to find that they required to be

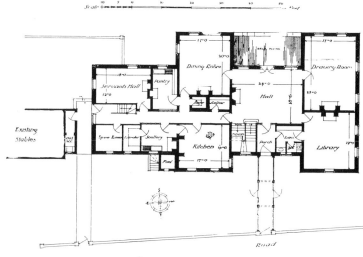

38.—GROUND PLAN.

39.—FROM THE SOUTH-WEST.

dusted daily, when the furniture of my mind was all undusted still, and I threw them out the window in disgust." We need not take so feverish a hate to household gods as did the "transcendental Yankee" of Stevenson's phrase, but it would be wise to accept his policy to the length of keeping them few and fit. Our forefathers were content to begin home-making with a little, and gradually to add a fine chair here and a bedstead there, each beautiful of its sort, and meanwhile to sit and lie on simple utilitarian things, till they all in their turn were replaced by more as beautiful. Perhaps it

40 —THE HALL AND STAIRCASE.

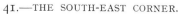

41.—THE SOUTH-EAST CORNER.

42.—DRAWING-ROOM FIREPLACE.

took a lifetime to fill the house worthily ; but it is precisely to this policy that we owe the lasting construction and decorative charm of the old furniture for which we compete to-day. The passion for filling a house immediately with complete suites of everything is partly responsible for the shoddy stuff that passes for Art furniture. There is at least comfort in the knowledge that posterity will have little opportunity to gird at us for our folly in acquiring such things, for time and use will resolve them into their original number of pieces before they can give evidence against us. The love of possession is not in itself an evil, provided that the aim is for quality and not for quantity. Great merit in furniture must always be sought in hand-made work, and there is a plenty of fine modern furniture to be bought if people will pay for it. Machine-made things may be, and often are, admirable, but it becomes an absurdity when a scrap of carving here and a patch of inlay there makes them masquerade as the work of a live craftsman. It is a good plan, therefore, to begin by acquiring (if funds are limited) plain, unornamented furniture, void both of offence and pretence, and gradually to replace it, as the exchequer allows, with examples, whether of fine modern work or of genuine old work, but all the best of their kind. Above all, the policy is to have nothing that is not actually needed. Once more to quote Thoreau, " at the present our houses are cluttered with furniture, and a good housewife would soon sweep out the greater part into the dust-hole and not leave her morning's work undone." This is as true to-day of England as it was of Concord in the eighteen-forties, and it is, therefore, with pleasure that one visits such a place as Bengeo House, where the furniture is aptly chosen and throws into relief, instead of smothering, the proportions of the rooms.

SUNNYMEAD, WADHURST.

DESIGNED BY MR. FRANK CHESTERTON.

The Planning of an Invalid's House—Ground Floor Bedrooms—The Cost of Building.

PERHAPS the most interesting thing about Sunnymead is its unusual ground-floor plan. Though designed, happily not for an invalid, but for a man with a liking for a downstairs bedroom which opens on to a loggia, it would be an ideal arrangement for an owner in ill-health, and may be considered in that light. The main feature of its arrangement is the little suite facing south. The ground floor bedroom is entered from the hall, but has another door to an inner and parallel passage, from which open a room that would serve for a sick-nurse, the bathroom, etc. In the event of open-air treatment being desirable, what more easy than to wheel a bed from the main bedroom through its folding doors into the loggia ? The latter also communicates with the sitting-room, which has its fireplace in an ingle. The room adjoining the kitchen is used by the present owner of Sunnymead as a study, but (still assuming a permanent invalid) it would serve as a housekeeper's or nurse's sitting-room. The kitchen quarters are good, save for the larder, which is windowed to the west instead of to the north, as is the better practice. Upstairs there are four bedrooms and usual offices. The house is

43.—THE ENTRANCE FRONT.

very solidly built, but despite the use of Dutch bricks, Mr. Chesterton succeeded in keeping the cost down to one thousand two hundred and fifty pounds, representing the very low price of sixpence a cubic foot. This economic achievement is, doubtless, due in part to the simplicity of the fireplaces and other fittings ; but when that is discounted, the success is none the less real. Moreover, the lowest tender for the building was set aside in favour of another and higher one, and presumably, therefore, the contract price was fair and reasonable for the work done.

44.—FROM THE WEST.

The question as to how far cubic foot prices are of value has been discussed in the Introduction and need not be restated here. This method of calculating comparative costs is of importance, however, in

45.—THE SOUTH FRONT.

46.—THE LOGGIA.

emphasising the all-important truth that sound and artistic building does not necessarily mean costly building. The oft repetition of old saws, however untrue they may be, drives their false doctrine into people's minds all too surely. Thomas Fuller cannot be held guiltless, for this is how he instructed his friends in the seventeenth century : " In building rather believe any man than an artificer. . . . Should they tell thee all the cost at the first, it would blast a young builder at the budding. . . . The spirit of building first possessed people after the flood, which then caused the confusion of languages. . . ." So much for

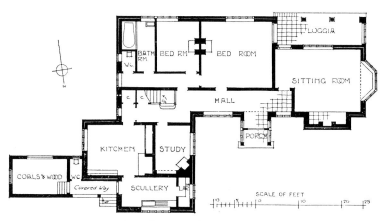

47.—GROUND FLOOR PLAN.

" The Marvellous Wisdom and Quaint Conceits of Thomas Fuller." The figures given throughout this book, however, may do something to stop the dreamer of house-building dreams from being " blasted at the budding."

But the exterior of Sunnymead claims attention. The entrance front is approached by a short drive, and we are impressed by the solid simplicity of its treatment. The chimney-stacks are massive, and, in particular, that to the right of the porch has an added size from its being raised on the sitting-room ingle. The porch is adequate, and the inner half of it goes to enlarge the hall, a neat point in planning. The bricks came from Holland, and are nine inches long for the main walls and seven inches for the chimneys, a well-chosen variation. Here and there tiles are built into the walls, not, as too often happens, as a fad, but in odd corners where it was normal to use them, because it saved the special cutting of bricks. The house groups well from all points, and gains gravity from its unbroken roof-line. The half-timbered gable on the south front is genuine timber-work, with filling a single brick thick, not a wall with oak on its face. The exterior woodwork is all in oak which has weathered to a fine silvery hue. The paths about the house are paved with irregular slabs of local stone, pleasantly water-worn Altogether, in the scale of the dormer windows, in the reasonableness of the bay that looks westwards and in the carefully thought-out massing of simple elements and play of natural textures Mr. Frank Chesterton has created an interesting house on sound traditional lines at a cost that does him infinite credit.

48.—PORCH AND CHIMNEY.

THE COBBLES, WALTON HEATH.

DESIGNED BY MR. L. STANLEY CROSBIE.

Thoreau on House-building—The Size of Verandahs—The Treatment of an Ingle.

THERE is a peculiar charm in what Thoreau has to say about house-building, for he had a knack of getting at the root of things. "There is some of the same fitness in a man building his own house that there is in a bird's building its own nest. Who knows but if men constructed their dwellings with their own hands, and provided food for themselves and families honestly enough, the poetic faculty would be universally developed, as birds universally sing when they are so engaged? . . . Shall we for ever resign the pleasure of construction to the carpenter?" We need not take Thoreau too seriously; but that he was honest with himself is clear from his record of the house he built for his own habitation at the cost of twenty-eight dollars twelve and a-half cents, and "Walden" deserves to be read if only for this story. Mr. Crosbie's problem in building The Cobbles was one that confronts many scores of architects to-day—to give to a house of small cost (it was built for seven hundred and fifty pounds, and at sevenpence a cubic foot) something of character without straining after effect.

49.—THE SOUTH FRONT.

He has succeeded, and though criticism finds its work to do, there is much that shows thought and taste. The verandah is the feature to which some small exception may reasonably be taken. It is only six feet wide and, therefore, too narrow to accommodate a table for any outdoor meal except afternoon tea. It is, on the other hand, forty-one feet long and, regarded as a shelter for those who watch a game of tennis on the lawn, unnecessarily spacious. In practice a verandah is not useful for the larger meals unless it is at the very least eight feet wide, and ten feet is a better minimum. If the verandah at The Cobbles had occupied only the central third of its present length, leaving the two outer thirds to be thrown into the nursery and living-room respectively, sufficient outdoor space would have been left for all ordinary purposes except the larger meals, and the floor area of the rooms by so much increased. On the other hand, there must be stated the arguments for a narrow verandah. In the winter, when the sun is low in its travels, the light is not greatly impeded, while in the summer the shelter afforded to the south rooms makes for coolness and pleasant shadow. On general principles, however, it seems better to provide a verandah or loggia with a short frontage and running back about ten feet, taking care to light the room which it adjoins by another window facing either the same aspect or another, as the rest of the plan may

36

determine. In other respects the house is admirable. All the living-rooms on both floors face the south, save only the study, which looks to the north, and so secures the most satisfactory light for writing and drawing. This avoidance of all but south aspects necessitates a long, narrow plan, and gives opportunities for architectural treatment which are more fruitful than with a more compact arrangement. It makes possible, for example, the three pleasant gables on the garden front. In such simple little houses as this it is only in the broad outlines of the building that any effect can be produced. Ornament and the richer sorts of craftsmanship are barred by considerations of cost, and reliance must be placed on right proportions, colours and textures. The roof is an important feature, and is very pleasant in its covering of old tiles. So uneven were they that it was thought well to bed them in mortar, even though that meant some strengthening of the roof timbers. The tile-hanging on the garden front is of a deep red, which accords well with the roof, and the brick walls are rough-cast. It is possible to get tired of this latter treatment, and for large and important buildings it is being less used now than a few years ago. It has, however, large practical advantages. Where cost dictates that the walls shall be as thin as is consistent with sound construction, it is almost essential for exposed aspects that the brickwork shall have its resistance against

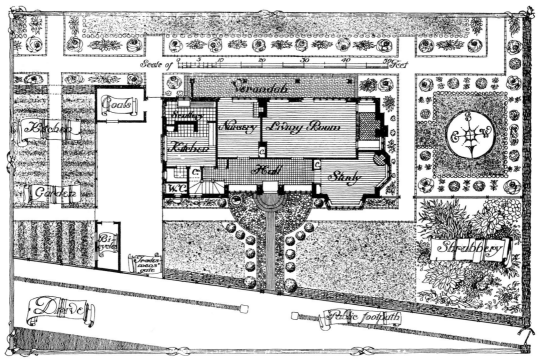

50.—GROUND PLAN.

rain strengthened by the protective coat afforded by rough-casting. Moreover, some colour contrast is desirable. In a large building, where, perhaps, porch and window dressings are of stone, the red in roof and walls finds thus relief and lightening. In a small house built all of red materials there is apt to be a hint of undue sameness. Internally, despite economies, there are touches of interest. The hall has a barrel-shaped ceiling, which veils the fact that it is partly in the roof. In the sitting-room some Dutch panels of oak, surround the fireplace, and the two slim columns of the ingle will be recognised as *ci-devant* bedposts. They seem a little thin, and something stouter would have been better. The ingle is a step higher than the rest of the room. This separates it as a sitting-place, but it is a feature of doubtful wisdom where there are little ones to trip and fall. It has, however, the advantage that the seats are wide close to the fire.

The staircase and upstairs passage are very well planned to absorb the minimum of room, while every odd cubic foot of space is utilised for cupboards. The four bedrooms and bathroom are necessarily small and partly in the roof, but light and airy. Here, then is a house which shows that, if Mr. Crosbie has, in Thoreau's words, " resigned the pleasure of construction to the carpenter," he has devised a home which has grown out of his " necessities and character." It shows him skilful in conceiving economies and happy in stamping his own home with an artistic quality which is as agreeable as are all those things which are not the result of straining after effect.

37

51.—THE LIVING-ROOM.

52.—THE ENTRANCE FRONT.

COLDICOTE, MORETON-IN-MARSH.

DESIGNED BY MR. E. GUY DAWBER.

*The Cotswold Traditions of Building—The Craft of the Mason—Stone Slating—
The Home of a Hunting-man.*

COLDICOTE is typical of the earnest cleavage to old traditions of building which is characteristic of the work of Mr. Guy Dawber. In a parliament of architecture none would have a better claim than he to sit as member for the Cotswolds. He has been a sedulous student of what is perhaps the most attractive manner of stone-building that England affords. There is an air of artless simplicity about these old manor houses and cottages that might tempt the casual observer to the belief that there is little to learn about their making. Two or three gables and a bay, plain square chimneys, a stone panel or two, and simple porchless doors —these are the ingredients. The minor arts are but slightly represented. Eaves, gutters and down-pipes are unknown save on the greater houses. Here was no outlet for the cunning craftsmanship of the leadworker, who not only at Knole and Haddon, but on many a cottage in other districts, set up pipe-heads which, gilt and painted, bejewelled fronts that were otherwise austere. The men who set their homes on these rolling hills were simple and straightforward masons, but that is not to say their art was meagre in invention. Nature, who yielded them rich store of stone from so many village quarries, was diverse in her gifts. The various strata of the lime-stone belt which reaches from the Dorset to the Yorkshire coasts comprise all the oolites and provide nearly all the build-ing limestones used in England. At some levels in the Cotswolds the stone comes out in great blocks, at others in rough shards, and a few rich pits yield the laminated sheets which go to make the slate roofs. These differences affect profoundly the nature of building from village to village, and bring a sense of infinite variety and charm. Tudor House, Broadway, for example, was built in the richest manner of the mason in coursed ashlar, with a finished surface. In other houses the stones would still be coursed, but in rubble, and with face left rough. In humbler homes they were laid at random as they came to the mason's hand. In a neighbouring district the thin, slate-like layers of stone, when used for wall-building, would produce yet another technique. In Northamp-tonshire the chances of variety afforded by the presence also of red ironstone suggested its alternation with bands of limestone; in fact, the possibilities

53.—THE PORCH.

54.—ENTRANCE GATE AND LODGE.

55.—FROM THE SOUTH-EAST.

are almost endless. The pictures of Coldicote show that Mr. Dawber has adopted coursed rubble as the most suitable treatment for the thin layers in which the local quarries, only two or three miles away, provide the stone. It is built without any dressing or cutting beyond what is needful to make the pieces roughly rectangular. By this means, and by raking out the joints deeply when the mortar is partially dry, a quality of surface and a texture are secured which not only suit the material but are of the essence of the local traditions. No dressed stone is to be seen anywhere but on the porch, which very properly is reserved for this dignity of finer workmanship. All angles and window dressings are in ordinary walling stone, but emphasised by the use of larger blocks. The chimneys are built in brick for reasons economical. Ashlar was ruled

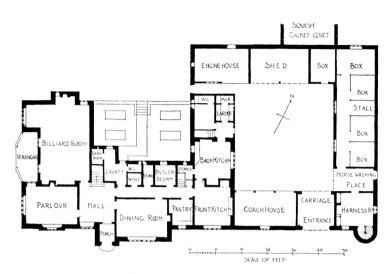

56.—GROUND FLOOR PLAN.

out on the score of expense, and rubble would have meant stacks disproportionately large. The treatment of the roof demands notice. The radical difference between the old Cotswold stone slates and the hard, blue Welsh slating to which modern builders have accustomed our unwilling eyes is in the rough texture of the elder work. Of late years there has been a tendency to forget the merits and possibilities of stone slates by splitting them too thin and too smooth, and by cutting their bottom edge neatly and accurately. This passion for fussy exactness destroys their chief charm, and it is refreshing to see with what success the older manner has been followed at Coldicote. There is no affectation or pretence, no attempt to imitate an old roof by copying the defects which the battery of Time inflicts. The material is used simply as it comes from the Eyford quarries, without wasting labour in reducing it to a mechanical precision which not only destroys its interest but means extra cost. It is supposed by some that care in building in the vernacular manner proper to any district involves costly workmanship. The precise contrary is generally the fact, for the unnatural finish of materials not only gives them necessarily a dreary air, but often involves utterly misplaced and expensive labour.

The plan of Coldicote is interesting by reason of its compact and self-contained character. A demure lodge guards the entrance to the drive. The entrance front of the house is a little east of south, and

57.—THE ENTRANCE FRONT.

58.—THE SOUTH-WEST FRONT.

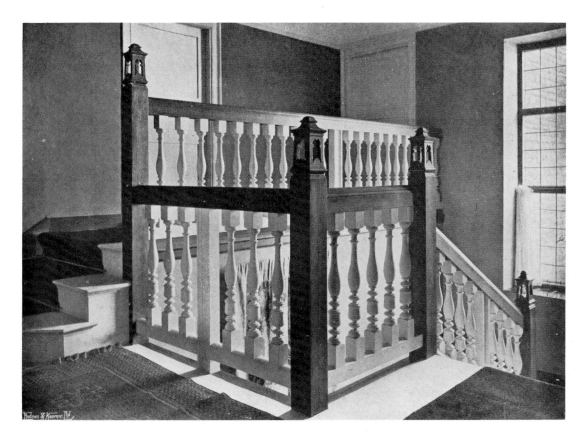

59.—THE FIRST FLOOR LANDING.

shows a long range of building. To the right is an archway to the stable-yard, flanked by a tower-like projection, and to the left the drive leads us to the main entrance. The hall is small but adequate, with the dining-room to the right and a parlour to the left. The billiard-room, however, is the main living-room, for it has a pleasant bay looking to the south-west and doors to a good verandah, while the fireplace is set in a comfortable ingle. As the room is over thirty feet long, there is ample sitting space after allowing for the billiard-table. Upstairs the bedrooms are spacious and pleasant, and an excellent feature has been made of the first-floor landing. Everywhere the construction of the house is solidly comfortable, and despite the abundant use of oak for floors, a pretty painted ceiling in the billiard-room, and modelled plaster-work in the dining-room, the cost of the house worked out at no more than ninepence per cubic foot. Masonry is ordinarily much dearer than brickwork, but Coldicote shows that, in capable hands and given good local conditions, it can be as cheap.

The house reveals by its general scheme the tastes of its owner. For a family consisting of three only the bedroom accommodation can be limited and the general plan simple; but in the home of a hunting-man the stable court must be well equipped. The latter is entered through the archway already noted, the gates of which can be locked. As it is entirely enclosed by buildings, it is sheltered from cold winds and safe from marauders. On three sides of it are the coachhouse, harness-room, loose boxes, garage and the engine-room, where electricity is generated for lighting and pumping. The kitchen quarters form its south-western side, and everything is accessible from the house and under immediate control. While the coachman and gardener live in the entrance lodge, there is a messroom and a man's bedroom in the stable block, so that someone may always be on the spot to attend to the horses. Nor has Mr. Dawber forgotten the unhappy lot of a sportsman prevented by frost from keeping fit in his accustomed way. On the north side of the stable block is a roofed squash-racquet court, which serves also in part to wall the garden and to protect it from the east wind. Here in wet weather or in frost is strenuous exercise to be had, and it serves also as a tea-room when outdoor entertainments are afoot.

Perhaps in nothing does thoughtless architecture so readily stand condemned as in its back elevations, when they are mean and fail to carry on the fair promise of the front. In old Cotswold houses there are no backs (in the sense of the old oft-quoted gibe about Queen Anne fronts and Mary Ann backs), and at Coldicote this good tradition has been faithfully followed. Coldicote might say of itself, as Abraham Cowley made old Somerset House speak when Henrietta Maria restored its shattered beauties after the Restoration.

As in kings we see
The liveliest image of the Deity,
We in their houses should Heaven's likeness find
Where nothing can be said to be behind.

It is a long and rather pompous way of putting a sound bit of architectural criticism, but it is abundantly true of Mr. Dawber's houses, that " nothing can be said to be behind." Coldicote can be surveyed with pleasure from every point of view.

ELM TREE COTTAGE, FARNHAM.

DESIGNED BY MR. HAROLD FALKNER.

A Convenient Plan—An Old Farnham Industry, Tile Making.

THE problem of the very inexpensive little country home is of perennial interest, and Elm Tree Cottage is an example of its solution which is commendable if not free from criticism. The plan shows both skill and thought. Because it was desirable to reserve the maximum of the frontage facing south for living-rooms, the entrance door has been put at the north-west corner away from the road front. In a house of such small dimensions it is best to utilise the minimum of space for the hall, and Mr. Falkner has contrived to do with only seven feet by four feet. This involves the entry of the study through the living-room, but that is a small disadvantage to set against the saving in passage-way. A very convenient feature is the dark room opening out of the study. The drawing-room is of good size with a bay window to the west and a little loggia, nine feet by four feet six inches. The latter just gives room for two people to sit down to tea, but it is a tight fit. As a door to the garden from the drawing-room is a valuable feature, and it is difficult to make such a door weather-tight unless it is roofed in some way, the loggia is justified. The corresponding projection at the east end roofs the cycle-room. A rather disturbing little break is made in the roof-line by the projection of the first-floor bay; but the amenities of the room are greatly bettered by the increased space and outlook it affords. The north front is happier in its design, but the triangular patch of tiling which forms the porch breaks up the roof. Had the slope of the latter been continued and the corner sup-

60.—SOUTH FRONT.

ported by a plain post, the effect would have been simpler and space for a good roof-cupboard secured in the west bedroom, but the porch would have been unduly lofty.

That Elm Tree Cottage has excellent features is clear when it is noted that it was built at the unusually low figure of fivepence per cubic foot. This is a very ordinary cost for workmen's cottages; but Mr. Falkner has contrived by economical planning and construction to find money for artistic albeit simple joinery and for good fittings. In the living-room, for example, is a well-designed barless fire, of make by no means inexpensive, and an oak mantel-piece. It is only by taking considerable thought that buildings like this can be cheapened and yet be structurally sound. Windows and doors must be made each in, say, two sizes only. The habits of the local builder need to be considered and his suggestions for small economies given a sympathetic hearing. The green hearth-tiles in the living-room deserve more than mere mention.

Of late years there has been a successful and, it must be admitted, a justified invasion of England by Dutch tiles, not only of the figured type, where slight sketches in blue of *genre* subjects, windmills, etc., are seen on a white ground, but of the glazed tiles in plain colours. The success of this importation was due to the fact that the tiles were inexpensive and hand-made, and showed a richness of colour and vitality in their surface which had almost died out in England owing to the abandonment of hand-making for the all-conquering

61.—NORTH FRONT AND ENTRANCE.

machine. The latter turned out a product of perfect smoothness and accuracy of size, which was highly respectable and totally lacking in interest. It was cheap, and had every demerit possible to tiles. The

62.—LIVING-ROOM FIREPLACE.

Dutch tile which largely supplanted it in the affections of architects has a surface mechanically imperfect, and for this very reason delightful. It had no affectations of antiquity, such as have made the very word "antique" of ill omen. By its depth of colour and by the reflections which played elusively over the uneven surface of its brilliant glaze, it brought back to remembrance the natural beauties of old pottery, which the dull regularity of the machine-made tile had well-nigh caused to be forgotten. Happily, English manufacturers have not lagged for many years behind their Dutch *confrères*, and it is now possible to get hand-made glazed tiles which are equal to the foreign product. The interest of the green glazed ware at Elm Tree Cottage is due, however, to the fact that it is of local production, and that its making has been carried on at Farnham, with some long intermissions, from the sixteenth century unto this day. On August 19th, 1594, Sir Julius Cæsar, Treasurer of the Inner Temple, wrote to Sir William More, Constable of Farnham Castle (the See of Winchester then being vacant). He asked that the bearer of his letter might have liberty, as in times past, to dig, out of Farnham Park, "certaine white cley for the making of grene pottes, usually drunk in by the gentlemen of the Temple." It does not appear from this whether the clay was turned into "grene pottes" at Farnham or elsewhere, and there is nothing by which they can now be identified, for they were doubtless of the ordinary late mediæval type. When Farnham pottery began again to be made, greens were not attempted; in 1886 there came an order to copy some French green glazed vases which had partly perished from the severity of English winters. Much experiment was needed before a glaze could be devised to suit the local " body," but the difficulties were eventually overcome. All colours of glaze are now employed on Farnham ware and a mediæval craft has come into its own again. The old claypits in Farnham Park have long been closed, and the clay now used is so different that new colours and glazes had to be devised The old method was to sprinkle copper or brass filings on the ware, after it was glazed but before firing. It is unfortunate that when a kiln, probably of Roman times, was recently discovered near Farnham during the excavation of some foundations, no fragments were found to prove

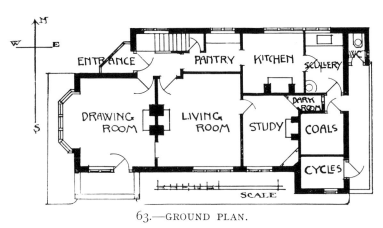

63.—GROUND PLAN.

that the same tradition went back fifteen hundred years even before the gentlemen of the Temple were so concerned about the continuing supply of their green pots. This is a diversion from Elm Tree Cottage, but not a useless one if it draws attention to the continuity of the lesser building arts and

64.---FROM DRAWING-ROOM TO GARDEN.

to the way these are woven into the mesh of English history. And so, to sum up, this little place may be set down as one very interesting solution of the problem of how may be provided three sitting rooms, kitchen offices, four bedrooms and bath room at a low cost. The exact figure is not ascertainable; but another cottage which Mr Falkner has designed near by, of practically the same plan but eight feet longer, cost five hundred and thirty pounds, inclusive of drainage and water supply.

SOUTH HILL, HOOK HEATH, WOKING.

DESIGNED BY MR. HORACE FIELD.

Felicity in Building—Thomas Swift on Surrey—A True Cottage—Conceits in Thatch—Simplicity Without Roughness.

T HE dictum of Sir Joshua Reynolds that art comes " by a kind of felicity and not by rule " is never more true than when it explains such an engaging thing as Mr. Horace Field's cottage. One is more ready to associate his name with work of a graver sort, where ordered forms and conscious rhythms play their own very excellent part. A thatched cottage built at the foot of a sharp slope, which is approached down a path so steep that from the gate one expects almost to touch the chimneys, demands, however, only the felicitous touch that gives simple grouping and pleasant outlines. Any formality in the elevation, any nice balancing of solids and voids, would be hopelessly defeated, save on the terrace front, by the wayward points of view which alone are possible to the observer.

Hook Heath is almost due west of Woking Village, and forms part of the higher ground which runs in a south-westerly direction from Maybury Hill to Pirbright Common. Although the elevation above sea-level is not very considerable, these rolling moorlands, with their sandy soil, heather grown, give a fine feeling of freedom and expanse, while the air is keen with the scent of pine trees. When the cousin of Dean Swift was a Surrey village parson at Puttenham, not many miles from Hook Heath, his enthusiasm for his home made him write it down " so healthy, as to deserve such a remark as the best pen could give it." Thomas Swift did not possess the literary gifts of Jonathan, but he was somewhat of a prophet. " Such is the salubrity of its air, as did those wealthy citizens

65.—THE WEST FRONT.

know it, who want nothing so much as health, I might say . . . that they would come and make a city here." Time has shown that this knowledge has come not only to wealthy citizens, but to many who are content in simple homes to enjoy the delights of Surrey heaths as well at Woking as at Puttenham, and in vastly greater numbers.

The photographs show how attractive is the situation of this cottage, which is indeed a cottage. Looking from the terrace front, one sees that the building is wholly protected from the north and north-east winds and almost entirely from the east by the hill and a generous grouping of trees. To the south and west the ground slopes away gently, giving opportunity for wide terracing, and affords a view across a large expanse

66.—THE GARDEN FRONT.

67.—FROM THE NORTH-EAST.

of well-timbered plain. Looking down from the garden gate, which is reached by a leafy lane from the heath, the full charm of fine thatching is apparent, and we note the pleasant conceits that are the prerogative of that ancient craft. At the points of the gables are plaited crowns, and on the ridge of the eastern dormer roof perches a peacock in straw, a quite convincing bird. There is a good deal of complaint made that thatching is becoming a lost art; but with such a recent example before us there is no need for undue pessimism. It should be noted, moreover, that these imaginations in straw are not a product of the drawing-board, but the spontaneous expression of the thatcher's pleasure in his work. It all looks very simple, the thick rich covering and the pleasing lines of the plaits that tie down the mass; but few are aware of the arduous work it entails. Many young men who are apprenticed to this work abandon it owing to its very tiring nature, and, indeed, it requires no small strength and resolution to do a day's work at it, especially in the sun. Mr. Field has not been afraid to vary his roofing materials, and has thereby avoided any sense of undue emphasis. The bay window on the north and the door-hood on the east are leaded, and the contrast between thatch and lead is very satisfactory. As we reach the bottom of the steep path we come between the cottage and the rose garden. The latter is prettily trellised, and the chains from post to post seek the invasion of ramblers, while a joyful little garden

68.—LOOKING NORTHWARDS.

god presides within on a sturdy pedestal. The door-hood is extended to the right to shelter a little paved space where one may sit and regard the roses. Above the door Mr. Aumonier has carved amid a trail of conventional leaves the pious legend:

Enter, dear Lord, mine house with me,
Until I enter Thine with Thee.

We go into a tiny hall, and its picture is worthy consideration because it points a notable moral. It is too much the habit in the architecture of cottages intended as the homes of cultivated folk to assume that simplicity must find its expression in rough brickwork and in coarse-hewn timbers. Time has tempered in old cottages the rawness of finish which came from lack of finer materials and ignorance of more genial methods. Refinement is, however, as needful an atmosphere in a cottage as in a palace, but it must be obtained by studiously simple means. The gracious severity of the two unmoulded arches and the judgment which used the slight recess as background for the enchanting little figure of Narcissus (from the original in the Naples Museum) make an appeal to our taste as immediate as it is inevitable. One may go far before seeing a treatment so satisfactory and so much in the spirit of cottage architecture, yet informed by scholarship. The floor is of red tiles, waxed to a rich finish. Opposite the staircase is a parlour, and facing the front door the big sitting-room. The west windows of the latter are high up, with bookshelves under, and between them is the door, which leads down two steps to Mr Field's study. This room takes the place of a verandah which was first designed,

69.—TRELLIS AND ROSES.

but it gives no idea of after-thought. Its little roof and chimney group to admiration with the main part of the cottage. As becomes its use, nearly half its wall space is taken by windows which look both westwards and southwards down a miniature avenue to the garden beyond. The garden door is placed in the passage between the study and sitting-room. The kitchen quarters are well arranged. As there are but three bedrooms upstairs, the maid's room is on the ground floor. From the kitchen there open the pantry and scullery, while the larder, with its north light, is entered from the latter. Throughout the interior one has the pleased sense that the furniture is exactly right for the cottage. There is no affectation of simplicity, but simplicity itself. The view of the west front from the garden is particularly attractive. As the bedrooms are all partly in the roof, there was an excellent opportunity for varying treatment of the thatch, which is carried over a little rough-cast gable in the middle and trimmed over dormers on each side. The brickwork is everywhere (except in the case of the little building which

70.—THE HALL.

contains the study) rough-cast and finished with a wash which has a hint of warmth in it. Nature has helped Mr. Field with the garden, which has its own note of quiet formality, heightened by the judicious use of treillage. The soil is sandy, for the site is neighbour to the heath, and wallflowers, Canterbury bells and dahlias each in their season take to such a home with a profusion almost riotous. Roses are successful; but that, no doubt, is due more to the skill which tends them than to the inherent qualities of the soil.

The homes which architects build for themselves are always of interest, because they represent the designer's mind unhampered by the special desires of clients, who sometimes are less knowledgeable than determined. One may go far, however, before finding a cottage which is so truly unaffected and charming, and where the graces of simple comfort sit so naturally, as in this little place that Mr. Horace Field has made as a refuge for quiet work tempered with golf.

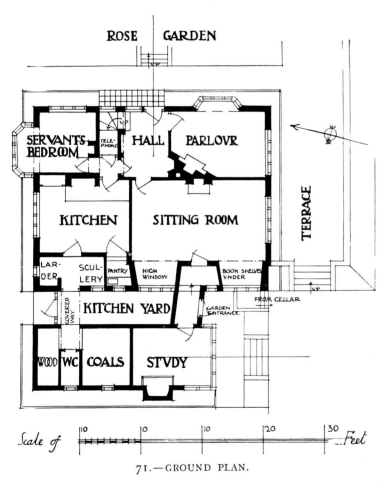

71.—GROUND PLAN.

A HOUSE AT SAPPERTON.

DESIGNED BY MR. ERNEST GIMSON.

*Autobiography in Building—Robert Kerr on " The Gentleman's House"—The Value of Simplicity.—
A Triumph of the Thatcher's Craft—Cotswold Masonry.*

MR. GIMSON'S home near Daneway, but in Sapperton parish, is another case of an architect building
for his own use, a circumstance advantageous to the result, which becomes the direct
interpretation of an idea. A thoughtful designer does not agree with Talleyrand that words
are given to disguise thoughts ; he conceives, rather, that not only words but even stone and
wood are his for the accurate and direct expression of thought, and he therefore uses his
professional experience to make every part of his house in accord with his mind. Such houses may
therefore be treated as if they were an autobiographical volume in which one may read their designers as
men with personalities, with decided aims, social and æsthetic, and with vigour of mind and body to
pursue them successfully. The text of " plain living and high thinking " has been taken for sermons
many in number and great in diversity. It is the corner-stone of this house at Sapperton, which rests

72.—THE WAY IN FROM THE LANE.

on it securely and truthfully; yet it equally fits many another and quite different superstructure. In this particular case simple habits and informed thought are to have an environment resulting from delicate æsthetic perception, and forming a dominating influence The house suggests that its designer's ideal must be that of the old, free village community, altered to suit an age of large organised masses and of wide humanitarian and intellectual intercourse. It seems to plead that there should be no extreme distinction of classes, no deep gulf between the mode of life of the highest and the lowest; but a pervading sympathy and neighbourliness of feeling, founded on a common intercourse in the various departments of labour in which all, in some one of its many forms, should be equally interested and engaged; and, above all, that those forms which are irksome and brutalising should be modified or abolished, for labour should be a delight and not a drudgery. Surely this house is "the material expression of its inmates' habits of life and turn of thought." It is severely restricted in its accommodation. Not only is no ornate feature introduced for the sake of ornament;

73.—THE GARDEN SIDE.

decoration is even absent from necessary features. But form and material, texture and colour have been so studied by an adequately trained eye that the whole thing is a joy-giving ornament to the charming spot of Earth selected for its site. It is amid "little glyns of difficult access," whose steep and twisting banks, clothed in timber, enclose the view and give a sense of privacy and retirement to a house which is really in close touch with Sapperton Village. Past its church and the spot where once stood its manor house, a lane horizontally bisects the hillside. At its end, and at the same pleasant mid-elevation, is spread out the cottage home, ample in its proportions and extent by reason of the sufficiency of its adjuncts—shedding and workroom, yard and terrace, garden wall and yew hedge. Though small, it is a complete settlement for a family, not a cube containing so many rooms set down gaunt and unsupported on a roadside plot. The designer has considered the general lie and also each special undulation of the land. He has used Nature's differences of level and peculiarities of curve to weld his homestead into the landscape composition and to give it purpose and distinction. The building stands at the top of its ground and looks down into the narrow vale.   Across a little raised forecourt we pass from the lane to the ample stone-tiled porch, which opens direct into what in old time would have been termed the house-place—the one and only sitting-room of the house.   It is amusing to contrast the mental attitude which has dictated this arrangement with that one more usual even now, and much more so fifty years ago, when Mr. Robert Kerr wrote his " Gentleman's House."   His favourite words are " propriety " and " impropriety."   To reach the former—even to understand how it is to be reached—is evidently a difficult task.   The latter meets you at every turn, and you are up to your neck in it if your little villa has not exactly the same disposition as the mansion " fit for the purposes of a man of rank."   Decent society will almost cut you if your kitchen doorway " exposes to the view of everyone the dresser or the cooking-range."   But the real test of a man's worth is his mode of going to his meals, which he should call " the act of proceeding to and from dinner." A doorway between dining and drawing rooms is a " grievous informality " which even an intervening lobby scarcely palliates, for " however small the house may be, to pass through a door of inter-communication or to slip out of one door and in at the other is always undignified."   What words, then, are there to express the case of a man who has positively abandoned " the act of proceeding to and from dinner " entirely ; who passes through no doorways at all, but merely moves from one chair to another in the same

74.—THE LiVING-ROOM.

room ?   Mr. Robert Kerr would have made short work of such doings.   " This is not a ' Gentleman's House ' at all," he would have explained, and he would have passed by on the other side in search of a " very superior house " where the drawing-room paper imitated white-watered silk, where the consoles of gilt composition imitated carving, and where the japanned iron coal-scuttle was adorned in front with a painted landscape and was called in the auctioneer's catalogue a " purdonium, liner and scoop."   There is, of course, no reason why a reaction from the horrors of a habitation planned, built and furnished under the inspiration of such principles should drive us as far along the road of simplicity as the house at Sapperton takes us.   Yet it is difficult to approach, enter and examine it without being pervaded by the feeling of its sufficiency, without realising that a single living-room may be a temple of elegance and refinement, while a " very superior house " may be a den of vulgarity and coarseness.   What component parts does the room possess to produce this feeling ?   A floor of exceptionally wide oak boards carefully selected for their grain and figure.   A white-washed ceiling divided into compartments by two oak beams, plainly chamfered and resting on stone corbels.   Low walls whose thickness is revealed by the recess of the mullioned windows giving depth for a seat.   A large open hearth containing logs that rest on wrought-iron andirons, while wrought-iron implements, perfectly simple and yet satisfying in design and craftsmanship, are set or hung around.   The book-filled recess and shelves imply the student, the spinet the musician.   There is practically nothing here which is not for use.   Not only is decoration totally absent from the fabric, it is scarcely represented by any of the objects in the room except the one bowl of flowers—proof of kinship with Nature, of intimacy with her profusely-given charms.   But this absence of ornamental superfluities produces no effect of conscious and militant Spartanism—no Trappist determination to mortify the flesh.   It merely gives full value and effect to the quality of the furniture and implements.   There is no elaboration or

75.—THE ANGLE OF THE HOUSE.

luxuriousness about them; they are almost austere. But they are all so right in their line and proportion, so finished in their handling and workmanship, that they fill in the picture, raise it out of the common and stamp it with character. The rest of the interior, kitchen and stairs, workshop and bedrooms, have the same merit and tell the same straightforward tale of their maker's purpose. Yet it is less the interior than the exterior of the house which arrests attention. This is partly because there is so much more of it. If the underlying principle demanded an interior which many might deem rather exiguous, the love of a free-handed use of material has created an exterior of considerable presence. The illustrations do it bare justice,

not because the photographer has at all failed in his art, but because the lie of the ground and the presence of trees interfere with the best points of view. The wing with its open shed resting on rough stone pillars, and having the workroom over it, gives a valuable extension to the building, which thus acquires an L shape, and the angle shelters the yard. The gable end of the living-room, standing above the garden slope, affords, with the tall, massive chimneys, the vertical lines which aptly break the general horizontal sense produced by the descent of the roof to a single storey height. This roof is an incomparable piece of thatching. The whole scheme and its every detail have been carefully thought out as a matter of design and grouping, while the actual laying, fixing and dressing of the straw manifest the high point which the art has reached in the thatcher's hands. The Cotswolds, with their natural yield of stone tiles, were, of course, never an exclusively thatched-roof district, as are so many parts of Devon, Dorset and Wilts. The real home of thatch is the down country, where cereal agriculture freely yielded what geology denied—a roofing material. Here, too, the thatch blends most perfectly with the landscape. The swelling outlines and suave hollows of the downs seem like the mighty model that was copied in the curves of the modest roofage of the habitations. But the Cotswolds were a wheat as well as a sheep growing region, and thatch was much used by the humbler folk, so that for a dwelling that aims at the expression of humility the roof of the cottage rather than that of the manor house is rightly adopted. Indeed, it would have been a real loss had this house lain in a place where its designer's correct sense of adopting local material would have forbidden the use

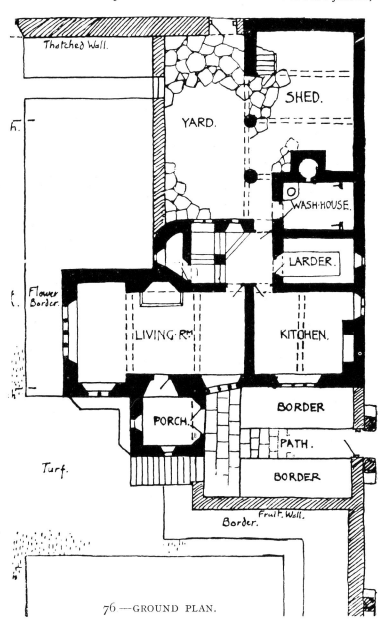

76 —GROUND PLAN.

of thatch. He has a full mastery over it arising out of his warm sympathy for it. He knows that to stint it is false economy, that, if dexterously wrought, thickness means duration as well as equable temperature within the dwelling. The straw has therefore been used with lavish hand, and its great depth at the eaves is most pleasant to see. But that is not all. From the thickness of this coating largely springs the excellence of all the roof curves. The quiet swell of the hoods over the dormer windows reminds us of a summer sea. They rise out of and fade back into the general lie of the roof imperceptibly, and yet they reach a considerable elevation at their highest point. The ample fold wrapping round the living-room chimney and pouring over the round-angled projection of the staircase again brings to mind the action of the main in its most friendly embrace of outlying rocks on the Cornish coast. The humping up of the central portion of the roof for the evident purpose of giving headroom in the attic, whose windows appear on each side of the ridge, is one of the many instances where advantage has been taken of a necessity to produce a desirable effect, while the weaving and pegging of the ridge gives a charming finish in the manner of a hem-stitched edge to sheeting or table-linen. A roof of such ampleness and substance, although not really as heavy as one of stone tiles, calls for solid-looking walls to satisfy the eye. The thickness of the walls and the massiveness of the masonry of the chimney-shafts may be precisely gauged by a glance at the ground plan, but the full sense of this is also given by their appearance as shown in the illustrations. The rubble stone of the walling looks like a slice out of a Cotswold quarry, and its use for the pillars of large diameter on which the wing roof rests completes the sense of adequate solidity. Where the windows are stone-mullioned, an ashlar of good grain and vein, not too smoothly finished, is used in a large manner. This comparative roughness of the masonry surfaces and the careful dressing of the thatch reveal a due sense of the value of texture. However great the thatcher's skill and finish, the straw will yield a surface of sufficient variety, and one on which light and shade will play a myriad of engaging pranks. But the mason's finishing tools must be used with judgment and withheld at the due moment. Here that judgment is rightly exercised and that moment is exactly caught. The care with which the external features and the general grouping have been thought out is well shown by the picture with the dovecote in the foreground, which forms the frontispiece of this book.

Need more be said to prove that the house is a success and that it was built by a man who knew quite well what he wanted and what effect he wished to produce, and has had the skill to realise it. There is nowhere the obtrusion of a good feature overdone, nowhere the jar of a bad one half hidden away. The whole is an *entente cordiale* between the utilitarian and the beautiful. There is no feature, no material, no workmanship that sets out to be ornamental, none that fails to be charming. The impression carried away is that the accommodation and the disposition desired were carried out in materials close at hand, and fell into the shape and assumed the appearance before us out of the sheer necessity of the case. It all looks as clear and simple as that two and two make four, and that is why it is a triumph. The road to success in the domain of art is apt to be through a very Slough of Despond. But it is the part of Art to hide the effort and the falterings of its footsteps and appear clean-footed and clear-browed at the goal of its endeavour. At Sapperton this has been done, and done without undue expense. In these days of processes and manufacture, when men's chief function is to turn a handle or stoke a fire, specialised handicrafts successfully exercised are apt, however simple the outcome, to be costly. But this house has been built at sevenpence per foot cube, and considering the amount and the quality of the material and workmanship and the special and individual characteristics of the work, this is encouragingly reasonable. It is not everybody's house. It is, in every sense, the home of its particular occupant, and that is its most priceless quality. But the general manner of it must warmly commend itself to all who look out, with intelligence, on to the problems of right living ; and the fact that building and furnishing of this kind may be seriously attempted by the man of moderate means for his necessary home, and not lightly played with by the millionaire for his occasional diversion, is a matter of wide and deep importance.

THE THREE GABLES, LETCHWORTH.

DESIGNED BY MR. CECIL H. HIGNETT.

The Disappointments of the First Garden City—Technique of Thatching—An Interesting Plan—The Problem of Small Gardens.

LETCHWORTH is a little disappointing. The name of " Garden City " calls forth the picture of a Terrestrial Paradise from which the Serpent, in the guise of the speculative builder, has been rigidly excluded But it would really appear that at Letchworth he has not merely glided in, but has been gladly received. There is a lot of very poor building at this first Garden City. The impression that anyone has been allowed to put anything anywhere is the first to be received. It is an impression which, fortunately, is afterwards somewhat modified. There has been a certain amount of town-planning —of rules and limitations as to building, of planting, road-making, spacing and general lay-out. More, perhaps, cannot have been expected of pioneers. Their experiment was venturesome, and this led to its being carried out in tentative manner, and with a good deal of submissiveness to the bad practices and sordid results which it was designed to correct. We must accept it as a step in advance, and not as the ultimate haven. That must be reached in the future by those who can mark the deficiencies but gain courage by the success of the premier undertaking. And there are successes to record. Such stalwarts as Mr. Baillie Scott and Mr. Geoffry Lucas, among others, have erected most pleasant little houses, while a great school commands real

77.—THE SOUTH FRONT AND THE GARDEN POOL.

respect by the dignified simplicity of its mass and the right proportion of its details. All these buildings entirely depend upon themselves for any amenity they possess. They have a very uninteresting setting that lacks trees and natural features. All around the station there is a large region that has this character. But there is something better to the south, and again to the north. Go a mile in the latter direction and you are among pleasant farm lands well clothed with giant elms in rows and groups. It is here that Mr. Cecil Hignett, rightly undeterred by the note of remoteness, or by the almost primeval condition of the track now called Croft Lane, pounced on a site for the charming thatched cottage he has built for his own occupation. Elms guard both the north and the east boundaries of his tiny domain, and it is between two of them that we find the wicket-gate and pass up the flagged way to the house. The characteristic of the elevation that faces us is the great sweep of roof descending unbroken from the ridge of the

78.—FROM THE NORTH-WEST.

79.—THE WAY IN.

58

house over the cycle shed and the porch. It is composed of fenland reeds and is fifteen inches thick. Nothing can be better than the craftsmanship of the men employed. Very often the sheer ability of thatchers is their worst snare. They are apt to be a little too anxious to exhibit their own cleverness and distress the eye with "ornamental thatching." They will put on layer after layer of reeds and shape the edge of each layer in various patterns. They are so pleased with their power over their material that they seek to give the sides of their dormers the straight appearance which they would have if carried out in slate or tile, and thus they lose the

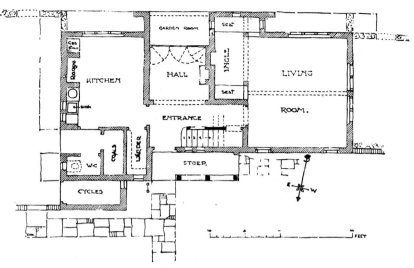

80.—GROUND PLAN.

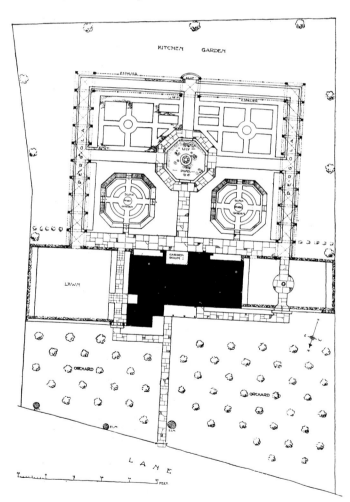

81.—GARDEN PLAN, SHOWING COMPLETE SCHEME, PART OF WHICH STILL REMAINS TO BE CARRIED OUT.

delightful curves and suave lines which are natural to thatch. Thanks to Mr. Hignett's supervision, nothing of this appears at The Three Gables. The ridge is neatly plaited, but is straight edged. There is no break in the roof-sweeps except the thoroughly easy and agreeable hipping at the gables and over the windows. The criticism might be made that there is a superfluity of upstairs windows, causing a restlessness of the roof-lines on the south side. Had there been no break except that of the central gable the effect would have been quieter, but the bedrooms would have lacked some of the abundant morning sunshine which they now enjoy. As now arranged, the bedroom over the living-room is so liberally windowed that, with the addition of door and chimney-piece, there is not much wall space left for bed and wardrobe; but for a sunny room one is ready to sacrifice something. He is captious, indeed, who has any other fault to find with this clever little dwelling. The plan is effective. Instead of squeezing in a drawing and a dining room, we find a large and picturesque living-room, and a hall and loggia, or garden-room. Each is rather small, but they may, in a moment, be thrown together to form one—an open-air room. The division between the two is composed of glazed doors, which fold back out of the way. A bench, which uses one of the doors as its back when the latter is closed, also folds away, and a perfectly adequate and convenient space to sit round a table for meals or work is provided. In such matters as the falling front of the coal-box, the top of which is a recessed seat, we get further examples of ingenuity, which

82.—THE HALL AS AN OPEN-AIR ROOM.

83.—THE LIVING-ROOM INGLE.

add much to the convenience of the cottage, and yet are carried out with such taste and reserve as to avoid all feeling of the complexity and mechanism of a ship's cabin. The illustration so well shows the hall and loggia thrown together that no further description is necessary. But a few points of detail should be noted. Red roof tiles have been aptly used in construction as a contrast of colour and texture to the rough-casting of the walls. They form corbels below the beam of the loggia opening and a drip course above it. The local pattern of tile is made to hang on its lath by three semi-circular teeth, and by placing this end of the upper tile of the drip course outwards (a device which one associates with Mr. Brierley), a slight ornamental value is given to this utilitarian detail. The windows are topped with the same arrangement. Tiles have also been freely used in constructing the fireplaces. That in the hall, where space was valuable, is a circle with a break in its ring of tiles at the bottom for the ash tray. The keystone projects upwards a long way so as to support a small shelf or bracket. The effect is not so thoroughly pleasing as that of the more extensive fireplace which runs right across the ingle in the living-room. In the centre is a large arch flanked by small ones, all carried out in roofing tiles, while paving tiles fill in the general face. These present the appearance of a diaper, such as old builders produced with cut flints and chalk. Red quarries are set up vertically, showing their face, and stability is given by filling the alternating spaces with half-a-dozen buff quarries laid horizontally,

84.—IN THE LIVING-ROOM.

and showing their ends. The general effect of colour and texture is very pleasing, although the designer is not quite satisfied that the crimson tone of the red tiles harmonises with the flame colour of the fire. The ingle is fitted with seats; that at the window end is long enough for use as a couch, and both seats are screened with a division which supplies bookshelf room, but has an aperture to see through. The general effect would have been quieter without the latter; there would have been more bookshelf room and the seats would have gained in seclusion and draughtlessness. The room has a beam and rafter ceiling. The rafters are whitened, but the beam is self-coloured. It is of elm, like most of the woodwork in the house. Elm is the local timber, and is therefore, rightly and representatively used. Its tendency to warp and wind, objectionable, no doubt, where high finish and classic perfection of line are needed, is no disadvantage where it is simply and massively used as in the present instance, while the tone and the grain are excellent. Well feathered and figured planks have been chosen for the panels behind the seats and in other conspicuous places, with good result. The furnishing of the room is apt. The gate-legged table, the rush-seated high-backed chairs, the fine oak dresser of Queen Anne type, liberally laden with a good collection of pewter, all help to make of this living-room a successfully realised conception. The same may be said of the rest of the house. The details are well thought out as parts of a general scheme. There is nothing cheap, in its evil sense, but nothing costly. The dwelling is a cottage and in nothing departs from the cottage spirit. The ledged elm doors, for instance, with T hinges stretching across the ledgers and with handles of good form but quite practical and inexpensive, are in no point other than one could wish or expect. Again, how neat and apt is the bedroom curtaining! The rods are of ashwood, the rings of bone and the curtain material is an indigo blue linen. The general effect of this in the whitewashed rooms is charming. But convenience has been fully as much considered as appearance. The kitchen is very fully fitted, and upstairs the bathroom leaves nothing to be desired; while the hot closet and linen cupboard arrangement next to it may well be envied by many housewives much more amply domiciled. The cost of the house was five hundred and thirty pounds, which works out at sixpence three farthings per cubic foot.

To the illustrations and plan of the house, a sketch of the garden scheme is added, because it offers a good example of an effective yet inexpensive lay-out. It affords considerable variety and interest, but is in scale with the size and character of the dwelling with which it is associated as a single composition. The area of the site is about a third of an acre. The house stands fifty feet back from the road, and the ground on this, the north side of the house, is planted as an orchard. East and west of the house are small lawns, but the real garden is on the south side. Here, centring with the garden-room, a parallelogram, eighty feet by sixty feet, has been taken, with pergolas as its east and west boundaries, while the south end has only low espaliers flanking its alley. In the middle of the scheme is an octagon lily pool with brick walls rising some two feet from the paved way that surrounds it. In the wall are four openings. As these might prove an attractive source of danger to the child that appears in one of the illustrations, wire protectors have been hooked on. The same octagon form is given to the little rose gardens that occupy the two quarters next to the house. For shelter as well as for effect they are sunk a couple of feet. The further quarters are laid out in beds cut out of the turf and dedicated to herbaceous plants. The work of garden-making has been mostly done by Mr. Hignett in his leisure hours. It has, therefore, been a source of much pleasure and little expense. Given a well-considered little design like this one, the difference of cost between carrying it out or having the featureless dulness of the usual villa plot is very trifling, but the difference in result is enormous. The Three Gables is a cottage, but, small though it be, it is a complete country home to be occupied with satisfaction to body and to mind.

THREE LITTLE HOUSES.

DESIGNED BY MR. P. MORLEY HORDER.

Thomas Fuller on Building Extravagance—The Doom of the " Desirable Villa "—Staircases and Halls—Compactness in Planning.

THOMAS FULLER is best known for his " History of the Worthies of England," but in another book, " The Holy State," he delivered himself of nine maxims " Of Building." The seventh may be quoted as a pleasant scrap of wisdom on the economics of domestic architecture in the seventeenth century : *" A house had better be too little for a day, than too great for a year :* And it is easier borrowing from thy neighbour a brace of chambers for the night, than a bag of money for a twelve-month. It is vain therefore, to proportion the receipt to an extraordinary occasion ; as those who by over-building their houses

85.—RHOSWYN COTTAGE : ENTRANCE FRONT.

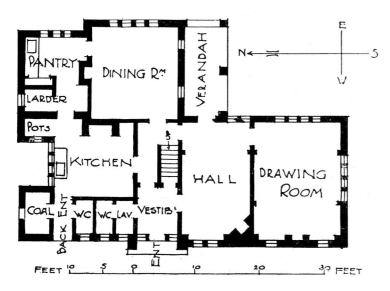

86.—GROUND PLAN OF RHOSWYN COTTAGE.

have dilapidated their lands, and their states have been pressed to death under the weight of their house." The judicious old cleric had doubtless pondered on the havoc wrought in Jacobean times by the craze for costly and ostentatious mansions. Not a few of the fortunes made by merchant venturers in the days of Elizabeth and her successor had been, as Fuller says, " pressed to death " by over-building. It is, perhaps, from those days that there sprang the notion that " Fools build houses for wise men to live in." However true that may be of a period of wild architectural extravagance, it is a proverb of crystallised stupidity to-day. Armed by its sanction, too many people abstain from building for themselves houses which would fit their taste and habits. It is an odd reflection, but out of ten men who would complacently purchase a ready-made house, it is unlikely that there would be one who would contemplate the buying of ready-made clothes. Yet the speculative builder flourishes exceedingly, and not only over the suburbs, but up and down the rural districts within reach of towns scatters his unlovely and thoughtless handiwork. It is not merely that clients connive at an æsthetic crime by encouraging the making of houses that affront the country-side and flout the building traditions of the locality, but in the long run it is expensive to the offenders.

It is safe to say that never was the smaller type of house better understood or more carefully designed than by the abler men of the present school of domestic architects. This will be readily agreed by those who read this book with care. The aspect of the question that is, perhaps, of most urgent interest is the economic one. It is obvious that many men abstain from building their own house for fear they are embarking on an amusement of uncertain costliness. They would rather commit themselves to the tender mercies of the purveyor of ready-made houses of which the cost is a known quantity. In this chapter are shown three typical houses, differing in treatment yet all characteristic of their designer, which have been built at prices much below the average cost of the ready made "desirable villa." That a man's house be different from his neighbour's is surely much to be desired ; it is more—it is inevitable if the architect be equipped both with capacity and a good conscience. Every site, even if it offers only a fifty-foot frontage to a suburban road, sets up its own conditions, and the variety of plan seems inexhaustible. Some line of view towards distant country, an old tree that one would not sacrifice, or the contour of the ground, suggests some new arrangement. Individuality may often be won by breaking away from the absurd idea that the house must be built up to the frontage-line of the road. There is no virtue in the notion, too widely accepted, that the "Chambers of Delight" (as an old book on building pleasantly calls the reception-rooms) should be in the front when the aspect calls loudly for the reverse arrangement. In the interior planning of a small house it is generally a mistake to try to turn the staircase into an architectural feature. With nothing has

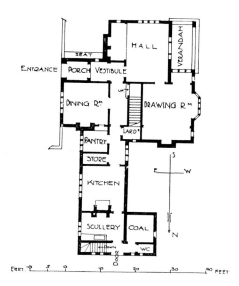

87.—GROUND PLAN OF THE CROFT.

Mr. Morley Horder been more skilful, in the three little houses now illustrated, than the way in which he has maintained the privacy of the hall as a living-room instead of confusing it with the staircase. The least expensive of the three, Rhoswyn Cottage, Gerrard's Cross, shall first be described. The cost of this simple and dignified little home was but seven hundred and twenty pounds, inclusive of fencing and of the brick path which makes so pleasant a feature of the entrance front. To secure a house with three

88 —THE CROFT, CHESHAM : ENTRANCE FRONT.

89.—LANE END: GARDEN FRONT.

90.—LANE END: HALL LOOKING INTO DRAWING-ROOM.

sitting-rooms and four bedrooms of good size (the drawing-room is eighteen feet six inches by thirteen feet six inches) it was necessary to devise a plan of peculiar compactness, so that every cubic foot of space served a purpose. Where one servant is employed and back stairs are, for every reason, impossible, the staircase must be arranged so that it gives access privately to the upper floor and takes up little space. Mr. Morley Horder has placed it in ordinary cottage fashion, between partition walls. Incidentally, there is no need for expensive stair carpet, as the stairs are hardly visible from any point, yet they are readily accessible both from the hall and kitchen quarters. The arrangement of the latter with respect to the dining-room is very neat. Serving is done from the kitchen through the pantry, where the mistress of the house can supervise china and the like and have her store cupboard. To save space, the usual scullery is omitted, but a recess for pots and pans preserves the comfort of the kitchen, where an admirable sink is provided. To reduce labour, the whole of the ground floor is laid with plain red tiles, save in the dining and drawing rooms. Both the latter have windows to the south as well as to the east, and a pleasant verandah faces both aspects.

What then is the explanation of the low cost, seeing that all usual comforts are provided ? Economy has been sought and found in every way. Externally there is an absolute simplicity of wall and roofing. The verges, etc., are all in plain tiles, and one notes the absence of external woodwork except in doors and windows, with a consequent low cost of upkeep. The fireplaces are ingeniously arranged so that only two chimney-stacks are needed, but the latter are built solidly and form outstanding features in the sober grouping of simple elements. The walls are hollow, built of local many-coloured bricks and the roofing is of dark handmade tiles. Internally the walls are distempered one colour throughout and the woodwork treated with a creosote stain and wax polished. Where hard woods

91.—LANE END : NORTH FRONT.

such as oak are denied for reasons economical, this treatment is sound and needs no upkeep. The cost of the house works out at less than sixpence per cube foot, a fair standard for a workman's cottage, yet none can deny that the house is refined and individual.

The next house, The Croft, at Chesham, involved an expenditure at the rate of eightpence per cube foot (this cube foot standard is by far the most informing), and it will be useful to enquire the reasons of the increase. They are in the main two. The plan of Rhoswyn Cottage was extremely compact, whereas here not only is the arrangement more spread and the grouping more diverse, but the materials are more costly, notably in the large use of old oak. The spread of the plan involves the need for four chimney-stacks as against two at Gerrard's Cross, and the external walling is of much greater amount in proportion to the spaces enclosed. The result is vastly more picturesque, and gives the general impression of greater size ; and yet the hall is only a little larger, the drawing-room, though of more interesting shape, has about the same floor area, and the dining-room is actually smaller. On the other hand, the extended plan in the Chesham house involves a much larger floor space absorbed in passages, which are reduced to a minimum at the Gerrard's Cross cottage by its very compact arrangement. Clients would save themselves some disappointment, and their architects much wasted labour, if they would, at the start, clarify their ideas as to their needs. Picturesque and irregular grouping makes for additional cost. It may very well be worth it, but architects cannot be expected to design a house thus treated which will work out at so low a cost per cube foot as a building conceived on simpler lines. Before leaving the Chesham house, attention may be drawn to the charming effect of the timber work, with its filling of brick mostly arranged in herring-bone, and to the agreeable sense of enclosure and comfort given to the drive by the low wall, which reaches outwards from the house.

The third, Lane End, is at Walton Heath. The plan is less spread than at Chesham, but more so than at Gerrard's Cross. The cost, therefore, might be expected to come between the two. It worked out at sevenpence halfpenny per cube foot, and would have been less but for the heavy expense of carting due to the distance of the site from the station. It must be understood, of course, that these comparisons are only possible or useful because the internal finishings of all these houses are on simple lines. Lane End is a good example of a successful small house built in obedience to a sound maxim, that the smaller the house the less assertive should be the materials, and the more economical of broken lines should be the design. The north front shows the dignity which follows the perfectly natural use of simple brick and tile. A pleasant variety of colour is secured by the judicious contrasts between the rough plum-coloured bricks which are used for the bulk of the walls and the bright red corners and dressings, while a touch of interest is given to the walls near the verandah on the south side by six bands of thin red tiles set with wide cement joints. The hall opens on to the verandah and dining and drawing rooms, yet it is cut off from the front door. The placing of the windows and their aspects are so well managed that, though they are small enough to give a sense of great comfort, the lighting is ample. The picture of the hall shows the simplicity which is characteristic of the whole house. The settle is open to criticism. It is an inexpensive feature and useful to ward off the draughts from the verandah door, but nothing will convince that it makes a comfortable seat. A good and economical treatment of window-sills is to make them, as here, of thick red tiles a foot wide. On the first floor are five bedrooms and above them a fine attic. The pictures hardly do justice to the garden, which was laid out by Mr. Morley Horder, because a wall now encloses the drive before the entrance and runs where the young shrubs appear in the view of the north front. The garden has grown up since the photographs were taken, and Nature has brought her softening graciousness to aid the designer's art ; but these early pictures, perhaps, do Mr. Horder the more credit, since the house speaks for itself without adventitious aids.

Lane End is, as its name tells, at the end of a pleasant byway, and looks on to the Heath. It is one of many houses which have sprung up since the Walton Links took so firm a hold on the affections of golfers, but none shows a greater convenience of plan married to sane and simple treatment at a lower if at so low a cost. The next chapter illustrates a larger house by the same architect. It is, perhaps, an even better example of the rigid economy which is compatible with interesting design, and shows a decorative treatment within the building more ambitious than suited the small scale of the three homes just described.

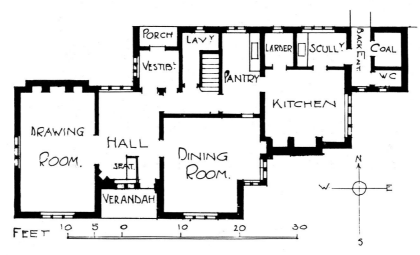

92.—GROUND PLAN OF LANE END.

INVERLEITH, NORWICH.

DESIGNED BY MR. P. MORLEY HORDER AND MR. A. G. WYAND.

A Frugal Expenditure—The Planning of Motor-houses—Adaptation of Old Panelling and Doors—Windows and Their Hangings.

WHEN discussing in the last chapter the economical aspect of Mr. Morley Horder's work, old Thomas Fuller was brought in support by the quotation of one of his building maxims. It is doubtless true that the conditions of modern life are responsible for the all but universal desire for inexpensive building ; but economy has always held an important place in the formulas supposed to govern architectural practice. Nearly all the literature of the art is based directly or indirectly on the writings of Vitruvius, who set out the principles of Greek architecture for the benefit of the cultivated public of Rome, at some date undetermined, but probably during the Augustan age. He lays down six elements of which architecture consists. The last, and for the present argument the most important, he calls Distribution—a not very illuminating word. He defines it, however, as " an advantageous use of the materials and the site, and a frugal expenditure in the execution," and he gives us a still clearer lead by setting down its Greek translation, " oikonomia," which is simply our " economy." One may be pardoned for quoting so threadbare a truism as " there is nothing new under the sun," for it is of interest to find an author of nearly two thousand years ago lecturing us like any modern architectural professor to his students. The house now to be described, Inverleith, Norwich, will be found a striking example of Vitruvius'

93.—THE GARDEN FRONT.

sixth principle—a frugal expenditure. It stands in the outskirts of that enchanting city, which perhaps may fairly boast more buildings of profound interest for its size than any other English town. Though the blighting hand of the ignorant restorer has not left it unscathed, it has been peculiarly fortunate in this way, and the recent reparation of the Town Hall shows how well such necessary work can be done, if wisely directed. The outskirts of the city are attractive. The road in which Inverleith stands is approached by a long straight avenue of fine trees, an example for the town-planner. The site of the house was entirely lacking in interest and gave no hint of privacy. The latter quality is of the essence of the intelligent treatment of house-planning, and has been well won by putting the entrance door in an inner court and approaching it by an arched entry. The north front, which one sees from the short drive, gives a satisfying sense of balance, and the bringing down of the main roof to form a hood for the archway affords a pleasant feature without any feeling of effort. The trades entrance to the left communicates directly with the scullery and obviates any need for cart and errand-boy to go through or into the entrance court. Until the advent of the motor-car, the tendency had been, for obvious sanitary reasons, to increase the distance of the coach-house and stables from the main building. A motor-house, if adequately protected from risk of fire, can, however, be included under the main roof, and in this case it adds greatly to the scale and importance of the building without

94 —NORTH-EAST CORNER, SHOWING ARCH TO COURT.

any countervailing disadvantages. The chief entrance in the court is very simple. It is emphasised only by the projection of the tile-hung work above the door, a treatment which seems a little bald. As we enter, a door in front leads to the kitchen quarters, and another to the right into the hall, which was planned of small area in order to allow of a large billiard-room. The latter is entered by a pair of wide folding doors,

95.—THE ENTRANCE COURT.

which have the effect of making the hall and billiard-room practically one room on occasion. The owner, Mr. Davidson Walker, also stipulated for a like treatment of billiard-room and drawing-room, and, as the picture shows, a long vista is achieved by the wide opening in the dividing wall when the doors are open. The particular charm of these three chief rooms is derived from their enrichment with eighteenth century panelling, doors, etc. It may be objected that their delicate conventions do not accord very happily with the character of the outside of the house, which seems to call for a decorative treatment within of conscious simplicity. The Norwich Union Insurance Company has recently built new offices of a massive and none too lovely sort, and these decorations are the discarded refinements of the old building. It happened, however, that Inverleith was well advanced before such delightful spoils became available. They proved too irresistibly attractive to be abandoned at the bidding of any formula of style. Great patience and judgment were shown in adapting the panelling to suit its new home. It came from lofty rooms, and a very drastic remodelling was inevitable. In the result it has been made to suit the new proportions with much skill. After the first hint of surprise at finding such rich work in a house otherwise so modest, it fronts us with an air of the inevitable, and is abundantly justified in its use. In addition to the panelling there are the mantel-pieces which the illustrations show, and some splendid old mahogany doors which just appear on the right side of the picture of the dining-room. Last but not least are the delightful carved mouldings which have been disposed to such rich effect on the drawing-room chimney-breast, and others (too delicate to show clearly) which ornament the door architraves. A word must be said of the ceiling decorations, which, though very slight, are of interest. Parts of them, to save expense, were done in fretted wood instead of plaster, and though such an unusual treatment needs particular discretion, the result is satisfactory.

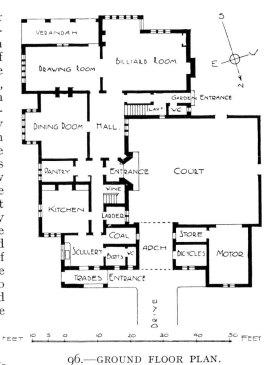

96.—GROUND FLOOR PLAN.

The arrangement upstairs will win the sympathetic admiration of the lamentable company which regards with disfavour the practice of going downstairs to breakfast. The morning-room is *en suite* with the principal bedroom. It would be possible (should such an idea ever enter the mind of the owner of Inverleith) for the first meal to be negotiated in a dressing-gown. A thoughtful housewife might object that breakfasting upstairs means extra trouble in service. As, however, the room is just at the head of the back stairs which lead down to the kitchen quarters, the criticism would be unreasonable. The further accommodation on this floor amounts to six bedrooms and a dressing-room.

The photographs were taken when the garden had been made only six months, and they consequently do not

97.—THE DINING-ROOM.

reveal the meaning of its lay-out. With a bare site, it is important so to subdivide the land that the lines of the house may be emphasised by being carried out to the boundaries. Time will produce this effect at Inverleith ; but, so far, the pink thorns, planted by the drive which leads to the arched entry, are little more than shrubs. A good proportion of the available space has been set aside for the kitchen garden. This just provision would have pleased old Thomas Fuller, who seasoned his last maxim of building with a healthy piety : " Gardens are to attend in their place. When God planted a garden eastward, He made to grow out of the ground every tree pleasant to the sight, and good for food. Sure, He knew better what was proper to a garden, than those who now-a-days therein only feed the eyes, and starve both taste and smell." The loggia on the garden front is unaffectedly contrived, and the better for having its east end glazed. There seems to have been a little lack of thought in the arrangement, on the east front, of the down-pipes, which make ugly upright streaks on the tile-hanging. The worst offender, however, is one demanded by bye-laws, which will not be denied. The same criticism applies to the corner by the front door, where the pipes are very obtrusive. Lastly comes the question of cost. The house was built for less than sixpence per cubic foot, an achievement on which the architect may be congratulated, for it is no more than the rate for a well-equipped workman's cottage. Nor can this result be attributed to construction erring on the side of flimsiness. So far from that being the case, the local bye-laws insisted that what would have been the reasonable construction above the first floor, viz., of timber with tile-hanging, should be set aside, and the full bye-law thickness of brickwork was used behind the tiles. The economical result may be attributed, to some extent, to the ground floor rooms being only eight feet high and the bedrooms being partly in the roof. Low rooms offer no disadvantages provided always that they are efficiently lit. At Inverleith the windows are adequate and the lighting and ventilation consequently leave nothing to be desired. Architects are often accused of making windows too small. This is not a question that can be judged on general grounds. In comparison with the dreary expanses of glass that the familiar type of villa has made normal, the windows at Inverleith may seem small, especially to anyone who does not realise how much lighting area may be cut off by unnecessary and generally costly drapery. It is only the ill-designed room that needs a plethora of hangings to create in it an air of comfort. Given the reasonable casement curtains that are seen in the pictures of the interior, the windows are of ample proportions for their purpose.

The low cost, then, should be attributed to careful planning and to the omission of elements which are essential neither to comfort nor to architectural fitness. Altogether, Inverleith may be taken as a good example of a house which wins its picturesqueness by natural means. It is free from any striving after the merely quaint, a snare into which has fallen too many a designer of small houses in the last few years.

98.—DRAWING-ROOM, LOOKING INTO BILLIARD-ROOM.

BROOKSIDE, CHESTERFIELD.

DESIGNED BY MR. PERCY B. HOUFTON.

The Cost of Masonry—The Question of Local Building Traditions—The Evil of the Builder's Draughtsman—" Roses in the Heart."

THE building traditions of Derbyshire are essentially those of a stone country, and the following of such traditions is of the essence of reasonable and right architecture. Builders of centuries gone by, before railway transit began the annihilation of distance, built in their local materials because they were to their hand, and none was cheap that came from afar. In these days, however, brick is nearly always the cheapest material, and that is sometimes true even in the heart of a stone country with quarries in the next field. The reason is simple : machine-made bricks are turned out with the minimum of labour, while masonry demands skill in quarrying, in shaping and in dressing, which usually more than balances the cost of carriage from a brickfield. This is especially the case where ashlar masonry is used ; with rubble, as at Brookside, the cost is less. That Mr. Houfton has not been put to great expense in building by the use of the local materials is clear from the low cost of his

house, which totalled only nine hundred pounds. This included drains, fences, gates and some stone paving, but not, of course, the levelling and planting of the garden itself. Brought to the convenient standard of cubic measurement, it works out at sixpence three farthings per foot, a figure which does credit to the designer's care and thoughtfulness. Had it been the case, however, that to follow the traditional masonry of the country involved an extra cost of, say, twopence per cubic foot, it is possible that Mr. Houfton

99.—ENTRANCE FRONT.

would not have faced a situation in which respect for architectural considerations dictated a money sacrifice of, say, the value of a room. Questions of this sort have to be borne in mind before any hard-and-fast rules are laid down about the employment of local materials. Cheap transit is a fact that cannot be explained away, and the assumption that bygone builders used local materials because they loved them best is at least an arguable one. If there is something intrinsically immoral about material foreign to the locality, many mediæval church-builders, who went for stone not merely to the next county, but to Caen, must be condemned as incompetent persons, poisoners of the wells of æsthetic truth. One remembers, too, that Purbeck marble shafts appear fairly often up and down the land. The truth is that the mediæval person did not bother his head about traditions and theories, and would be very much astonished to hear all the subtleties with which modern writers credit him. When he wanted a good piece of stone or wood, if he could afford to get from a hundred miles away a better one than the next field afforded, he sent for it hot-foot without prick of conscience or any emotion except pleasure in getting good stuff. If, then, he did not mind paying more for good brick or stone from another county, why should our architectural consciences shudder at paying less ?

As the result of confused thinking, a good deal of criticism has been written on this question of materials which is not far removed from cant, for the real crux is not in the stuff, but in the way it is used. To employ stone in a brick country, or brick in a stone country, is no crime ; the folly begins when a type of house which took its character in one county from the nature of the local materials is repeated in another county where a different type had evolved. It is not the materials themselves, but their handling, which make for architectural folly or wisdom. Red brick is capable of very elastic and various treatments. If it is cheaper in a stone district than stone, it can be plastered, not to imitate stone, but to give the same general colour effect in a landscape where red is not customary, or it can be simply colour-washed. In some districts timber was always scarce, and half-timber work there becomes a foolish offence against local methods, whatever they may be, as well as a construction which belongs definitely to the past almost everywhere in England. "Half-timber" becomes credible when it is literally half timber and half brickwork. The building bye-laws of some districts require a fixed thickness of brick wall, whether there be timber with it or not, in which case the timber becomes a sheer superfluity.

100.—THE PORCH.

It has been Mr. Houfton's skill and good fortune to build in a credible local way at a low cost ; but architects must not be scolded because they have not built as their forefathers did, until, first, the views

101.—THE SOUTH SIDE.

of their clients, and, secondly, the provisions of the bye - laws, have been ascertained. The country-side is admittedly covered with houses that offend against every canon of sense, whether common or artistic. Let it be remembered, however, that not one-tenth of the houses of England are, even now, built to the designs and under the superintendence of architects. While ninety per cent. of English homes are hashed up by a local builder with the aid of an unqualified and half-educated draughtsman and sold to the public that says, " I know nothing about architecture, but I know what I like," the present state of things is not likely to improve.

But to return to Mr. Houfton's house at Brampton. The masonry is of a greyish brown stone of the same formation that yields the blue York stone, but from the top beds, which give thin pieces suitable for rubble. From lower beds in the same quarry come the bigger blocks which are dressed for quoins, etc. The roof is covered with new red tiling, which is patched with black, a circumstance due to the exposed tiles of the stacks having weathered as they awaited use. A pleasant vitality is given to the western slope of the roof by the apparent sagging which is due to the tilting of the tiles at the verge. This practical method keeps the water from being blown over the edge on to the gable-end. The little dormer gables are tile-hung, which helps them to maintain their character as part of the roof. The plan is admirable, for the minimum of space is absorbed in passage-ways. The living-room has recesses at either side of the fireplace, five feet by seven feet, one of which takes most of the piano out of the floor space of the room, and the other is to be fitted up as a tiny study. Such recesses give a feeling of partial privacy which is better than nothing, and at least delimit the sphere of untidiness for the musical and literary members of the family. The floor is of oak boards nailed on three inches of coke breeze concrete, with four inches of ordinary concrete below. From this room to the garden there is a door, which is protected from the weather by the south wall being continued thirty inches eastwards as a screen ; an excellent idea.

It should be noted that the kitchen, living-room and principal bedroom all have windows both to the north and south. This is good not only for the excellent light afforded, but because the window away from the prevailing wind can be opened for ventilation. A good feature is the masking of the trades-men's entrance from both front and back garden by screen walls, which with the boundary wall of the site make a miniature kitchen court. Upstairs the bedrooms number four. Mr. Houfton has experimented with his joinery, using great elm planks for doors. They do not succeed if left plain, owing to serious shrinking and warping, but seem satisfactory when waxed. The garden is delightful. It was a wet, unhappy site, gashed by a great ditch ; but levelling and draining, joined with good design in its lay-out and fine existing trees, have made

102.—FROM THE EAST.

a very pretty, homely place. The paths are of generous width and paved with big stone slabs, as is the coping of the terrace wall on the south front, which is made needful by the rise of the ground southwards. The device on the lintel of the entrance porch deserves a word. Mr. Houfton had been considering what should be carved there, when he was called to Caunton Manor, Newark, the old home of the late Dean Hole. The famous rose garden recalled to his mind the Dean's aphorism that " He that would have beautiful roses in his garden must have roses in the heart." Where a definite idea can be reduced to so few words as this, it is difficult for decoration to tell the same story to as good effect, but the designer rose to the occasion. On the lintel the local mason carved for him four Tudor roses, within an outline which, though much conventionalised, represents a heart. By such a pretty fancy the treasures of the garden find a spiritual expression in a symbol, which remains through the dead months of winter to keep alive the "roses in the heart." It is precisely by such little subtleties of decorative meaning, which convey nothing to the passer-by, that an intimacy is established with a home that belongs to one's self and not to another.

God gave all men
    all earth to love,
But, since our
    hearts are small,
Ordained for each
    one spot should
    prove
Beloved over all.

The idea is at the

103.—THE LIVING-ROOM.

heart of home-building, and has inspired the renascence of country architecture. This enthusiasm is partly due to a revived interest in the artistic side of building, but it has its roots deep in social life and in the possessive instinct which finds expression in the tag, "An Englishman's home is his castle." On other men's houses we may not carve, and do not want to carve, the monogram that is dumb to strangers but eloquent to us, a poignant date, or roses reminiscent of a kindly epigram. It is in the home which is our own, the "spot beloved over all," that such innocent intrigues of sentiment are not only allowable, but becoming, and it may be doubted whether anyone has found a whole content who lacks the right to carve his roses on his lintel.

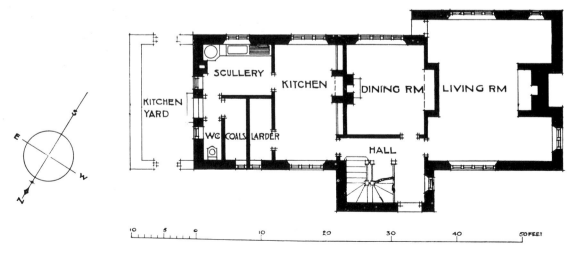

104.—GROUND PLAN.

THE OLD POUND HOUSE, WIMBLEDON.

DESIGNED BY MR. GEORGE HUBBARD AND MR. ALBERT W. MOORE.

An Appropriate House-name—Eighteenth Century Traditions and Their Influence To-day—Pepys on Regular Elevations—Literature and Architecture

IT is rarely that a new house in a London suburb can by its name ally itself with local customs so reasonably as does The Old Pound House. One often notes a group of houses which, with a large patronage of the trees of the field, take to themselves the style and title of The Oaks, The Elms and The Beeches, with never an acorn or a broad leaf in sight. Some kindly philosopher should write a guide to the wise calling of houses, and so save the builder from being driven to many an odd shift when adding to his local habitation the dignity of a name. The old paternal rules for the due ordering of Wimbledon Common, however, served Mr. Frank Bullock better than any imaginative flights. Opposite the entrance to his house is the old pound, into which they used to drive the cattle that strayed about the common, and we may hope that its stout timbers will long remain to make this pleasant house-name something more than a memory. The house will be familiar to the many who motor from Putney to Kingston, its cheerful red front looking across the common. A feature of the gate piers is the use of iron cradles to support the stone balls, an interesting variation of design. The mass of the house is of dark red Crowborough bricks, with dressings of a brighter hue. In the big pediment there are carved a cartouche and swags and the stout wood cornice is pleasantly adorned with egg and tongue and dentil mouldings.

From either of the entrance gates one notes the happy proportions and quiet ornament

105.—THE ENTRANCE FRONT.

of the main doorway, with the door itself well recessed. We enter through a vestibule into the hall with the stairway facing us. Round this hall the reception-rooms are grouped. To the right are the drawing and morning rooms, both with bays looking southward on the garden. The former also is windowed to the west, and the narrow opening which adjoins the front door has a practical value, as it lights the piano, a need not always considered in the planning of drawing-rooms. It is an example of the importance of considering the satisfactory placing of usual furniture when the arrangement of doors and windows is being committed to paper. The dining-room, though entered from the hall, has its second service door separated from the kitchen only by the width of a passage.

76

106.—FROM THE GARDEN.

107.—FROM THE SOUTH-WEST.

The latter leads also to the billiard-room, a single-storey addition with a top light, which groups admirably with the main block. The arrangement of the ground floor is very satisfactory except for one feature. To pass from the trades entrance, wine and coal cellars, etc., to the front hall necessitates going through the kitchen. This not only involves the disturbance of culinary mysteries, but, as there is no servants' hall, lessens the amount of privacy and quiet which it is reasonable to accord to servants. With this type of plan it is clear that something has to be sacrificed, and the extension of the serving passage to the trades entrance would have meant a slice off the billiard-room. All planning on a restricted site is a matter of compromise, and it may be that of two inconveniences the least has been chosen. The entrance to the garden from the hall is under the stairs, and a very agreeable garden it is.

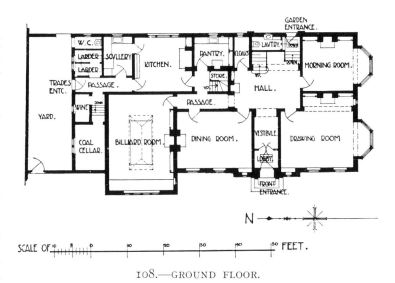

108.—GROUND FLOOR.

The sundial is reminiscent of Time's destruction, for the baluster which supports it came from old Kew Bridge. The south front is simple and symmetrical, with its two tile-hung bays, but on this side and on the east the proportions are rather marred by the very large dormers, which tend to overpower the roof. This is in some sort the defect of their qualities, for they make the attic rooms very light and spacious, but it would, perhaps, have been better to omit their pediments so as to lay on them the minimum of emphasis. The house cost in 1903 five thousand and eighty pounds, inclusive of motor-house, boundary walls and gardening works. It boasts ten bedrooms and dressing-rooms on its first and second floors, and the contract price works out at elevenpence per cubic foot.

Considered from the point of view of design, The Old Pound House is a sign of the architectural times. The tendency of to-day is to cleave more closely to the quiet traditions of the late seventeenth and early eighteenth centuries. The Gothic revival was a necessary movement that lifted architecture out of the dreariness of stucco and of those thin refinements which alone justified the era of Nash and the vapid respectabilities of Regent's Park. Mediæval ideas, however, were too remote from the current of modern life to make them feasible as an enduring inspiration, save in such root principles as the right use of materials,

109.—DOORWAY AND PEDIMENT.

and the large genius of Eden Nesfield, George Devey and Mr. Norman Shaw gradually broke away from the use of Gothic forms and found outlet in the grave field of the Renaissance. This tendency continues to stiffen, and, in so far as modern architecture can be said to have any definite purpose, we are moving in the direction of another eighteenth century. An American critic has recently reminded us that an age of ardour must always be succeeded by an age of law, to keep the foundations

110.—THE HALL AND STAIRCASE.

sure. The Gothic revival provided the ardour, and we are watching the growth of something like a new law, which attaches increasing importance to symmetry and sobriety. The general current of modern taste is curiously like that of Pepys' day. In 1662 he wrote : " Up to Hinchingbroke, and there with Mr. Sheply did look all over the house, and I do, I confess, like well of the alteracions, and do like the staircase, but there being nothing to make the outside more regular and modern, I am not satisfied with it." It is precisely this plea for an " outside more regular " which is influencing both architects and the public generally. The Gothic revival was in some sort a necessary sequel to the Romantic revival in literature which we associate with the Lake poets. The force of the latter revival seems spent, and the world is so set on the practical pursuits of sociology that there is in sight no fresh impetus likely to produce a new school of romantic literature. Until such a school arises it seems unreasonable to suppose that architecture will get any fresh start, and, indeed, it is doubtful whether any is wanted. The present need seems rather to gather up the threads of the sound traditions of building that were broken at the end of the eighteenth century, and to look askance on the various new gospels of design which are preached from time to time, only to find their place in a kindly oblivion. There is ample room for experiment in the right use, on traditional lines, of the many new materials which science is continually providing for the exercise of the designer's invention. For the present, at all events, English architecture is in need of nothing so much as rest, so that it may absorb into current practice such of the results of fifty years' chaotic experiment as seem to have some elements of permanence. This is true particularly of domestic architecture where the practical needs of house-building do not call for the solving of engineering problems, such as may be met by new employments of steel and concrete. These will, it is to be hoped, bring into being architectural treatments which suit their nature ; but enough is known of them to make it highly doubtful whether they will ever displace masonry and brickwork for the building of country homes. The place they may fill in the construction of city buildings, already an extensive one, is another and separate problem, both in construction and design, and, as it is unrelated to the subject of this book, need not here be discussed.

THE HURST, FOUR OAKS.

DESIGNED BY PROFESSOR W. R. LETHABY.

A Beautiful Mantel-piece—Montaigne on Libraries—Restraint in Furnishing—The Spirit of Adventure in Architecture.

THOUGH the most devoted lover of Birmingham cannot say much by way of praise of the city itself, the near country-side is full of beauty, whether in the gentle leafy lanes, which are characteristic of so much of Warwickshire, or in the sterner upland country about Sutton Coldfield. Though distant only about eight miles from the heart of the city, the country atmosphere is singularly well preserved at Four Oaks, a happy state of things due largely to the great expanse of Sutton Park. This supreme pleasaunce of the Midlands is owed to the foresight and generosity of Bishop Vesey, who was born thereby in 1452. A friend of Wolsey, and Bishop of Exeter, he did not hail with any favour the rigid Protestantism of the early years of Edward VI., and he retired to his native place, where he built himself a house. His benefactions to Sutton were well-nigh endless, but of them all the greatest has been well

III.-- FROM THE SOUTH-WEST.

called " that wonderful experiment in municipal socialism," the gift of Sutton Park to the people. The vast acreage of the original gift has been whittled down by enclosure and dishonest grant, but it remains a marvellous prospect of coppice, moor and pool. The site of The Hurst is in Lady Wood, and a more ideal situation for a house could scarcely be found.

The house is built on an L plan, with its entrance near the north-west corner of the principal arm. Going through a small porch, we come into a spacious vaulted hall, the delightful simplicity of which appears in the accompanying picture. Nearly facing the entrance are the doors to drawing-room and library, while at the end folding doors invite to the dining-room, and through it, by a flight of steps, to the garden beyond. The main features of the drawing-room are the exquisite marble mantel-piece and the fine plaster-work, the latter by the hand of Mr. Gimson. When one remembers the orgies of pilasters, consoles and shelves which Early Victorian architects dignified with the name of mantel-pieces, this simple thing strikes the eye with a sense of gratitude. The quiet alternation of green and white slabs and the austere little mouldings that form the inner and outer frames give a feeling of large satisfaction, while, above it, the dull white and the

112.—THE SOUTH-EAST CORNER

113.—THE GARDEN AT THE HURST.

rich, low modelling of the plaster foliage give a pleasant relief both in colour and texture. The library is a good room, and, as becomes its purpose, has a bay. Lovers of Montaigne will say that no room can be a true library without a bay, though perhaps they will not go so far as to demand the true Montaigne quota of three. The library at The Hurst falls, too, below the standard of the château of St. Michel de Montaigne, in so far as it is not in a tower ; but if it does not enjoy that " farre-extending rich and unresisted prospect " which so delighted the wisest and most detached of Frenchmen, even his fastidious taste would have approved the trim yews and rich lawns which form the outlook at The Hurst. It is difficult to read with happiness in disagreeable surroundings. Some heroic souls can adjust their attention to serious books in a railway carriage ; but such detachment is denied to most. Few readers worthy the name are content to have only one or two books within reach ; in fact, a library is the place for this employment. " There," as the seigneur of Montaigne writes, " there is my seat, that is my throne. . . . There without order without method, and by peecemeales I turne over and ransacke,

114.—THE HALL.

nowe one booke and now another . . . and walking up and downe I endight and enregister these my humours, these my conceits. . . . There I passe the greatest part of my live days, and weare out most houres of the day." It is not too much to say that this library at The Hurst is just such a room where one could (in the enchanting words of Florio's translation) endight one's humours. Nor is this happy atmosphere due only to the grave and pleasant art of Mr. Lethaby. The house has been furnished by Colonel Wilkinson with that wise reticence that is at once so rare and so desirable. It is too often the case that furniture and ornaments smother a room, and the intention of the architect in its proportions is buried in an aggregation of chattels. It is the old story of not being able to see the forest for the trees. It is not necessary that we should imitate the Japanese economy in this matter, and let a mat, a low table and a bronze vase with a branch of cherry blossom serve us alone as household gods ; but we can at least let the mind of the builder of our home be revealed, and this has been done at The Hurst. The pieces of furniture are few and fit ; no pictures are seen save those that are beautiful and rich in their own right. On looking up the stairs from the hall one sees only the cast of a head on the wall ; another space is provided only with a little piece of an illuminated MS. simply framed. By such restraint each little treasure gives fully of its own richness, and throws into strong relief the large simplicity of the architecture which frames it. The dreadful over - furnished state of most houses is due perhaps more to a lack of moral fibre than to a double dose of original sin in matters artistic. Who is there who does not look with

115.—IN THE DRAWING-ROOM

inward grief upon some picture that is hung because it is a gift? Are there none who writhe under the dreadful brilliance of a cabinet containing useless silver objects, the penalty of marriage? There are few things from the pen of De Quincey finer than the essay on " Murder considered as one of the Fine Arts." It remains for some great spirit, goaded by the burden of possessions as innumerable as they are useless, to pen some splendid epic in praise of burglars who can relieve the oppressed (as they relieved this writer) of a whole cupboardful of costly gimcracks. Of objects rare and beautiful in themselves there is no lack at The Hurst, but they are not obtruded on the eye, and the house remains a home, and does not become a museum. In particular there are a few fine harpsichords which recall the history of bygone virtuosi.

Of the dining-room no more need be said save (in Pepysian phrase) that it is answerable to the dignity of the rest of the house. Its bay fronts the east to catch the morning sun, and there is a window to the south. The corridor and upstairs rooms are of the same admirable lightness as the ground floor, and a charming touch is the picture of a fallow deer done on the panel of a door by the architect himself. When we go to the garden and survey the elevations of the house we are at once struck by the sober and masculine character of Mr. Lethaby's art. He is one of the few men living who can at once create real architecture and write about the subject of his preoccupations in luminous fashion. It might be thought that by now everything that could usefully be written about the art and mystery of building would already be on record; yet Mr. Lethaby recently made a pronouncement on the spirit of adventure in architecture which has set people thinking. Here is a fruitful saying: " True originality is to be found by those who, standing on the limits of the sphere of the known, reach out naturally to some apprehension and understanding of what is beyond; it is the next step in an orderly development." The Hurst is a comparatively early work of his design, but it exhibits that combination of reasonableness and originality which we expect from him. The simple roof-lines, the quiet masses of the bays, the curved heads of the windows and the restrained touch of gaiety in the diamonds of green tiling which adorn the chimneys make up a whole which is eminently satisfying and expressive of sober strength. Mr. Lethaby has not set out to astonish us, and there is no one feature which calls aloud for notice. It is representative of the time. It presents to us no spirit of romance, but stands confessed a simple, modern home. As its creator has said, " When poetry and magic are in the people and in the age, they will appear in their arts, and I want them, but there is not the least good in saying ' Let us build magic buildings. Let us be poetic.' " What delights in The Hurst, then, is its honesty of purpose and the success with which it fills its place.

Of the garden a few words must be said. It forms a beautiful frame for a notable building. The yew

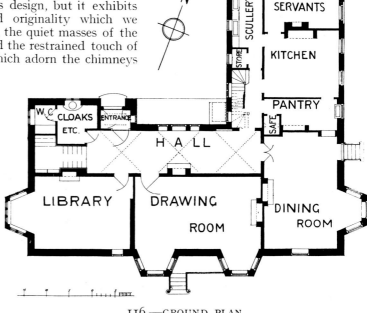

116.—GROUND PLAN

hedges are in perfect verdure, and the grassy terraces lead to a pond of flowers, a gentle gradation. Everywhere there are masses of blooms, and most of all in the great border by the south front, which flings its perfume through the library windows. There is enough restraint in the use of shrubs against the house not to mar its features. The main terrace is upheld by a fine retaining wall with simple buttresses, in the corners of which many exquisite shrubs might be grown. Here is a fitting home for choisya, myrtle, escallonia and ceanothus, none of which seems to fill its rightful mission in the life of the garden save in such situations. If there is one doubtful feature in the gardens of The Hurst it is the spotty quartette of shrubs which stand sentinel by the little pond, for they rather mar the dignity of the greensward. As becomes a true garden, there are surprises, and one comes on a little rose garden, the more pleasant for its stone flagging. All these beauties, whether of house or banks of flowers or trim hedges, find their fitting background in the trees which bring the old forest life of Sutton to the very door.

POYNDER'S END, NEAR HITCHIN.

DESIGNED BY MR. GEOFFRY LUCAS.

The Use of the Minor Building Arts—An Architectural Expression of the Simple Life—Breadth and Scale in Building—The Right Garden Framing of a House.

MR. GEOFFRY LUCAS is perhaps best known to the public by his work at the Hampstead Garden Suburb. It shows him as an architectural economist, winning his effects by simple dispositions of mass, roof-line and gable, and with small aid from the minor building arts. At Poynder's End he was free to call in those crafts which bring diversity and with it richness. It is a house most simple in arrangement, yet with a large dignity. The broad span of the roofs, the solid way in which the bays jut out and the gravity of the gables are emphasised by a restrained use of varied textures. The north-east bay is sheeted with lead, a feature not merely decorative, but highly practical in resisting the penetrative power of driving rain. The gable above it is weather-boarded, and the natural edges of the unsquared planks give an agreeable yet reasonable air of irregularity. This device for adding interest to outside boarding was very successfully employed by that great, but too little known, architect, the late George Devey. Below the larger gable of the north-west front is a long row of casements divided by two blank spaces, which are plastered and treated with incised decoration. It will be noted, however, that these enrichments and the rather massive wood mouldings at the top of the bays serve only to throw into relief the prevailing sense of simplicity. It has been said that it is not mere æsthetic beauty but the quality of expression which entitles any work possessing it to a place among the things to be regarded as fine art. This is peculiarly true of domestic architecture. It is not enough that a house shall please the eye and be convenient and well built. We are entitled to expect that it shall express some definite mental attitude in its owner.

Mr. Hugh Exton Seebohm, for whom Poynder's End was built, is a student of social conditions and impressed with the importance of simplicity in living. The term "simple life" is perhaps best avoided, as it has come to connote some rather farcical aspects of a reasonable position. To other interests Mr. Seebohm adds a taste for serious farming, and this site of one hundred acres, about three miles from Hitchin, includes an old and picturesque farmstead where lives one of the farm hands. While

117 —LEADED BAY AND WEATHER-BOARDING.

118.—ONE END OF THE HALL.

119.—THE ENTRANCE FRONT.

Mr. Lucas has refrained from giving to the building any imitative flavour of the traditional farmhouse, the simplicity of its arrangement reflects the tastes of its owner. This needs to be taken into account when examining the

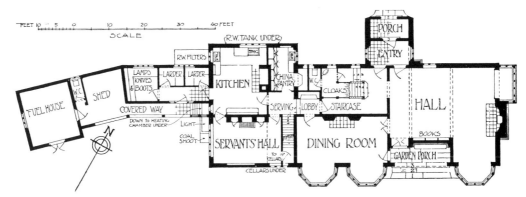

120.—GROUND FLOOR PLAN.

plan, which presents some unusual features. The carriage drive approaches the house from the south, which explains why the office wing is not in line with the main body of the house. The porch is in the smaller gabled projection on the north-west front. It opens into an inner porch-like space called the entry. To the left a door opens to the hall, and to the right another to the foot of the stairs and the passage to the kitchen quarters. This is a development of the rather barbarous custom of letting the porch give direct on to the hall when it is the main living-room. The dining-room opens out of the hall and has also a door to the serving lobby adjoining the kitchen. The hall is of impressive proportions. The two illustrations of it show respectively the fireplace end and the return end with the dining-room and staircase framed in the open doorways. The panelling is simple and effective, and the fireplace of generous size, with a pleasant lining of tiles arranged edgeways in herring-bone. The square bay facing the north-east and the octagonal bay look out over a magnificent sweep of country to all sides save the west, stretching away even to Sandy and Wrest Park in the far distance. The bronze casements have been glazed with plate glass divided into sheets

121.—DINING-ROOM AND STAIRCASE SEEN FROM THE HALL

of reasonable size instead of with the smaller leaded lights used in the upper rooms. This seems a sound compromise with the idea of single sheets of glass, which are best for seeing the view, but do not give a fitting sense of enclosure. The dining-room is also rich in windows, and has a door to the garden porch, or loggia. Both these rooms are lofty, and give in some measure the feeling that their scale is over-large in relation to the plan. The hall has rather a barn-like air. It is frankly a little bald. This would have been avoided if there had been some sort of screen (however openly designed) between the two parts into which it seems naturally to divide itself. The floors and doors here are all of oak, and the latter are fitted with thumb-latches of polished steel. The sense of massive architectural well-being is heightened by the staircase, with its treads of solid elm and sturdy balusters. On the first floor above the porch is a delightfully treated study, while three of the bedrooms benefit by the bays being carried up to the eaves. The second floor provides a great workroom.

When we regard the exterior of Poynder's End as a whole, we are struck by the natural and easy way in which Mr. Lucas has arrived at an interior notably light and airy without interfering with a due proportion between solids and voids. The entrance front in particular is characterised by an admirable air of breadth. The large light-giving capacity of projecting bays has enabled him to leave his main wall spaces but little broken. Breadth and scale are two of the most valuable qualities of architecture, and both have been achieved on the entrance front. It is enough to imagine the effect of comparatively big windows inserted in its two gables to see how valuable is the right proportion between openings and wall space. Large openings would have destroyed the sense of breadth which is afforded by the gables, and accentuated by the bulk of the chimneys. Of the garden there is little to be said. The site slopes away rather sharply from the house on one side, and offered opportunities for terrace and yew hedge and wall that would have added greatly to the amenities of the building. A scheme has been prepared by Mr. Lucas, but not yet carried out. When it is, the hint of bareness which gives to the grouping something of *gaucherie* will disappear. The more civilised the type of architecture (and Poynder's End, for all its simple plan, is a finished product and shows no small scholarship), the more needful it is to provide by gardens of formal type a middle world between the house and the country beyond. One looks for some spreading of the influence of the architecture to its immediate surroundings. The dim distances of rolling hills and plotted fields need the garden as a foreground of ordered beauty. It is just in such a situation as Poynder's End, where the wide outlook gives the sense of a large freedom, that the view seems to demand in the immediate surroundings the repose of quiet lines and conscious art.

122.—THE STAIRCASE.

MIDDLEFIELD, GREAT SHELFORD.

DESIGNED BY MR. E. L. LUTYENS.

Horace Walpole on Deliberate Trees—Mass, Symmetry and Proportion—Repose in Architecture—Dutch Brickwork—A Notable Plan—Charles Lamb and Staircases.

MIDDLEFIELD is an example of purely country architecture, and one cannot imagine it anywhere but on English soil. It stands on a site as yet absolutely bare, and looks southwards down a gentle slope over a characteristic but, it must be confessed, not highly attractive stretch of Cambridgeshire farm lands. The gardens are so far on paper only, and the building, therefore, owes nothing in its pictures to the charm which Nature adds with a setting of tree, shrub and flower. The house sits starkly on the ground, but pergolas have been schemed, which will creep out from the loggia and from the other end of the south front to enclose a garden. It is in such early days of the surroundings of a house that one remembers with sympathy the irritation of Horace Walpole. " The

deliberation with which trees grow is extremely inconvenient to my natural impatience. I lament living in so barbarous an age, when we are come to so little perfection in gardening. I am persuaded that a hundred and fifty years hence it will be as common to remove oaks a hundred and fifty years old, as it is now to transplant tulip-roots." He wrote this in 1748, and his limit of time is passed by twelve years, yet the promised specific for ready-made forests lingers. Perhaps, however, he did not expect it in a large sincerity, for he also prophesied whole groves of humming-birds and tame tigers taught to fetch and carry. In any case Middlefield is so far nothing but a house, and if it is an ordeal to show it without the framing which is due, the success which it achieves is at least owed to no external aids. Mr. Lutyens has probably done nothing more austere, nor indeed can one imagine a country house relying more exclusively on the qualities of mass, symmetry and proportion. There is nowhere an external moulding but in the windows and doors, which are of extreme simplicity, and in the subtle line of brickwork which marks the slight recessing of the lower part of the projecting wings on the north front. Perhaps an observer will look for relief in a carved tympanum here or a keystone there, and missing it will bring against Middlefield a charge of baldness. With such a criticism one could not argue, but it would be based on a large misunderstanding of the principle which seems to have inspired the design. Were it made, it could best be met as Pope Julius II. was countered when he complained that there was no gold on the painted figures of the Sistine Chapel. " Simple persons," replied the painter, " simple persons, who wore no gold on their garments." It has been always the finest types of small

123.—THE ENTRANCE DOOR.

domestic architecture which disappoint the unthinking critic by lacking gold on their garments, buildings which have won their place in our affections by the very fact of being " simple persons." Such houses, like the people whom they represent, have the gift of repose, and it is precisely in that sense that Middlefield will impress the thoughtful. The perfect suavity of the lines of the roofs, which are kept in harmonious and unbroken planes, the masculine tower-like bulk of the three chimneys, the windows few but large, the dormers with their angles swept in generous curves so that they grow organically out of the roof—all these things produce an effect of extraordinary repose.

124.—THE ENTRANCE FRONT.

The detail picture of the entrance door gives some hint of how the mass and outline are helped by the texture of the bricks and tiles. The house is not large, and its scale is made the greater by the smallness of the bricks. They came from Holland (needless to say, they are hand-made) and are only seven inches long by one and three-quarter inches thick. There is a charm about Dutch bricks which it is difficult to explain. Though they are well made and hard, their faces have that hint of cushion shape which lets the play of light send a ripple of colour over the wall. The wide white joints, more plentiful than in normal English brickwork, help to give a roughness of texture which adds vitality to the surface. Happily, English brick-makers are realising that for buildings that belong to architecture the day of machine-made bricks is over, however useful they may be in engineering works. Already hand-made bricks have been produced which touch a very high level of achievement, and there is a growing tendency to improvement. It need not be doubted that the study of the methods used in Holland, where the tradition of hand-making never died out, will serve as a stimulus to bring the English clay-worker to the same level of perfection. This use of foreign materials at Middlefield, whatever sober reflections it may raise as to the backwardness of an English craft, is not an extravagance, for the total extra it involved over the cost of native bricks was only sixty pounds, an amount which must be less than the increased cost of carriage. This is another example of the effects

125.—FROM THE SOUTH-WEST.

which are to be got simply by wise choice of materials ; for no small part of the charm of Middlefield would be lacking had the bricks been of ordinary size and inferior texture.

Now as to the plan of the house. It is often supposed by the unthinking that there is some special cleverness in houses that are broken up into odd nooks and corners, features that are externally emphasised by turrets, chimneys and gables of queer shapes, placed in an irregular fashion. Some suppose, in fact, that such exercises serve best to exhibit an architect's ability. Nothing is further from the truth. The combination of symmetry outside with well-shaped rooms conveniently disposed within needs far more thought and skill. Middlefield is an example of large success in this direction. The entrance on the north front opens into a long hall, which has no pretensions to being more than a convenient passage-way. From it is entered the whole suite of the ground-floor rooms. The kitchen quarters are to the east, the study and garden-room to the west, while the dining, drawing and school rooms face due south. Particular attention must be drawn to the hygienic virtue of the plan, a quality to which far too little attention is ordinarily given. By opening a few doors and windows at the same time, perfect cross-ventilation is secured and the free air will blow through the house. This is an advantage often lacking where rooms are grouped round a main hall. The same simplicity which informs the exterior is carried into the treatment of the rooms. The fittings throughout are of the plainest and least expensive. In the drawing-room a little

126.—FROM THE NORTH-EAST.

127.—THE STAIRCASE PILLAR.

128.—IN THE DRAWING-ROOM.

more elaboration has been allowed in the mantel-piece, but even that maintains the prevailing note of gravity. The doors are all of two panels only, and the lock handles are very small round knobs. The windows in all the rooms except the attics are sliding sashes, for the site is so wind-swept that casements would have been hopelessly inconvenient. The sash-bars are half round in section, and their stoutness adds no little to the general

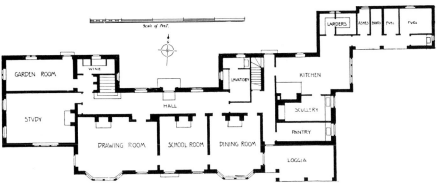

129.—GROUND PLAN.

effect. Some people have the idea that heavy bars cut off too much light, and this may be true of town houses with little windows. At Middlefield, however, there is not a room in the house but is lit not only well, but brilliantly. The loggia is conveniently placed with doors from the dining-room and from the kitchen quarters, and makes a fine open-air meal-place. The day nursery is above the dining-room, and has a casement door opening on to the flat roof of the loggia, which some day is to have railings added, so that it may serve as an outdoor nursery.

Not the least of the difficulties involved in a symmetrical plan is the adequate lighting of the main staircase without interference with the balance of the windows. This has been accomplished by placing the bathroom window in the corresponding projection on the other side of the front entrance. The gaiety of the main staircase is a brilliant foil to the gravity that rules everywhere else. There is a touch of way-ward fancy about the use of a single twisted pillar that sends the mind back to the letter that Charles Lamb wrote to Coleridge in 1800. He had received from Cottle a copy of that worthy bookseller's epic " Alfred." " When he is original," writes Elia, " it is in a most original way indeed. . . . Serpents, asps, spiders, ghosts, dead bodies, *staircases made of nothing, with adders' tongues for bannisters.* What a brain he must have ! "

It would be a libel to liken Mr. Lutyens's delicately-turned balusters to adders' tongues, but the pillar suggests just that delightful hint of extravagance in design which brings Lamb's criticism to the memory. That is not to say that tradition has been flouted, for a doorway at King's Lynn of 1708, attributed to Henry Bell, has a pair of twisted Corinthian columns which strike the same attractive note. The staircase itself is somewhat unusual in its equipment, and would not be convenient where old people lived. In some places—Birmingham, for example—no staircase is permitted to be built which lacks a hand-rail on the open side, or a wall-rail on the other. Neither is to be found at Shelford, and the ascent would offer considerable difficulties to the infirm. That, however, is a small point, to be corrected easily enough by fixing a wall-rail, or, better still, a stout cord running through ring brackets. The outstanding fact remains that in a house notable for breadth and sobriety Mr. Lutyens has given rein to his fancy and produced a feature which offends against no rule of reasonableness and yet entertains us hugely.

Middlefield is altogether a shining example of the admirable results which come from a mastery of line and proportion. As one drives to Shelford from Cambridge, the eye is tired by the range of architec-tural mediocrities lining the pleasant roads that lead from the town with its fine colleges to the open country. Here, however, is a home to which one turns gratefully as to the shadow of a great rock in a weary land

HOMEWOOD, KNEBWORTH.

DESIGNED BY MR. E. L. LUTYENS.

A Study in Gables—Ionic Pilasters and Vernacular Traditions—The Fusion of Architectural Styles—The Buildings of "The New Republic"—A Richly-furnished Garden.

THE last chapter showed a house but recently built, which lacked the kindly setting which Nature gives. In Homewood we have an earlier work of Mr. Lutyens—it was built in 1897—and the garden frames the house to admiration. If Middlefield is a study in hipped roofs, Homewood owes its beauty to gables. Nothing could exceed the welcoming charm of the entrance front. A short drive brings us from the road to a square gravelled space before the entrance which is marked by a delightful round hood. The vestibule, with a lavatory opening from it, is unprotected by an outer door, and indeed there is no need for one. At its end, a door facing us leads to the kitchen quarters so that the servants need not enter the hall when answering the door bell, and a door to the right gives the visitor entrance. The rooms are rather low, yet perfectly light. Very delightful are the quiet dignity of the staircase ascent and the treatment of the first-floor landing, as the pictures abundantly show. It is, however, rather in the handling of the exterior that Mr. Lutyens's enchanting art is so strikingly apparent. The

130.—THE ENTRANCE FRONT.

131.—FROM THE WEST.

132.—THE SOUTH-EAST FRONT.

south-east front with its loggias is a conception of extraordinary grace. There is a hint of the South African stoep in the broad space in front of the dining-room windows. No roof hangs over the latter to keep out the sunshine, as the pair of loggias stand clear at the sides, and nothing checks the view from the windows over the quiet rolling landscape.

The brilliance of the design of this front is in the neighbourhood of Ionic pilasters to the simple elements of roof and gable, which are the essence of a treatment characteristic of farmhouse traditions. Like so much that Mr. Lutyens does, it was an experiment that few would have dared to make, and fewer brought to satisfactory achievement. People sometimes talk as though architecture had come to an end, as though there is nothing to be done except to copy the work of our forefathers. This garden front of Homewood is a small, albeit delightful, thing in itself, but it is symptomatic of much. It proves, what people are slow to believe, that in the new arrangement of traditional forms, perhaps themselves of widely differing provenance, there is room for infinite originality. We do not want new forms, but new light on the old, a new perception of their possibilities, and it is precisely this illumination which the work of Mr. Lutyens affords. Happily the days are gone when they talked of " pure styles " and the work of some periods (notably English of the fifteenth century) was dismissed as " debased." In Mr. Mallock's *New Republic* the makers of modern taste were happily touched off for us under pseudonyms which concealed little. Walter Pater was made to masquerade as Mr. Rose, and if the portraiture is a little malicious in its delicate parody of the Pateresque position, Mr. Rose's dicta are luminous even when they are exaggerated. A sly hit is made at æsthetic posing, by now almost entirely buried under a mound of ridicule. Mr. Rose was expatiating on the joys of

133.—IN SHARP PERSPECTIVE.

upholsterers' shop windows : " I seem there to have got a glimpse of the real heart of things ; . . . indeed, when I go to ugly houses, I often take a scrap of some artistic cretonne with me in my pocket as a kind of æsthetic smelling salts. . . ." This is simply admirable fooling, but in his pontifications about the architecture of the future, about the buildings which should glorify the metropolis of the New Republic, a note of serious truth sounds clearly.

" If you will just think of our architecture, and consider how that naturally will be——"

" Yes," said Mr. Luke, " I should be glad to hear about our architecture." (Luke was Matthew Arnold.)

134—STEPS AND SOUTH LOGGIA.

135.—FIRST FLOOR LANDING.

136.—THE SOUTH-WEST FRONT.

"How that naturally will be," Mr. Rose went on, " of no style in particular."

"The deuce it won't!" exclaimed Mr. Luke.

"No," continued Mr. Rose, unmoved. "No style in particular, but a renaissance of all styles."

This should not be read as a plea for eclectic imitations, but rather for an organic fusion of differing motives. It was precisely this readiness to use all elements that made Sedding so successful with Holy Trinity Church, Sloane Street, and it appears to be in the same spirit that Mr. Lutyens applies a Greek order to the front of a vernacular English cottage, and achieves a certain success. In his later work he has played on the same string in a more assured fashion, but never in a more winning way than at Homewood. A further word by way of description must be added. The boarding of the great gables has weathered to an exquisite silver grey, through which the grain of the elm is wonderfully pictured, and on the sunless north front the dripping rain has marked the boards with bands of greenish stain. On the south-west elevation fig trees and peaches flourish, protected from the winds by the raised lawn.

137.—GROUND PLAN.

Over one loggia pavilion a broad-leaved American vine climbs freely, and even in late September the garden is brilliant with colour and rich with quick scents. As one walks round the house every step shows a fresh picture, and the low spreading roofs fall into a new grouping. For all its diversity of mass and the shadows which its broken outlines throw, there is an underlying gravity which comes of the considered symmetry of every front. Add to that the subtle massing of colour the simply whitewashed brick at the base, the broad spread of silvery boarding and the medley of red roofs, and Homewood stands revealed as the notable work of a notable man

138.—THE SOUTH-WEST FRONT.

ROSEBANK, SILCHESTER COMMON.

DESIGNED BY MR. MERVYN E. MACARTNEY.

Concerning Cottages—Gardens the Architect's Province—Mr. W. Robinson's Criticisms—Formal and Natural at Rosebank—Frogs in an Italian Garden.

WHEN Samuel Taylor Coleridge took to satirical poems, he generally wrote dreadful doggerel ; but in one effort, " The Devil's Thoughts," there are buried some crystals of savage wisdom. His Majesty, risen from his brimstone bed, visits his snug little farm, the Earth. Among his observations :

He saw a cottage with a double coach-
   house,
    A cottage of gentility !
And the Devil did grin, for his darling sin
    Is pride that apes humility.

It would be harsh to apply " S. T.C.'s " criticism too closely, but it makes one think that the name cottage is often applied rather foolishly to buildings of some pretension. Such a shaft would fall very wide if directed at the delightful little place built by Mr. Macartney on Silchester Common. It is a real cottage in size and equipment, but with all the refinement in simple things that we are entitled to expect in the work of the surveyor to St. Paul's Cathedral, who is also the historian of a great period of English architecture. Mr. Macartney is a discerning enthusiast for the art of the English Palladians, but in this cottage he has adhered to the simplest traditions of local building. Nowhere, however, is he more in his element than in garden design. It was Chambers who wrote in 1759 of the craft in England : " Ornamental garden-ing, which in Italy, France and other countries of the Europeon Continent constitutes a part of the architect's profession, is here in other hands, and with a few exceptions, in very improper ones." This criticism continued to be just for about a century, but for some years now architects have been coming into their own, and it is to men of the ability of Mr. Reginald Blomfield, Mr. Lutyens, Mr. Macartney, Mr. Inigo Thomas and others that we must largely attribute this happy renaissance.

139.—RAMBLER AND CREEPER.

There are still many devout lovers and masters of gardening who think the incursion of architects into this domain has been marked by unfortunate results ; but they are

140.—THE GARDEN ENTRANCE.

in a dwindling minority.   The battle is really joined on the distinction between " formal " and " natural " gardens.   Mr. W. Robinson has written pungently about " frivolities of paper plans," and to his rare sympathy and insight, which come of vast knowledge and experience, all respect must be paid.   In his enchanting book, " The Garden Beautiful," he has dealt with many architects who were also garden-designers on the traditional Irish method of " When you see a head, hit it."   Specially did he rend the memory of Nesfield

141.—THE SOUTH ELEVATION.

and Barry under the common condemnation of "broken-brick gardeners." It is fair to say, however, that most wise architects who concern themselves with gardens are as keen as Mr. Robinson himself to join the beauties of woodland with those elements of formal gardening which bring Nature into right relation to the house. The ordinary garden-lover has no opportunity to avail himself of what De Quincey delighted to call "forest lawns," and must fall back on the formal garden as the best treatment for strictly limited spaces. At Rose-bank Mr. Macartney has achieved a peculiar success in a setting especially favourable. He began with an ideal site on the edge of the common, covered with pines and purple heather. His ability has been exercised in making the garden beautiful and cultivated in itself, while yet in keeping with its framing of the wild, like a gem in rough but rich setting. He has kept before him the

142.—THE DRAWING-ROOM GABLE.

143.—THE LONG WALK.

simplicity of the cottage which it serves, and has been careful, while creating a garden of considerable extent, to keep it unpretentious and its many parts in scale with the building. It is a pleasaunce in a wood, unsophisticated for all its skilful design. The bird's-eye view shows how skilfully the natural and the formal have been mingled. On the edge of the common is a simple iron entrance gate hung to brick piers, which are supported by curved wing walls. The structure with its wide flat roof gives something of the feeling of a lych-gate. As we enter, the straight path stretches away in the distance—its vista emphasised by the sundial set where four paths meet—and ends in an indeterminate background of woodland. Right and left are close-trimmed hedges of yew. As the eye follows the main walk it lights to the left on a little old cottage, heavily thatched, which has been preserved for the gardener's use. The walk is gay with a broad herbaceous border, and behind it a holly hedge serves to screen, now the practical precincts of the kitchen garden, and now wide spaces of purple ling. The sundial comes at the corner of the tennis lawn, which is stolen from the heather and framed in pines. Right and left, paths stretch away and disappear into the wood. As we return to the house, openings in hedge and trellis lead us to new countries. To the right is an orchard lawn, strewn with windfalls in early autumn. Everywhere pergola and trellis are richly covered, and a fine feature is the pier-like extension covered with blossom which juts out from the front of the house. The bowling green is sunk about eighteen inches and girt about with a loose-built brick wall, its reds and blues weathered in streaks of green and gold. In the late summer days the walls of the house can scarcely be seen, so rich are they with the creepers that enfold this garden habitation, but the little gable to the left gives the needed touch of variety. The roof-line is restrained and simple as can be, but one cannot help regretting the need for rather disfiguring yellow chimney-pots — a sacrifice to fitful winds. Berkshire is well wooded, and timber therefore takes its fair place in the construction. The east gable is covered with tarred weather-boarding, and for the gutters cast iron has been eschewed. They are made V-shaped of two narrow boards, and very simple and practical they look and are. This device is found in the greatest of all timber counties, Cheshire, but it is now rare in the South of England, though it can be seen at the Charterhouse. In Friesland not only gutters but even down-pipes are made of wood, just as in the stone country of the Cotswolds down-pipes are sometimes fashioned laboriously of stone. The illustrations are eloquent enough of the rich way that Nature has seconded the designer's ideas; but the greatest beauty of this place is seen where the art has been most conscious—in the tiny Italian garden. In the little sunk square, framed in low fruit trees, is a round stepped basin of stone. In its midst presides a battered little god; gold-fish swim among the lilies; but pleasantest of all is a great family of frogs. A score and more were counted, ranging from a pale yellow through bright golden brown to a grey-black. Some were swimming with the slow leg stroke and hands behind the back that is the despair of the mere man who delights in water sports. Others sunned themselves on the step or perched immobile on the stems of water plants. Had the garden been devised for the shade of Aristophanes, it could not have fitter denizens.

144.—THE ITALIAN GARDEN.

The cottage itself is small, but has been smaller. A drawing-room was recently added; originally the sitting-rooms were two only. Everything is liable to the faults of its qualities, and beautiful as are pergolas and trellis when rich with leaf and blossom, if close to the house they destroy the view. The floor line of the added room, therefore, was raised five steps above the ground-level of the house, and the little undercroft so formed serves as a cellar. This room has nothing above it, so opportunity was taken to treat the ceiling as a barrel vault, which gives a pleasant touch of the unexpected. From its windows one can see over the wealth of growing things towards the common. The dining-room and study both have doors to the garden. The former had its walls painted a brilliant post-office red. The fireplace is lined with little terra-cotta bricks about four inches by three inches by three inches, ornamented with fleur-de-lys, lions and double-headed eagles in delicate relief. They are tree translations of an old example, probably Dutch or South German, which can be seen at the Brewers' Hall, Antwerp. They have this advantage over tiles—they cannot fall out. If tiles are properly cemented in, they should not become loose; but in practice they often do. If bricks be used, however small, they can be built in solid fashion and will never give trouble.

Upstairs there are four bedrooms and a dressing-room. They do not call for particular remark, save that the best bedroom in the overhanging bay has a pleasant polygonal ceiling. This enables part of the roof space to be used, and thus adds to the cubic air contents of the room at a trifling cost and with marked increase of effect over an ordinary lean-to treatment.

Altogether this cottage is an admirable example of a home for week-ends and for the holiday month. The rooms are small, but the cost of building was small also—seven hundred and sixty pounds, which works out at a shade over six-pence halfpenny a cubic foot. The situation could not be more delightful. On the edge of a common fringed with old thatched cottages and but a short walk from the excavations of Silchester, the only perfectly explored Roman town in Britain, there are riches of natural beauty and antiquarian interest at the very gate. But the cottage has this grave disadvantage—with such a garden in which to dream away a holiday, it is possible that even the interest of a long-buried city would hardly tempt one to forsake the shade of hedge and pergola. Rather one would seek to earn Evelyn's benediction as a Hortulan Saint.

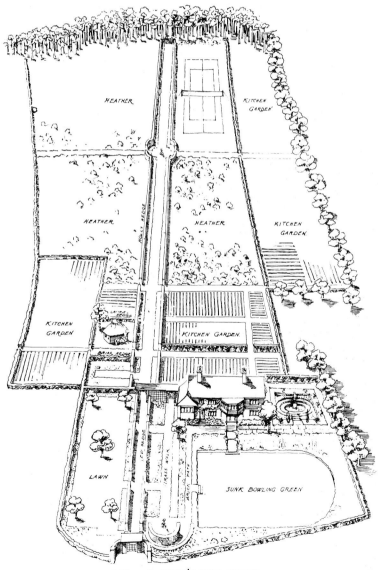

145.—A BIRD'S-EYE VIEW.

GILHAM'S BIRCH, ROTHERFIELD.

DESIGNED BY MR. E. J. MAY.

The Sussex Traditions of Building—Modern Needs in Planning—A Man's Sitting-room—The Dairy and Its Lighting—Sussex Hearths and Firebacks—Iron-casting in the Weald—A Wheelwright's Gate.

GILHAM'S BIRCH is to be regarded as an example of an admirable devotion to vernacular building, untinged by imitation of local characteristics which have lost their significance. A *bon mot* by Mr. Lethaby may help appreciation of the architectural quality of this house. He had been poking gentle fun at the passion for building houses to look like old farmsteads and cottages, and quoted a story told by Mr. Gerald Horsley. Passing down a back street in London, the latter saw a card in a grocer's window, " Fine jam, good *strawberry flavour*, 4d. a lb." Mr. Lethaby assumes very rightly that it is not the flavour of architecture we want, or the suggestion of age, but the intrinsic beauty which comes of building in a reasonable and traditional way to suit modern needs.

146.—THE NORTH-WEST CORNER.

Gilham's Birch has long been a place of habitation. There stood on the site a cottage, which, from the evidence of the fireplace now illustrated, must have gone back some hundreds of years. They say, indeed, that Cromwell's soldiers were quartered there in those days of stress. The stone jamb has its corner rounded by the sharpening of the knives of many generations, and the oak beam which crosses the recess is also a memory of the original homestead. Local tradition associates the place with William the Conqueror, hence Gilham's (Guillaume's) Birch ; but that is a dim byway which need not be pursued. The main fact is that Mr. May has succeeded in imparting to the house a purely Sussex character, while yet it is in no way an imitation of an old farmhouse. The massing of the roofs is of a greater irregularity than the old builders employed, and for a very sufficient reason. The arrangement of the elder homesteads of Sussex was on more primitive lines than suits modern life, and the greater complexity of plan is revealed by the increased elaboration in the grouping. Mr. May was designing a house to serve the purposes not of yeomen, but of gentle people. Four sitting-rooms minister to the comforts of modern life ; and, in particular; a man's room immediately by the entrance porch and cut off from the three other living-rooms is a measure of large convenience. Here business may be transacted with callers whom it is inconvenient to introduce into

147.—A STUDY IN SUSSEX ROOFING.

148.—SOUTH FRONT.

149.—FROM THE ROAD.

the more private part of the house. The provision of this room makes a projection which breaks the lines of wall and roof. Again, in a country home a dairy is a valuable addition, and it is desirable to light it from the coolest aspects, north and east. This makes another projection in the plan, with its consequent break in the mass of the house. By the same token the other kitchen offices work out the modelling of the south-east end of the building, and the loggia makes its mark on the south front. Modern planning thus dictates a grouping which is delightful, not only because it is pleasant to the eye, but because it is the reasonable and natural expression of the inner character of the house, and at the same time carries on the local traditions of brick-building and tile-hanging. There are happy Sussex touches in the little gables which make a finish to the hipped roofs, while the fine colour of the local bricks makes a pleasant background to the garden which has grown up since the house was built in 1904.

It is good to sit in the hall, with its great open hearth in an ingle which is lighted by a little window from the south. There are three things which are of the essence of the old home-building in the Weald —a great hearth, a great chimney and Sussex oak—and this ingle shows them all. The hood of the fire is large, but its ornament unaffected, and it makes the fire burn well. The most characteristic Sussex feature, however, is the old cast-iron fire-back, and when one is writing of Rother-field is a good occasion to make some reference to a delightful bygone craft.

Some eight miles distant is Burwash, in whose church is the well-known grave-slab of John Colins, a work of the fourteenth century, the earliest-known example of mediæval iron-casting, and perhaps itself a memorial to the first of a family of founders. Grave-slabs are, however, rarities in iron, and it was pro-bably the Sussex men who took to making those earliest cannon which Edward III. employed in Scotland. From then onwards to the eighteenth century, when a Rotherfield iron - master, dying in 1708, left half his fortune in a stock of iron guns, the men of the county did well with the making of cannon, and it was the burning of the forests to feed their furnaces and

150.—THE HALL FIREPLACE.

the lack of coal when wood was gone which made the industry desert the South. We are concerned, however, now with less deadly things—fire-backs. From the first use of chimneys they became obviously useful, for fire will destroy both stone and brick walls, and the old passion for making the useful beautiful soon led to their being ornamented with coats of arms and the like. As the Gothic manner died with the rebirth of classical ideas, wreaths, crossed palms and little Biblical or classical scenes served to decorate their surfaces. It is one of the latter scenes in a framing of floral pattern which protects the brick chimney at Gilham's Birch, and very good it is to see the old back filling its function with continuing usefulness. A word of warning may be added here to the address of the amateur collector. The forger of antiques has not been unmindful of this, a valuable field for his employment. A skilled Sussex antiquary has lately confessed that both he and a Sussex museum have discovered that two of their respective treasures are identical in details which leave but little doubt that some very modern founder is the richer for their enthusiasm.

An interesting feature of the original trade in heraldic fire-backs was that people seemed to have bought them bearing the arms of anyone they fancied. One Giles Moore, a parson of Horsted Keynes, in the middle of the Weald, kept a diary from 1655 to 1679. He several times mentions purchases from the local ironworks, but the following most concerns us : " An iron plate for my parlour grate with Mr. Michelbourne's arms upon it, ten shillings " ; and again, " for a plate cast for my kitchen chimney, weighing 100lb. and 3qr. marked G.M.S., besides two shillings given to the founders for casting, thirteen shillings." The good rector seems to have realised that the ironfounders' life is a thirsty one. Perhaps the oddest thing about the iron-foundries of the Weald, the most important of which were at Mayfield, Heathfield and Lamberhurst, was their limited range of production. Andirons went with fire-backs naturally enough, grave-slabs and cannon have already been mentioned, and their activities seem to have gone no further. The iron railings of St. Paul's Cathedral, which gave Wren such a lot of trouble, seem to have been a sporadic case of taking up a new idea, and the Lamberhurst folk charged eightpence a pound for them as against a penny for fire-backs and a halfpenny for ordnance.

But to return to the house. Of the dining-room and drawing-room no more need be said than that they are pleasant, well-lit rooms, all furnished as becomes the house, and the same is true of the five bed-rooms upstairs. Not the least notable fact about Gilham's Birch is one that does honour to Mr. May's economic skill—it cost less than one thousand two hundred pounds, which represents only sevenpence farthing a cubic foot. The garden makes a happy framing for the house. The approach is by an entrance gate which speaks for itself in the picture. The site stands so high above the road that the garden is held up by a retaining wall of the local freestone of creamy tone with streaks of gold. The path to the porch is sunk between two banks and flanked by dry stone walls rich with plants of every sort. The brick steps are set round an old millstone, and the path leads on with random flagstones. The gate itself is worthy of note, the handiwork of an old wheelwright. Mr. May holds (and this example makes one inclined to agree with him) that a satisfactory gate is no work for a joiner, that it does not lend itself to being made at that craftsman's bench. A wheelwright is a man accustomed to the working of curves and to following the natural disposition of his material. Hence the agreeable outline of the top rail and of the brace. Another good feature of the garden is the big stairway, built, not too carefully, in the local stone, which leads from the rustic pergola down to the lawn. We leave Gilham's Birch with the feeling that Mr. May has created not an imitation of an old farmhouse, but a home in little for a country gentleman of to-day.

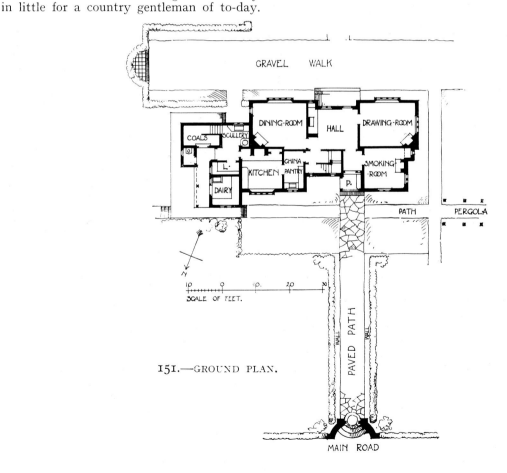

151.—GROUND PLAN.

THE THATCHED COTTAGE, LLANWERN.

DESIGNED BY MR. OSWALD MILNE.

A Cottage in Fact—Tile-work in Walls—A Sease of Material—The Training of Builders—
Reasonable Simplicity.

THE Thatched Cottage at Llanwern, Monmouthshire, occupies a site close to a road on the west and has a south-eastern slope and outlook from the rather bare meadow in which it stands. There are woods on the other side of the road; the forest-land of Gwent rears its altitudes to the north; to the east, across the lush meadows that border a trout stream, rise the lesser but picturesquely broken slopes of the grandly timbered park of Llanwern; while to the south a peep is obtained down to the rich pasture tract that borders Severn Sea. Much planting of trees, setting of orchard, building of terraces, making of borders and laying down of lawn have taken place, so that the

place is rich in hope; and the good soil and mild climate have encouraged such growths as already give the pleasant little domicile a settled air. It is called a cottage, and the simple lines, the low elevation, the long sweeps of thatch perhaps entitle it to this description as it is at present understood, for the dictionary informs us that the term was "formerly applied to a hut or hovel, now to a small, neat dwelling." Hut or hovel we have not before us; neat dwelling we have, and though it has three sitting-rooms of adequate size, yet it may rightly be called small, as it was designed for a lady with one servant, and has only four bedrooms. Nowadays the artisan prefers to dignify his tenement by the name of house, and the cottage is become the residence of the well-to-do

153.—A TERRACE WALK OF ROUGH FLAGGING.

who seek simplicity in their mode of living. Simplicity, of a thoroughly educated and tasteful kind, rules at Llanwern; it was strongly in the architect's mind when he designed it, and has been realised by the owner in her treatment of it. And so, despite its parlour and its dining-room and its "own" room, it is in the spirit of the cottage, and the purist in language will permit the designation. Cottage,

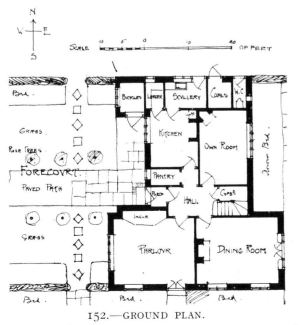

152.—GROUND PLAN.

however, is a word that is suffering sadly from a sort of fashionableness, and is being contorted out of all semblance of its right application by house agents. Not long ago a leading London firm advertised for sale " a reproduction of an Early English Cottage residence." Early English, indeed! This would be a " hut or hovel " in real earnest, and a study of it would surely teach us much of how the villein lived in Plantagenet times. Unknown though it was to the late Mr. J. R. Green and to M. Jusserand, it would seem that the villein's dwelling contained " billiard room, hall, loggia, four reception rooms, winter garden, small private chapel, eleven bed and dressing rooms, bath, three staircases and ample offices." The only point on which information is denied us, and that is disappointing, is the precise spot where the original of this egregious " reproduction " is to be found! Luckily, at Llanwern, there is no reproduction. We have a thing which belongs to to-day ; a little home in full accord with the best traditions of old cottage building, and yet accepting modern teaching in material, manner and disposition when these promise to add to comfort and convenience. From the wicket gate set in the road hedge a flagged way bordered by grass plats leads us to the hooded entrance door. The walls of the house are of lias limestone, dug out near at hand, and, therefore, used without stint. Of many tones from yellow to brown, it has to be used as it is dug out, for its weather-resisting power depends upon its retaining its surface. It therefore appears

154.—THE ENTRANCE.

in many sizes and of rough texture, the largest and squarest lumps being reserved for the quoins. Over the windows it is set up on end to form a low relieving arch, and the space between that and a narrow projecting drip-stone above the wooden window frame is filled with red roofing tiles. Such tiles have become, with many architects, a favourite material for obtaining by simple and inexpensive means an occasional change of tone and texture, and Mr. Milne has much recourse to them. Where as here they are used to fill putlog holes they appear as insignificant insets in the walling, the stonework of which already exhibits such diversity of size, colour and surface that these small spots of tile go near to destroying the due sense of breadth and restfulness. But in other positions the tiles are introduced with aptness and success. As a string-course they carry the line of the door-hood along the massive structure of the neighbouring chimney and again appear on it higher up in order to help the rough stone to fit round the panel of arms and to make a level platform from which the brick shaft springs. In the roof, in the larder and below the floor-level they are

155 —THE COTTAGE AND ITS TERRACE.

ventilating louvres, while set herring-bone-wise they form the back of the parlour fireplace. Thatching in Monmouthshire has been held to be a lost art, and we are apt to hear that corrugated sheets must replace straw as the covering of hay and corn ricks. These difficulties are frequently much of people's own making. There has been a submerging of the influences which produced the whole race of handicraftsmen by a general contentment with mechanical methods and effects. The drawing-board architects of the nineteenth century knew and cared little for the subtle effects derived from

156.— IN THE PARLOUR.

the right choice and manipulation of materials. The instinct of the craftsman for colour and texture withered from neglect, but it has not entirely perished. That under proper culture it will rapidly revive is proved by the results obtained at the cottage we are studying. Llanwern is a perfectly rural parish, with

157.—THE DINING-ROOM

a sparse population, but it is on the edge of, it is threatened with invasion by, a modern mushroom growth of industrialism. Nothing can be newer—newer in the most repellent phases of newness—than Monmouthshire's big town of Newport. Its network of streets, its miles of buildings, never at any one point display any attempt towards acceptable domestic architecture. What is not vulgarly showy is sordidly mean, and all has the same machine-made look. Architect, builder and workman have been in the grip of the modern monster, and its iron has entered into their soul. And yet at the call of Mr. Milne, a Newport builder, who has no doubt taken his modest part in defacing God's earth with rows of " desirable " tenements, and has not so far known or recognised that anything different was desirable or possible, set to on the right lines. Mr. Case went through Mr. Milne's plans and specifications, and saw his way to carrying them out for the modest sum of six hundred and fifty pounds. Perhaps he hardly knew what he was in for, and what time and trouble it would take him and his men to call back lost ideas and habits and to build after the manner of their forefathers. But if they had to use their faculties and be on the alert rather more than the average Englishman of to-day cares for, they succeeded perfectly and they liked it, and the Thatched Cottage is a job in which Mr. Case feels some pride. It is a little flower of the field amid the great crop of coarse artificial growths that environ it. And this he has come to recognise. He sees there is something in it, that the very simple means, good and unpretentious, by which the right effect has been produced and a character given to this dwelling which nothing near it shares, is perhaps a thing which should be aimed at. A seed has been sown which may germinate and wax great.

The contract price of six hundred and fifty pounds at once proves that no costly materials and no complex workmanship were demanded. In these respects it is a cottage indeed. Everything is of the plainest. There are no mouldings to the windows. The doors are ledged and fitted with quite ordinary hinges and latches. The fireplaces are built in with stock bricks, and the least possible woodwork has been used for chimney-pieces. If, then, the result pleases, it is not from elaboration. It is just because it is meet ; because the sense of scale has been thoroughly preserved. Every form and proportion suits its neighbour and suits the whole. Every material is allowed to be itself, and all seem to belong to the same family. A single mode of expression has been used throughout, and if it is not a grand one it is entirely wholesome. It says that " poor and content is rich and rich enough," and it spreads around it its self-evident contentment with its own lot in life. It fills you with the same feeling and convinces you then and there that it has enunciated a reasonable doctrine. Marble halls are right enough when their possessors are able and willing to live up to them. But playing at them with cheap scenic imitations is neither comfortable nor wholesome, while little vulgar efforts at introducing a semblance of their qualities in the jerry-built villa are sheer depravity of the reprehensible type that is stupid and ugly. Llanwern Cottage makes no pretence of representing an exiguous form of existence. It is spacious, convenient and well fitted, but at the same time its simplicity and straightforwardness encourage natural conduct. If you wish you may perfectly well be found baking the scones and boiling the water with an apron on, and the visitors will feel that to lend a hand is an enjoyment. Such action fits in with the picture and suggests self-help, although the whole setting speaks of ease, taste and comfort. A few additional expenses, such as an oak floor for the parlour and an oak staircase, were ventured on after the first estimate was sent in, so that the whole cost, including the architect's fee, reached a sum between seven hundred and fifty and eight hundred pounds. The whole cost, including that of the drainage, etc., worked out at ninepence halfpenny a cubic foot. The furniture is perfectly apt. It consists almost entirely of Welsh farmhouse pieces collected with great judgment. They are the products of small self-providing communities. A neighbour has made them for a neighbour. Mechanical methods and wholesale principles have not touched them even with a breath. Like the home they suit so well they seem to be the immediate output of the head and hands of individual men and to have taken on something of their personality.

A HOUSE AT AMBERLEY, SUSSEX.

DESIGNED BY MR. DOUGLAS MURRAY.

A Difficult Site—Old and New Materials—Concerning Chimneys—The House-place.

THE river Arun bisects Sussex from north to south, and flows through some of that county's choicest lands. It waters a country of rich flats and moderate elevation during its upper course. but long ere it reaches Arundel on its way to the sea it encounters the South Downs, and has to make many a bend and circuit to enable it to pass through this barrier. This lends much picturesqueness to its valley, on the edge of which, looking southward on to the down-encompassed vale, stands the subject of this chapter. Crossing the bridge from the West Burton side and rising from the river, the road on its way north-east to Amberley Village skirts the Down above the slope which the house and garden occupy. This lie of the land has been seized upon to give character to the setting and

laying out of the building and its environment. It has been done very successfully, though the necessity of duly treating a difficult piece of ground without outrunning the available sum was no easy matter. It is coping with difficulty that breeds skill, and though, of course, a bottomless purse could have produced bigger results, the great merit and interest of this little place is that, in mass and in detail, it possesses charm and distinction and has not been expensive. The entire cost of house and grounds, including paving, turf-

158.—THE SOUTH OR GARDEN FRONT.

ing and fencing, of everything, in fact, down to the smallest detail, was £2,126 17s. 11d. The house itself cost eightpence farthing a cubic foot. It stands thirty or forty feet west of the road and is approached from it diagonally down a broad flight of steps and along a pathway of local stones, flat but unsquared, which leads to the door at the back or north side of the house. Westward of this door, the office wing springs out of the main block of the house at an angle corresponding with the angle of the entrance steps from the road. The precise direction of the fall in the land made this the line of least resistance, occasioned the least movement of soil and building of retaining walls, and was, therefore, the most economical scheme. A note of pleasant originality joined with practical utility was thus obtained.　It was not a conceit artificially dragged in, but a business-like arrangement that came about naturally.

Though quite recently erected, it has no look of rawness, because it is very largely composed of old material.　Bricks, tiling, and timbers of demolished buildings in the neighbourhood were available, and

159.—THE ENTRANCE OR NORTHERN FRONT.

were gladly seized upon and used with judgment and success.　The great roof, typical of the county's ancient homes, shows a slight wave and has a mellow tone.　The old oak timbers of the southern gable and of other projecting parts lend an air of venerability to this youthful structure, and the effect is well carried out by the rough finish of the plaster.　As circumstances permitted this look of premature age to be given to the exterior in general, it seems rather a pity that the desired effect should be marred by the use, in the occasional weather-boarded portions, of painted deal of the most smooth, finished and mechanical modern sort. Paint and regularity combine to create a dissonance. The whole aspect lacks harmonious completeness. There is a want of loving relationship between the members, a slight hostility of the parts, as if they rather resented their enforced juxtaposition. This would have been avoided by using rough-sawn elm for the weather-boarding, which, in two seasons if not in one, would have assumed a wavy irregularity of line and a silver greyness of tone giving an air of close affinity to all the materials used. This treatment, owing to the inevitable winding of this wood, calls for felt between it and the wall behind if the latter is composed of 4½in. quartering filled in with brick, but the expense is small, and it has been used for the upper floors of quite cheap cottages for farm labourers. The house is of so engaging a kind, and so much taste and feeling have reigned over its contrivance, that importance is given to the least jarring note, to a defect which, in the general run of houses, would escape detection. That is why the chimney of the low office wing catches the eye as it should not. The great stack at the east end, with its three elaborate shafts, is admirable. It has presence, size, balance. It draws due attention to its honourable function of serving the principal rooms. Equally good and appropriate is the more massive stack that rises out of the main roof further westward. But where the modest part of the house is reached, no feature should attract attention by the saliency of its proportions. Stuck centrally on the ridge of the humble outhouse roof, the single shaft, shooting up high and slim, asserting itself by its diagonal setting on its base and by its enrichment of many mouldings, is certainly out of place. Its presence, rising through and above the pergola, as seen in the view taken from the west garden, was so distracting in an otherwise delightful composition that it has been effaced down to its plain square base. If the illustration of this is compared with that in which it is retained, the advantage of its removal will be clear. Of course, the present base is not of itself sufficient for the prac-

160.—THE HOUSE AND ITS SITE.

tical purpose of carrying away the smoke, but it should be raised as little and as simply as possible.

The southern elevation and terrace have a considerable space between them and the road, which is not at right angles to the house. This space is separated from the terrace by a retaining wall, and the growth of hedge and trees will soon give shelter and privacy to the garden. A broad flagged way runs along the south front and there is access to it from the house through an open-sided room or loggia. Beyond the house, this flagged way passes under a pergola of rough timbers—a wall sheltering it on the north—and then reaches a flight of steps descending to a lower garden of mixed flowers, fruits and vegetables. As regards the interior, the plan of the ground floor will explain itself without much description, especially as an illustration of the main living-room is also given. The conception of the plan tends towards a reversion to the house-place of old-time dwellings of moderate size, such as Gervase Markham figured and described in James I.'s time. There are, indeed, at Amberley an entrance or vestibule and a dining-room ; but the main feature is the room which occupies the whole east end of the house. It is in two sections on different levels. It is principally lit by a five-light casement window to the south. Its north side is open to the upper section, which is balustraded off except where three steps give access to it. At the back of this section rises the main stairway, while an ample, many-mullioned oriel occupies its eastern side. Space, incident and variety are thus given to the room, which must be a most pleasant one to live in, though there are some who would prefer the additional privacy of the stairs opening from the vestibule. This is a matter

161.— FROM THE WEST OR LOWER GARDEN.

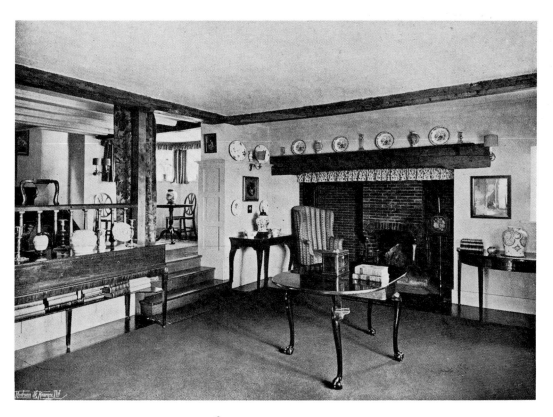

162 —THE LIVING-ROOM.

for individual feeling. Certainly the present arrangement is the more picturesque, and this stair is only meant for the use of the occupiers of the room out of which it rises, as there are back stairs at the other end of the house. The main stairway, moreover, is shut off at its summit by a door which opens on to a gallery 30ft. long and 10ft. wide, having a great bay window over the front door and a fireplace opposite to this feature. It therefore fulfils the function of an additional sitting-room, and also affords an air of spaciousness to the upper floor. From it the four principal bedrooms are entered. Through an arched opening at its west end a cross passage is reached leading to the ample bathroom and the well-contrived hot-linen closet, housemaid's accommodation, etc. Here, too, are the back stairs rising from the kitchen and continuing up to the attic bedrooms. The interior finish is simple and pleasing. The plain but well-proportioned panelling and the doors and chimney-pieces are kept white, and above them the walls and ceilings are washed white also, the latter being occasionally broken and relieved by old oak beams. The furniture, the china, the pictures, the implements are also in many cases old, and in all cases are well chosen with precise reference to the character of the rooms and to the effect desired. There is throughout a happy conjunction of the old and the new. The spirit of the past is here, yet rigid archaism and self-conscious eccentricity are wholly avoided.

163.—SOUTH-EAST GABLE.

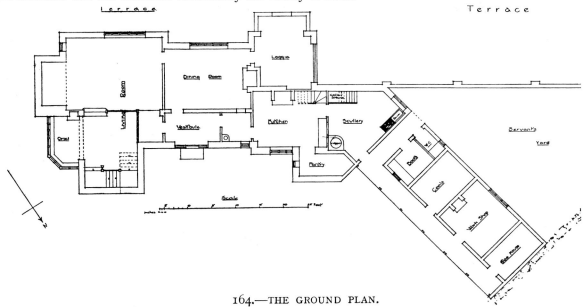

164.—THE GROUND PLAN.

LUCKLEY, WOKINGHAM.

DESIGNED BY MR. ERNEST NEWTON.

The Influence of Norman Shaw—Planning, Symmetrical and Otherwise—Plaster Cornices—Trellis Staircase Railing—The Baluster—Bedroom Windows.

THERE is a story—no voucher is given for its truth—that an enterprising critic set out to write a history showing the development of domestic architecture during the second half of the last century. After some labour in collecting and sorting his material, he concluded that the task really narrowed itself to a survey of the work of Norman Shaw and of those he influenced. While this view is too exclusive, and does some injustice to many eminent men such as Philip Webb who have left our architecture the better for their achievement, it is worth recording. The students whose earliest inspirations were guided by Norman Shaw make a long and distinguished list, and among them was Mr. Ernest Newton. His work early took on, and with consistence has maintained, a delicate individuality which separates it from that of his contemporaries.

During the thirty years that he has practised on his own account the fashions of architecture have been many and changing; but Mr. Newton has pursued his way unaffected by the foibles to which many able men have turned for a time. In all domestic work there are two opposing tendencies in planning. The one is to devise an arrangement of rooms solely with regard to the nature of the site and the habits and needs of the future occupants. This means that the elevations may have, more or less, to take care of themselves. They are the natural outcome of the plan and are governed by it. The result, however admirable in its own right, is likely to be deficient in balance. At its best this method of planning produces a picturesque array of features, among which each projection or gable reveals and emphasises the plan. From the outside the building is full of the charm of the unexpected, and it is only by acquaintance with the inside that the external irregularity is seen to be justified by the fitness of the interior. At the worst this disregard of regularity produces an incoherent mass which reveals no sense of purpose. At the other end of the scale is the plan which

165.—THE ENTRANCE.

is governed by the proportions of the façades. The style adopted perhaps postulates a middle door of entrance and an equal number of windows at each side of equal size. The elevations are the fixed element, and the rooms have to be planned to fit them.

The middle course (and the *via media* is dear to our architecture as to other things English) is to equip one principal front with that balance and proportion that give to a building the great quality of restfulness, and let practical needs determine the rest of the plan, even if it involves some irregularity in other elevations. Of this middle course Luckley is an admirable example. Mr. Newton has employed a ground plan that is a favourite with him, and that commends itself for dignity and convenience. It is in outline a traditional English arrangement, commonly called the H plan. Popular over a long period, it is here adapted to strictly modern needs. In effect it consists of two narrow parallel wings, in one of which are the sitting-rooms and in the other the dining-room, kitchen and other offices. Connecting the two wings is a narrow body, which includes not only the main staircase, but a corridor from drawing-room to dining-room, serving the pleasant function of a processional path for the rites of English hospitality.

The illustrations show that Mr. Newton has allowed the entrance front to have one wing wider than the other (thus giving ample space to the kitchen premises), and has elected to get his symmetrical effect

on the garden front, which is the chief elevation. On the right one sees the kitchen offices set back, but the two wings, with their orderly arrangement of bow windows and pairs of triple lights above, stand out clearly balanced. The projecting windows compose happily with the curved and pillared portico. This latter feature is repeated exactly on the entrance front and is characteristic of Mr. Newton's work. The house is here at its narrowest, and on arriving at the entrance the visitor looks through both porches

166.—PORCH AND GARDEN FORECOURT.

on the garden court. It is in such small details as the paving of this court that a just sense of the value of materials makes itself felt. The footways are covered with large red quarries and the way to the lawn is flanked with spaces of rough flags in the wide joints of which rock plants flourish.

The general view from the garden is eminently satisfying. The house stands on the site of an earlier building, well bowered in trees. The walls are built of Sussex clamp bricks whose purplish tone is lightened by bright red dressings from Wrotham. The tiles are of the dark hand-made sort that give a homely texture to the roof and weather quickly in uneven tones. Dignity is given by the bold dentil course that supports the eaves and runs round the house, save where it stops for a projecting chimney. There is no effort to interfere with the natural position of the chimney-stacks as determined by the plan, and the central placing of the staircase in the connecting stroke of the H puts the middle chimney a little out of centre as seen from the garden front. This is all to the good. A lesser designer would have played tricks with his bedroom planning in order to avoid this irregularity. As it is, the chimney is a naive index of the upstairs arrangements to those who have the eye to mark them.

Mr. Newton is an old friend to the varied uses of lead in architecture. The half-dome roofs of the bays and the curved hood of the porch are covered with the characteristic English metal. Elsewhere, as at Red Court, Haslemere, the architect has given an added charm to these dome-shaped roofs by finishing them with a deep square gutter in cast lead, drained by a stout lead pipe with traditional ornament. Here the scheme of treatment is on simpler lines, and the gutter and down-

167.—EAST CORRIDOR, LOOKING TOWARDS HALL.

pipe are of plain cast iron. Before going indoors we must note the stables, which lie to the left of the carriage drive and group pleasantly and frankly with the house. In the old foolish days of Capability Brown and even of his more intelligent successor, Humphry Repton, stables and the like were tucked away behind screen walls, as though they were disreputable adjuncts to " the gentleman's house." A

168.—THE GARDEN FRONT.

169 —PART OF THE DRAWING-ROOM.

170. —THE HALL.

saner view of things as they are leads us to-day to regard such outbuildings as deserving architectural treatment in a frank way that will bring them into obvious and wise relation with the main building. This has been done in sound fashion at Luckley.

The interior has the same quiet dignity that the outside presents. The sitting hall is panelled in oak by the fireplace, which is screened from the passage-way, and the beams show. The overmantels, both here and in the drawing-room, have the triple arches which are so favourite a decorative motive with Mr. Newton. Throughout the house there is an absence of cornices, or of any ornamental ceiling treatment, except in the drawing-room, where there is an unobtrusive coving. The way that modern architects have freed themselves from the tyranny of the plaster cornice is altogether to the good. The layman may not realise that even modest cornices add about five per cent. to the cost of a house. It is not many years ago that the suggestion of omitting the cornice in a sitting-room, even of a suburban villa, would have been thought an outrage verging on the indecent. To-day they are still used to excess, but the wise architect omits them unless he can employ them without having to save on the quality of materials elsewhere, as used often to be done.

The fireplace in the drawing-room is in a recess, lighted on the left by a bull's-eye window—as happy a feature inside as it is in the external elevation. The staircase has simple rails of a wide trellis pattern, an agreeable variation from the usual baluster. We have come to regard the baluster as an essential architectural feature, but it is one of the few elements that we owe to the Renaissance. The history of Roman architecture may be searched for it in vain, and the same cannot be said of broken pediments and other devices which are commonly attributed to the revival of classical art.

A hint of practical value is given by the ventilation of the bedrooms. In the days of the Gothic revival there was a return to mullioned and transomed windows. The transom had this practical value, that while the lower casement was hinged sideways, the upper one could be hung at the top to open outwards. There is obviously no more wholesome way of ventilating a bedroom than by such a transom light. However, transoms are, if not impossible, at least absurd, with rooms of ordinary height, and give a needless emphasis to the horizontal lines. The device at Luckley is to divide the metal casement into parts, the upper third hinged from the top and the lower two-thirds opening sideways. The metal fillet connecting them is not noticeable from the outside, so the causes both of ventilation and sightliness are served. The general impressions one takes from the house are that it is imposing in a reasonable way for its size and accommodation, and that the design is throughout sincere and coherent. That economy has been considered is clear from the cubic foot cost, which was no more than sevenpence halfpenny.

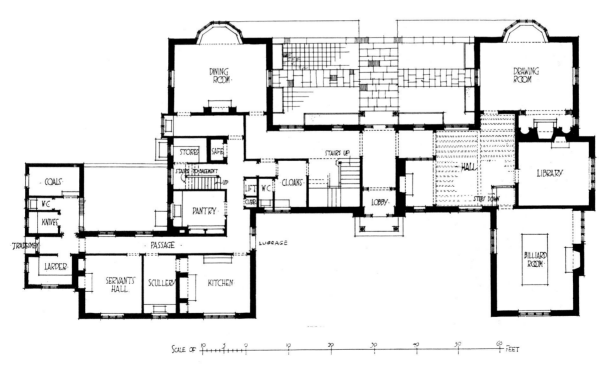

171.—THE GROUND PLAN.

LONG COPSE, EWHURST, SURREY.

DESIGNED BY MR. ALFRED POWELL.

*Mediæval and Modern Ways of Building—Sgraffito Work—A Cure for Porous Stone
Walls—Thatch and Heeling.*

A BUILDING of which G. F. Watts said that it was the most beautiful in Surrey has obviously qualities of value. Long Copse, Ewhurst, won this praise from the veteran artist, and though the dictum seems rather in the vein of hyperbole, when one remembers what Surrey boasts, none will deny the house a large merit. When the ordinary person contemplates the building of a country cottage, there are two courses open. One is to go to a local builder, describe the accommodation needed, give vague ideas as to materials, and trust to the Englishman's luck to muddle through. That way lies extravagance and dissatisfaction, and generally a building that is an astonishment and a hissing. The other is to employ an architect and let him see the house built to his plans by a builder. The " architect and builder " method, if an unhandy phrase may be forgiven, is partly the outcome of social conditions, but largely of the artistic revolution which we call the Renaissance. In mediæval times architecture was an art little conscious of rules, and doubtless impatient of rulers. The

172.—THE VERANDAH WITH SGRAFFITO DECORATION

owner of the building, were he layman or cleric, had probably a larger knowledge of the building arts than the average client of an architect to-day. It is true that the sum of technical knowledge then available was markedly smaller. The complexities of building bye-laws, often futile and always hampering, were unknown. Materials were simpler and fewer and, save for great buildings, limited to those that the neighbourhood supplied. Certainly, for small houses and in the country the architect was unknown and the very name did not appear until 1510. His place was taken in great buildings by the master of the works. For little houses the owner contracted direct with the master-mason of the village, talked over plans with him and the carpenter, and settled details with the smith and plumber. All this was possible when the process of building was unconscious. They built in the customary way. Style developed steadily for five centuries, but eclecticism was unknown. A man in the fourteenth century built as he did because he lived when he did, and not because he liked his style better than some other. With the Renaissance things changed, and learning and culture got mixed up with building. The time had gone for a man to build as his father before him— in the light of a great tradition. He must build in the Roman manner, after reading Vitruvius and Palladio. Thus

173.—THE HOUSE SEEN FROM THE GARDEN.

design became the business of the cultivated man who could understand hard words, and craftsmanship took a subordinate place. It would be as foolish as it is useless to regret the change. Without it we should have had neither Inigo Jones nor Wren ; but, as in all upheavals, there were great losses to set against the compensating gains. The architect did not kill the crafts, but he maimed them. Responsibility was taken from the master-craftsmen, with the result that their hands lost much of their cunning.

Long Copse, apart from its intrinsic beauty, has the special claim of our interest that it was built in the mediæval spirit. It was designed, in consultation with Mrs. Mudie-Cooke, by Mr. Alfred Powell, and he acted as master of the works. He bought all materials, and the craftsmen (save the plumbers—an entertaining exception) were University men who worked with him. Between the owner and the craftsmen, therefore, stood one man only, who both devised and wrought, instead of the usual two—an architect who designs only and a builder who hardly ever works with his own hands. The result is instinct with simplicity while free from affectation. The site is ideal. On the south-west slope of Pitch Hill, between Gomshall and

174.—THE DINING-ROOM.

Cranleigh, a clearing has been made in a delightful wood, and there nestles this thatched homestead. Immediately in front of it the garden slopes down the hill and the long copse flanks the site, while the lower lands towards Cranleigh spread themselves out like a map, and Hindhead opposes its heights in the distance. The building gives that sense of vitality which is the evidence of healthy growth. Simple as it is in plan to-day, it began even more simply. Mrs. Mudie-Cooke's idea was to have a little country retreat of the purely cottage type, with a single living-room, into which the entrance door gave. This was well enough in summer, but winter brought devastating draughts. It was impossible to add a porch without interfering with the curved wall in which the circular stair is set, and thus making an addition which could not fail to disturb. An extra room, marked on the plan " dining-room," was provided by converting the original kitchen and building a new kitchen and offices beyond. At the same time there were provided additional bedrooms on the upper floor and a verandah by the outer door of the dining-room. Sgraffito work is little used in England, but on the back wall of this verandah Cavaliere Formilli has scratched a picture of peacocks in light red and white. It sounds an ambitious treatment for a cottage verandah, but the straightforwardness of the technique and the reasonableness of the subject make it a desirable decoration by a skilful hand. The plan of the entrance front is made especially interesting by its break in wall-line at the circular stair. One unsatisfactory feature of this otherwise delightful stairway is a lack of headroom, a little thoughtlessness which could easily have been avoided. It was a happy notion to emphasise the position of the staircase in the body of the building. There is a tendency in modern architecture to pursue the quaint and to invent features for their appearance sake. Here, however, is a legitimate practical need organically emphasised in the plan, a sober piece of building which yet has a marked decorative value.

The construction throughout is massive and traditional. The walls are of the local sandstone, of a warm yellow and two feet thick. Though the stone (as usual very soft when quarried) has now hardened from exposure, the searching gales from the south-west drove the rain through the outer wall, despite its fortress-like thickness. It is useful to know that the painting of the outside with water-glass, a colourless and cheap liquid, stopped the pores of the stone and cured a very trying fault. The technique of the masonry is admirable. Note the strong and sober effect of the mullions flush with the wall on the outside and splaying slightly inwards. On such a building one feels the simplest moulding would have been a blunder. The chimney treatment is bold and adequate. The original cottage was content with a single central stack, but the addition necessitated a second, which groups with its fellow admirably.

The original roof idea was to tile, but for the cottage as first built Norfolk thatchers came with their reeds, and a beautiful roof they made. The addition was roofed with Horsham stone, better perhaps than the thatch, for heeling is vernacular in this neighbourhood and thatch is not. There is a tenderness about the way the moss and willow weed grow on this stone roof, that seems Nature's benediction of the use of local things. The interior is simple and dignified. Nothing but oak is used for beams, flooring and doors, and the great timbers are rough from the adze. Some of the uprights are left in the round, stripped of bark, but unsquared. This seems just to overstep simplicity and to plunge into the crude, for the saving of labour and material involved in omitting the squaring seems too slight to make it worth while. The whole of the woodwork construction was arranged so that the timbers could remain exposed. This allowed them to be cut from the green tree and used straightway without seasoning. The trees were chosen to give in their natural shapes the required curves for the roof principals. For the joinery work, such as doors and windows,

175.—THE SITTING-ROOM.

only thoroughly dry wood was used. The walls are whitewashed, and the house is innocent everywhere of both paper and paint.

The furnishing is of a grave and simple sort throughout. Many of the pieces are old, and, where new, they accord with the cottage atmosphere. The fireplaces in sitting-room and dining-room are open, with wood fires burning on plain stone hearths. In the case of the sitting-room the fire is very wisely supplemented by a hot-water radiator at the far end, which is worked from a stove built in the thickness of the outer wall of the dining-room. The installation is absolutely inoffensive in appearance and has the great practical advantage of keeping the house well aired during the winter. After fire, a word as to water. Wells are a difficulty on Pitch Hill, and there was much vain digging at Long Copse. Resort to the hazel twig and the spirit of divination had happy results, and in the one hundred feet well there is always forty feet of water at the driest times, when neighbouring wells yield nothing. The domestic arrangements are of peculiar simplicity. There is no accommodation in the house for servants, who have their quarters in an adjoining thatched cottage—another aid to the owners' pursuit of perfect quiet. The whole of the upper floor, with its five bedrooms, bathroom, etc., is thus available for the family and guests. Behind the servants' cottage is a long range of stables, etc., for the owner has not yielded to petrol, but still thinks horses are of the essence of country life.

It is after one has spent a day in and about a house of this kind that one is tempted to define the distinctions between building and architecture. Here is a successful example of the return to traditional ways of building, a return which is clearly possible to-day. It has none of the complexity of the conscious style ; it is not, in fact, architecture. The elevations grow simply and reasonably out of the plan ; the plan has not been contrived to lead up to effects, but is determined by the site. There is no conscious irregularity on the one hand nor contrived balancing of architectural elements on the other.

Long Copse does not give the feeling of having been devised. It seems rather to have happened. For the simple domestic building this is high praise, but hardly excessive. The experiment of departing from usual methods has been justified ; but Mr. Alfred Powell and those who worked with him were not usual men, and they were not working for an usual client. For the ordinary man to depart from customary ways is a desperate enterprise, and Long Copse in its success is but the happy exception to a wise rule which is based on experience.

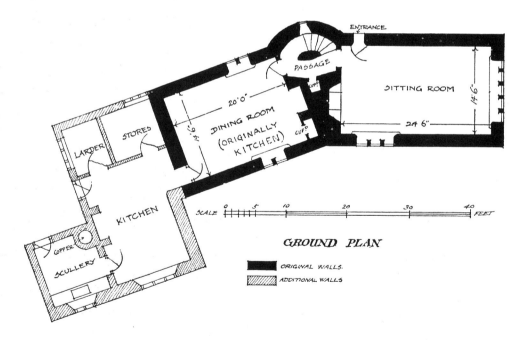

GROUND PLAN

WEST CHART, LIMPSFIELD, SURREY.

DESIGNED BY MR. E. TURNER POWELL.

Surrey Traditions of Building—Galleting—A Man's Room—Tile-Hanging—The Use of Old Materials.

ALTHOUGH Surrey does not boast any compact woodlands of very large extent, it is one of the best timbered counties in England, and nearly twelve of every hundred of its acres are covered with woods and plantations. It is to this characteristic that the site and surroundings of West Chart owe some of their beauties. So far back as the Domesday Survey the largest wooded tract in Surrey, outside those in the Royal possession, was one held in Oxted by Eustace, Count of Boulogne, which is described as worth a hundred hogs from the pannage. This luxurious quota of oaks, the acorns they gave and the noble herd of swine they fed have gone into the limbo of forgotten things ; but enough trees of pleasant growth are left to make Limpsfield a very agreeable place in which to build a home.

Surrey is peculiarly a county of domestic architecture, and for many reasons. It lacks great towns and rich industries and, in consequence, great public buildings. Southwark, indeed, had its palaces, but time and the receding tide of fashion have destroyed them. Other great palaces, like Richmond and Nonesuch, are known to us only from the pens of long dead draughtsmen, and though such places as Loseley and Sutton testify to Surrey's one-time wealth in great houses, it is perhaps of its smaller architecture that the county may most reasonably boast. It is unquestionably the favourite county for the homes of those who work in London, and this eminence in the favour of Londoners is no new thing. As far back as the reigns of Elizabeth and James I. the servants of the Court aimed to make enough (by means perhaps not always fanatically honest) to ensure retirement to a small estate in Surrey. To them, and to the latter race of wealthy citizens of London, we owe the numerous small houses which fixed the type of local architecture. It is therefore a happy event when the designers of modern houses are found following straitly in the paths of their forerunners and building in the traditional way.

The district is rich in building materials. It is more a brick than a stone county, but it is by no means poor in the latter. From the hills south of Guildford is quarried the rich brown stone called Bargate, and though not ordinarily fit for fine dressing, it has a strong texture, and is eminently suitable for walling. The rough shapes into which it ordinarily breaks when quarried make it convenient to build it with wide mortar joints, a use that brought in its train the delightful practice of decorating the joint by sticking in it little scraps of other stone, generally ironstone, a trick which goes by the engaging name of "galleting." The Romans

177.—THE PORCH.

employed this black ironstone for cubes in their mosaic floors, and it is used to-day for paving with admirable effect. The bricks and tiles of Surrey have the great advantage of a touch of iron in their composition, which gives that richness to the red that can nowhere be bettered. In the habit of tile-hanging walls this county and its neighbour, Sussex, strike their most characteristic note. It is not, however, a practice of great antiquity, for Mr. Ralph Nevill, who has given much study to the subject, is not inclined to date its introduction earlier than about 1700. The shapes of the tiles are many, but the most usual, except

178.—SOUTH-WEST CORNER.

179.—NORTH FRONT.

the simple oblong, is the rounded end. Where this weather tiling was used there was obviously a difficulty at the corners of walls. The ingenuity of later days has adopted the angle tile, but originally it was the practice to stop the tiles against a corner post of oak. So much by way of rough outline of the more usual Surrey building methods of bygone days. Let us see how Mr. Turner Powell has maintained the customary ways. West Chart is perched so high on the side of the hill—the doorstep is only a little under six hundred feet above sea-level—that a winding carriage drive had to be made, which brings us up at the north-east corner. Confronting us is the great kitchen chimney, built partly of stone and partly of brick, the masonry joints being galleted with the black ironstone that was excavated on the site. The varied views that strike the eye as the porch is approached conspire to give a sense of breadth and comfort. The house is long and low, and the roofs of a rather flat pitch, which is accentuated by the breadth of the dormers. The porch is a charming feature, built of stout oak posts on dwarf stone walls, and roofed with Horsham stone (or, to give its correct name, " heeling "). The porch steps are of ironstone, and its ceiling rudely plastered. At the north-west corner is a loggia, whence may be seen as fine a view as any place so near London can afford. Straight across the valley northwards is the long range of the northern downs of Surrey, to the left is Caterham and due west is Box Hill. It is not too much to say that the outlook is magnificent.

Continuing our survey of the house, we note the broad overhang of the roof on the west side, and tucked under it a window bracketed out enough to prevent any loss of light. The feature of the south side is the big weather-boarded gable which hangs over the paved space, and makes it in practice another loggia. Note, too, the modest little window in the western face of this big gabled projection, with its sill much lower than the long ranges of casements each side of it. This is the babies' window, of which more anon. The south loggia also has the ironstone paving, which is here enlivened by being laid round an old millstone. At the

180.—FROM DRAWING-ROOM TO HALL.

south-east corner is the low roof of the motor-house, which groups delightfully with the main building. So much for the exterior, which is a true descendant in the line of Surrey traditions, and so admirable in its sort that one is loath to criticise. It may, however, be said that there is just a little tendency to overdo features in themselves attractive. To the left of the porch there is some confusion in the management of the roof.

The next question of interest is the plan, which is very much like that of Gilham's Birch, also illustrated in this volume. Mr. Turner Powell evidently shares with Mr. E. J. May a liking for that excellent device, a library or man's room to the right immediately the house is entered, with the dining and drawing rooms on either side of the sitting hall and facing the south. West Chart is a larger house than Gilham's Birch, and there is consequently a passage running right through from the entrance hall to the trades entrance. The folding doors between the sitting hall and the drawing-room enable them to be used as one room if desired, as may be seen from the illustration. Attention is drawn to the brickwork above the drawing-room fireplace, which perhaps may be recognised as a glorified trimmer arch, which carries the hearthstone of the room above. Perhaps it is laying rather too much emphasis on a not very important structural feature, but it is an entertaining dodge. The sitting hall has a comfortable ingle with a little window to the south. In the latter is a fine scrap of old glass of a very tender blue from Hever Castle. The door from the hall to the south loggia opens in two halves horizontally, like a stable door—a very practical device. It enables the air to come in freely when the upper half is open, but keeps out the autumn leaves when the wind lifts them up into little whorls. The dining-room has a great open brick fireplace, with the timbering showing above and plastering b e t w e e n , while the red of the brick is brought to a fine richness by bees-waxing it. A variant of this construction is in the library, where the fireplace is built of iron-stone, and the wide joints are galleted with scraps of red tile, a simple device which re-verses the usual prac-tice and makes an agree-

181.—FIRST FLOOR LANDING.

able touch of warm colour. The servants' quarters are both spacious and practical. The kitchen in particular is lighted to perfection, and the china pantry opens out of it conveniently, as well as the scullery.

182.—DINING-ROOM FIREPLACE.

One big cupboard is fitted in a novel fashion, with a long rack for brooms, which usually are doomed to be thrown into corners, and, themselves the ministers of tidiness, are themselves untidy. A short passage at right angles to the main one leads past various offices to the motor-house, a convenient a r r a n g e-ment, for if the car be housed in an adjoining shed, a dash across the yard in pelting rain does not endear people to motoring. W e s t Chart boasts a hot-water system, worked not from the kitchen range, but from a separate boiler, and this serves the radiators in the motor-house. These are the more needful as this house is of one storey only and has an open roof. We return now to the main staircase, which, as it takes up little space, rather baffles the camera; but the picture of the first-floor landing gives some idea of the fine solidity of the oak framing. The stairs themselves are well constructed, the treads being of waxed brick and the risers of oak. Stairs altogether of brick are a mistake, because the edges are bound to break away in time; but this compromise seems a reasonable one. Here, too, must be mentioned a very ingenious use of the space under the stairs. It was not practicable to employ it as a cupboard opening to the inside, so rather than it should be wasted, it was turned into a tool cupboard with a door to the garden, and very convenient it is. Even in the small area of the stairs two fine clocks reveal themselves, evidence of the owner's (Mr. George Frederick Forwood's discriminating taste in clock collecting which makes ignorance of the time at West Chart of no excuse. The first-floor rooms are all particularly fresh and airy, and in the day nursery one sees the meaning of the babies' window noted from the outside. The sill is level with the floor, so the young people can sprawl about safely and yet see what goes on in the garden. Here and elsewhere Mr. Turner Powell's practical instinct flowers in a plenitude of cupboards, a virtue on which one need not tire to dwell, for it means a reduction of the furniture with which the floor must be cumbered.

Altogether West Chart does its designer credit. He has combined competent planning with pleasing treatment in the vernacular manner proper to Surrey; but it is fair to let the reader into one of the secrets of the old-world effect which has been won. The house with its garage cost nearly three thousand pounds to build (which means a shilling a cubic foot), and this includes the cost of a fine old barn bought at East Grinstead, the old oak timbers and roofing tiles of which were taken to Limpsfield and used in the building. By care and ingenuity the curved braces and the solid posts have been worked in to fill a new function at West Chart, and how naturally and well may be seen in the pictures of the landing and the dining-room fireplace. A good deal may be said in condemnation of taking new materials and treating them so that they put on a spurious air of age, for such a policy is simply that of the maker of "faked" furniture. When, however, an old barn has fulfilled its career of usefulness as a barn, and must come down to meet the ends of a more enlightened method of storing the kindly fruits of the earth, surely no better use can be made of its bones and skin than to build them afresh into a habitation which will enable them to renew their youth, while it benefits by their solidity and beauty.

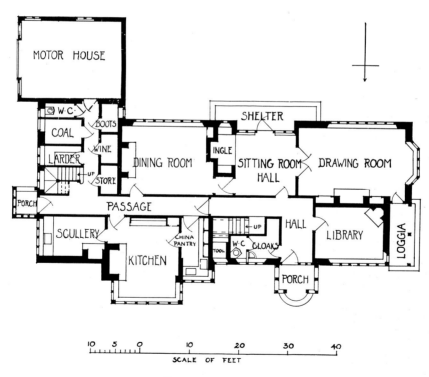

183.—GROUND PLAN.

FOUR BEECHES, BICKLEY PARK, KENT.

DESIGNED BY MR. C. H. B. QUENNELL

Roof Lines—An Excellent First-floor Plan—A Low Cost of Upkeep.

THOUGH Four Beeches is a charming little place, consistently fitted and furnished, it is not one of those rather eccentric houses which architects occasionally erect for themselves as representing somewhat experimentally their aims and views. Mr. Quennell wisely decided to house himself in a dwelling which in size, cost and character would neither burden him while he possessed it, nor make it difficult to dispose of, if he ever wished to part with it. It is a small house on a small piece of ground, and perfectly reasonable and normal in design, disposition and cost. Yet it possesses quality. The site had two characteristics. Its eastern edge dropped rapidly on to a well-wooded prospect, and it possessed a little clump of fine beech trees. Had these occupied the space towards the back of the site, and so formed a decisive lawn feature, it would have been better. Still, there are elms at that spot, and the beeches, rising from the south-east corner and hanging over the road and house, group charmingly and shade the house in summer from the hottest sun. The house stands on a bank above the road, and, except for a low retaining wall, is open to it. The absence of the usual ornamental fencing and laurel thicket gives a welcome air of a country farm rather than of a suburban villa. To the eye the general effect produced by this elevation is that of long and low walling surmounted by a little-broken and ample roof. The illustration does not quite reproduce this, as the camera, owing to the nature of the ground, had to stand below and look up at it. In the matter of colour, too, photography necessarily fails to do justice. A hand-made and sand-faced brick has been used. Though hard and durable, it has open pores and uneven surface, giving texture and inviting the tone and growths of Nature. It is also exceptionally agreeable in the matter of colour. the prevailing red being of many shades, from a suggestion of yellow to the purple-brown of a burnt end. One can trace the varied action of the fire in the kiln—the licking of the live flame here, the prevalence of a mere dull, smoky heat there. To roofing, walling and woodwork Mr Quennell gives due attention, both as

184.—SUNDIAL AND TRELLIS SHELTER.

185.—FOUR BEECHES.

186.—THE PARLOUR.

to what is used and how it is used. Ornamentation is practically absent from his elevations, but form and material are so presented that this absence is perfectly acceptable. As regards the east elevation, it must be confessed that the breaking of the roof line by two of the bedroom windows is unfortunate. The building rules of the local authority required windows of this height. To have raised the walling of the house 18in. would not merely have added to the expense, it would have destroyed the whole of the proportions, which depend on the accentuation of the horizontal lines. But there was an alternative. In houses which are kept low and where the bedrooms are part of the roof space, surely the gable ends are the place for windows. True, in this case the open aspect was to the east, and the gables only look on to the neighbours' plots. But the end bedrooms might have had top light and air from tall, narrow windows in the gables, while a long, low window, such as appears over the porch, would have given the morning sun and framed a charming view. A generous fenestration of the bay flanked by an extent of plain

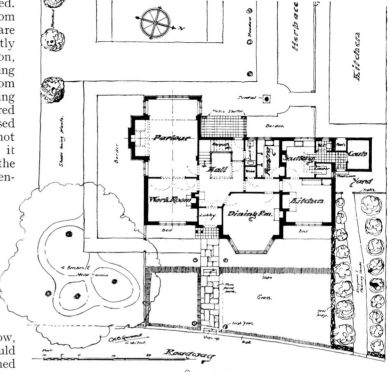

187.—PLANS.

wall would have more completely realised the conception of lowness and simplicity which was aimed at. So much informed thought has been expended on the house that the least jarring note is noticeable.

188.—PART OF GALLERY AND CORRIDOR.

Let it at once be said that none will be found when we cross the threshold. The interior of the house is really very good indeed. Perhaps the cleverest point here is the contriving of the landing and bedroom passage. In a quite small dwelling, where the utmost available accommodation is the chief aim, this section is too often planned on the barest utilitarian lines —hardly efficacious and certainly mean. At Four Beeches it is thoroughly gay and inviting and makes a charming picture. Yet the effect is obtained by very simple means and with no addition to cost or sacrifice of space. The stair rises from the west side of a good square hall and is amply lit by a four-light window containing examples of painted glass. Its last step is reached so as to allow admission to the bathroom and lavatory department, entered through an archway, while a second archway leads to the northern rooms, used as day and night nurseries, and, therefore, shut off by a gate. A passageway runs round the upper part of the hall far enough to allow access to the south-west bedroom, and its support by a column rising from the first newel-post below is very effective. The only oak used about the staircase is for the upper member of the hand-rail and for balls on the newel-posts, added since the photographs were taken. The rest of its woodwork —indeed, almost the whole woodwork throughout the house—is of deal treated with Carbolineum, an effective preservative, which gives the wood a pleasant grey-brown tone, and is so thin that it does not obscure the grain of the wood. Attracted by the landing, we have entered the house somewhat in aeroplane fashion and must now go downstairs to the sitting-rooms. To the left, when the front door is entered, lie the workroom and parlour, connected by folding doors, so that on occasion a single floor space 34ft. long can be obtained. The parlour is a very pleasant room, a comfortable appearance being given by bringing down the ceiling in the bay window and the chimney recess. In the centre of the latter is a cove where an electric lamp is placed, which sheds ample light around the fireside without anywhere catching the eye. The ceiling is decorated with set squares of ornamental plaster, and the general expanse has been left with a rough trowelled surface, an excellent idea seized with more zeal than judgment by the workman, who carried it out with a little exaggeration.

The dining-room, with pleasant china-filled dressers, has the morning sun streaming through its great bay window, and looks out on the wooded landscape, where the nearer houses are all agreeable examples of Mr. Quennell's designing. A service door from the dining-room leads immediately to the kitchen and offices. All the arrangements here are thoroughly well thought out, and the pantry and kitchen sinks are set in great slabs of teak. Upstairs, the bathroom, though small, is charming in appearance and quite luxurious in fittings. The bath has its douche and the basin its shampooer, while an ample airer assures the warmth and dryness of the towels. The walls are lined with hand-made Dutch tiles, with their mellow look and pleasant undulations of uneven glaze. They are plain white, except that here and there a little subject piece in blue is let in to attract and amuse. If we find perfect "simplicity" about the house, there is nowhere any unwise saving leading to later trouble. Durability has been considered ; the treatment of the woodwork and the use of green glazed tiling for the inner side of the window-sills are examples of how the cost of upkeep occasioned by need of repainting and renewals is kept at a minimum. Together with this practical virtue there are little touches on all sides telling of the informed taste which has ruled not merely the general design,

189.—LOOKING INTO THE PARLOUR FROM HALL.

but also the small details. The panelling of the doors is extremely quiet and effective. They are fitted with wrought-iron latches of the Norfolk type, which strike one as perfectly appropriate. They are so plain and simple that they attract no attention, but, if examined, they will give pleasure as being the product of handicraft and not of the machine. The casement fasteners are of the same school. Homely pieces of old furniture are set about the rooms, and one really fine Italian walnut-wood cabinet is to be found in the parlour. But there are also good examples of modern make, and all the furniture in the guest chamber is from Mr. Quennell's designs. They are agreeable in appearance, good in workmanship, reasonable in form. It is to be hoped that there is a large future for distinctive furniture designed by able architects, and made under sound conditions such as those that obtain in the Lambeth workshop where Mr. Quennell's furniture was made. When people revert to the old view that a little that is good and quiet is better than a plethora of showy rubbish, both their rooms and their minds will be wholesomer.

A final word as to outlay. The cost per cubic foot amounted to eightpence only, so that it is seen that a roomy house of excellent appearance and sound construction, with all the adjuncts of modernity fully represented, has been obtained at a low cost—moreover, this cost included the making of the garden—in a district where the London rate of wages prevails and hauling and carriage expenses are somewhat higher than they would be in the town itself.

WOODSIDE, GRAFFHAM

DESIGNED BY MR. HALSEY RICARDO.

Sir George Sitwell on Garden-making—The Choice of a Site—Colour in Architecture—Workrooms for Mind and Body—An Open-air Bedroom—Mr. de Morgan's Tiles.

TWENTY-THREE years ago Mr. Halsey Ricardo came upon a pine-bowered site at the foot of the Sussex Downs and was conquered by its beauties. Straightway he set about preparing it for the house that he built there only five years since. During those eighteen years of interval Nature was also making her long preparations for the building that was to follow. Too often one sees houses, in themselves perhaps beautiful, thrown down, as it were, on a barren field where the eye aches for a sense of shelter. Such houses seem to be accidents that might have been prevented, awkward intruders in a landscape which can retaliate only by making them look thoroughly uncomfortable. It is not the least of the charms of Woodside that it reflects the mature thought of its maker and owner. Mr. Halsey Ricardo has written no little of things architectural, and his words always arrest. His large knowledge and a taste highly individual are thrown into relief by a literary style vivacious to the point of rollicking. The art he serves he finds a jocund mistress. When he has a homily to read us of external colour decoration, he must needs wear the mantle of Landor and let us hear imaginary conversations with Alessi and Perino in Andrea Doria's Palace. Out of a rich vocabulary his criticism gathers pungent yet kindly force by the aid of what Rossetti called "stunning words." So much by way of saying that the designer of Wood-

190.—THE SOUTH-EAST FRONT.

side has views, and strong ones; yet the house does not show, save in a restrained way, that devotion to chromatic treatment which we associate with Mr. Halsey Ricardo. But we must get back to the site. The first work was to level and terrace it, and plant it about with those shrubs which love best the sandy soil of Graffham. Azaleas begin the flowering year, rhododendrons follow, and they in turn give place to kalmia. Arbutus, magnolia and tulip tree have taken to their home in strong profusion. Happily, few of the trees needed to be felled. The figure of the site suggested that the main front of the house should look to the south-east. West and north it was fully protected by a fine forest of Scotch firs, which fill the air with their sharp fragrance. To the east this wise preparer for the future house planted more trees, so that now there is protection on all sides save the garden front, whence one looks out over the rolling country to a distance of wooded hills.

191.—EAST CORNER.

192.—LOOKING SOUTH-WEST.

The slope is quick and the terraces called for retaining walls, which were built forthwith. At the same time were planted the yew hedges of the upper lawn, which enhance the garden's air of age. Thus field and hill-side have slowly turned to garden, and when one sees the red light of the setting sun through the wood, as it touches the pine stems to a slow flame, the sober beauties of this Sussex home and its setting become impressive even to the casual visitor of a summer evening. Mr. Ricardo has not dragooned Nature, but has slowly tempered her disorder, and she has rewarded him with prodigality. When Sir George Sitwell wrote " On the Making of Gardens," he told us " The great secret of success in garden-making is the profound platitude that we should abandon the struggle to make nature beautiful round the house and should rather move the house to where nature is beautiful." Not one in a thousand can view the question in such a lavish spirit of abandonment. Better far the profound foresight which this chapter records. It is one of the trivial disadvantages of a wooded site that photography meets with difficulties. It is practically only the main garden front facing the south-east to which the camera can do justice. It will be noticed that the mass of the building steps up, as we face it, from left to right. This was done of conscious purpose to balance the upward slope to the left, which is better seen in the picture, " Looking South-West." The elevation is severely plain, both in form and colour. The preacher of colour has restrained his hand, but for reasons obviously

193.—THE HALL.

sound. In cities the need of it is clear, for half the year their aspect is grim and dreary, and " the only refreshment t h e eye gets " (Mr. Ricardo is quoted) " is in the glimpses of the sky over-head, the shop windows and the hoardings." The colourist's claim for streets gay with large surfaces of brilliant hue need not be fol-lowed here, the more so as the well-known house in Addison Road is a monument to Mr. R i c a r d o's v i e w s. In t h e c o u n t r y " the need of artificial c o l o u r is less insistent ; we have but to open a shutter or draw a curtain, and we disclose a painted window. We look out on a garden of living enamel." In an England of perennial colour the builder is wise not to compete with the green and scarlet, gold and russet, with which Nature has enriched him. At Woodside the exterior boasts nothing save the red of tile and brick, while the jalousies are a strong green on which time and weather will develop a blue bloom. The outlines of roof and gable are grave and balanced, so much so, indeed, as vaguely to suggest an institutional character, which a little wars against its domestic realities.

One feature of the front may be noted as unusual : the sloping rain-water-pipes connecting the two pairs of pipe-heads. It is customary and perhaps better to use in such a case a horizontal box-shape gutter ; but there was a desire to avoid too great emphasis of horizontal lines. In any case the pipes, though of ample capacity for their work, look small and trivial in comparison with the big, simple pipe-heads, which bear the initials of Mr. and Mrs. Ricardo. The chimneys are of a fine solidity and group pleasantly with the gables, while the railing of the balcony gives the needed sense of substance and safety. A word may be said of the colour of the rough-cast. It is a rich cream, and has stood for five years quite unharmed, whereas it is usual after such a period to note some small shabbiness. This satisfactory result is due to the lime being slaked with boiling water. It causes the ochre, which is added to produce the creamy tone, to amalgamate with the plaster and wear well. If the slaking is done with cold water, the colouring is apt to wash out. The inside of the house is extremely simple in arrangement. We look from the entrance porch through the small hall to the garden, with the drawing-room and dining-room left and right. It might be said that a little too much floor area has been absorbed in vestibule and passage, and that the kitchen is of rather sumptuous proportions compared with the dining-room ; but when a man designs a home for himself, he knows his own requirements accurately and is likely to depart in some things from normal methods. Precisely such a personal need has produced the delightful garden-room, which serves Mr. Ricardo for a studio, where he may work undisturbed and cut off from the rest of the house. If the work of the mind is done in the garden-room, labour of the body has its place in the workshop, which has no door to the garden front, but is entered from the kitchen court. Upstairs there is another sitting-room, with a spacious balcony which has sometimes been used as an open-air bedroom. On the first floor are four bedrooms and the like number on the second floor, and all may be described as large. They have this supreme advantage in common— that every window frames a view.

Though the exterior is conceived on lines almost austere, with an entire absence of modelled decoration, and with the simplest and broadest colour treatment, the picture of the drawing-room shows that Mr. Ricardo has a joy in ornament rightly placed. The plastering of the deep beam, with its decoration modelled by Mr. Ernest Gimson, is natural and charming, and in happy contrast to its soft whiteness is the brilliance of the tiled fireplace. It is only fair to Mr. Ricardo to point out that the decorations of the house are incomplete. The picture-rail, which gives a hard horizontal line, is merely temporary, and the intention is to fill the space between the top of the tiles and the ceiling with more plaster-work. Unhappily, too, the monochrome of the illustration can give only an idea of the pattern but none

194.—DRAWING-ROOM.

of the amazing richness of colour that belongs to Mr. William de Morgan's tiles. It is probable that few of the thousands who delight in " Somehow Good " and the other novels from the able pen of Mr. de Morgan realise that they are the product of the elder years of an artist whose early association with William Morris proved so fruitful. Together they worked in the painting of stained-glass windows, and out of that developed the tiles which have made the name de Morgan justly famous. Most of those used at Woodside are of the early days when the house in Queen Square, Bloomsbury, saw the revival of so many aspects of decorative art that are now taken for granted. It is not too much to say that the early de Morgan tiles have entirely caught the spirit of the splendour that belongs to old Persian work. In some of the examples that front the fireplace at Woodside one looks into pools of colour that are like the transparent living blue of the deep sea. It is a melancholy reflection that though people talked a deal about Mr. de Morgan's work, it was not supported by adequate purchase ; and there is a limit to the labour and expense to which an artist can go for an unappreciative public. Told shortly, the secret of the effect of these tiles is in the depth of the glaze. This is impossible if they are made in the ordinary way of compressed dust, for the glaze splits the tile. It is a cumbrous and costly business to form the " biscuit " or body of the tile by the wet process, but it renders possible the richness of the glaze which will make the name de Morgan remembered among the great ones of the Decorative Revival. How powerful was his personal influence is very clearly seen by comparing the tiles made originally by him with those later examples by his workmen who followed his methods, but lacked his immediate supervision.

Mr. Ricardo found it necessary to make up his sets of the earler examples with some later ones. The latter are still good, but the master touch is lacking. However, old and new blend well, and the tiles in their framing of Istrian marble form a sumptuous picture. It is not always that an architect who is greatly concerned with the artistic side of his work busies himself with those structural trifles that collectively add so much of comfort to the home. Woodside is full of what may be not disrespectfully called " dodges." Here are a few of them. It is often alleged with justice against curtains that it is needful to make windows much larger than they should be, because a proportion of the light is blocked out by the hangings. Mr Ricardo provided recesses in the architraves into which the curtains go when thrown back ; in fact he recognises them as part of the architecture and provides for them. Too often they are an after-thought and look it. It has been said that sliding sashes are so called because they usually will not slide. This sticking is often caused by the part of the frame on which the sash works being painted. If it be made of teak, even a hardened painter is likely to leave it untouched. Wooden casement windows are more liable to admit wet than sashes ; if, however, they shut against flat iron slips, screwed to the frame and projecting a little from it, the risk of a pool of water on the window-sill is greatly reduced.

Then as to floors : It is usual on the ground floor to leave a space of 6in., or more, between the concrete foundation and the floor-boards. The space thus provided has to be ventilated from the outside, and in any case forms a needless arena for the Olympic games of mouse and cockroach. If the concrete is struck to a level surface and painted with pitch the boards can be nailed directly to it and the result will be a much warmer floor. The backs of the wooden skirtings are usually nothing but vermin galleries ; if worked in solid cement that nuisance is avoided.

A word as to heating : In the ordinary way the heat, once it has passed from the fireplace, is lost up the chimney. At Woodside the fires of the drawing-room and hall are back to back. An inlet from the outside air is brought between them, zigzags to and fro, and delivers a good volume of heated air into the hall at no extra cost. There is no space to describe a clever idea for disposing of the grease from a scullery sink, but enough has been written to show how carefully the details of construction have been watched. One fact must be added—that the house, including a great rain-water tank of 8,000 gallons, was built for £2,600 which works out at a cost of ninepence halfpenny per cubic foot.

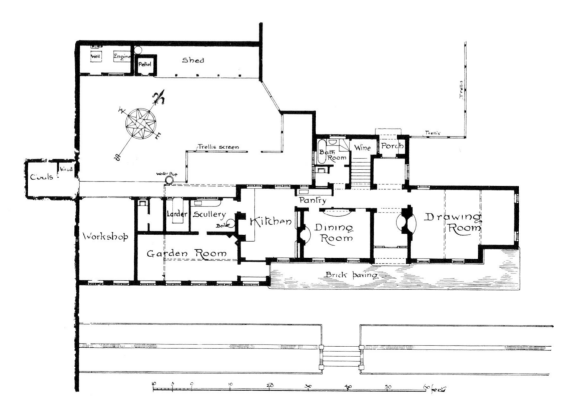

195.—GROUND PLAN

ROSEWALL, WIMBLEDON.

DESIGNED BY MR. M. H BAILLIE SCOTT.

Suburban and Country Houses and Their Differences—The Limitations of Suburban Planning—The Functions of the Hall—Open Fireplaces.

SUBURBAN houses built on small plots of land create problems of planning which are absent from country houses where sites are not only larger but more widely spaced. It is worth while to consider the influences which have created the average home of this sort, the more so as it has resisted, much longer and more stubbornly than any other, the rise in the tide of better taste. Domestic arch.tecture in England shows us its long story of development by innumerable houses of many periods and of all degrees of importance, but these examples are mainly in the country. The economic changes of town life have swept away nearly all the old city dwellings, and even where the outsides remain, whether untouched or restored, the interiors have usually been remodelled. Most of the remain ng town houses of any antiquity which stand as they were built date from the seventeenth century or later They are the outcome of Renaissance ideas both in arrangement and design ; they belong to modern life, and differ markedly from the ordinary town house of the Middle Ages. Until the industrial development of the nineteenth century created a vast and prosperous middle class, there were practically only the two types — the country house and the town house. Increased prosperity meant the creation of a third type— the suburban house, which neither needed the severe economies in extent of site which the value of city land made necessary, nor allowed the prodigal enclosures possible in rural districts. The

196.—THE GARDEN FRONT.

Great Exhibition of 1851 may be taken as a great symbol of the industrial and commercial might of England in Early Victorian times. It none the less marked the lowest depths of æsthetic degradation to which this or any other country had fallen or could fall. It was, therefore, in an atmosphere the most unpromising that the suburban house increased and multiplied. Itself an outcome of our industrial supremacy, it seems to have gathered during half a century nearly every element of the unloveliness which gave the greatest impetus to its increase. It was Goethe who called Gothic architecture a petrified religion. It would be fair to say that the suburban house which took its character from the Great Exhibition was a petrifaction of money-grubbing. Nor was it merely that the houses were ill-proportioned and sometimes built of such intrinsically ugly material as white brick. Their builders too often sought to hide by ornament the want of art. Ornament may be offensive, when it is in itself good, if it be overcharged and placed in a meaningless way. When, in addition to being ill-placed, it is vulgar in feeling and mechanical in execution, it can create nothing but a sense of disgust.

Here, then, is the gravamen of the indictment against the bulk of the English suburbs. They are a wilderness where vulgar ornament is the weed that has choked architecture. If it be true that a nation gets the government which it deserves, it may be agreed that the people of English suburbs got as good an architecture as they could appreciate. The revival in domestic work which we associate with the names of Norman Shaw and Eden Nesfield has taken many years to reach the suburban house, for the architectural education of its public has proved a slow process. One of those two great artists used to say that when he was a young man he could get no work, and when he was old the public would not leave him alone. Now, however, there are scores of architects who devote to the problems of the suburban house a wealth of ingenuity and a real artistic power. These qualities show that the more enlightened folk who desire to build for themselves not only deserve, but can get, suburban houses which will hold their own and honoured place in the story of English building. Among such is to be placed Rosewall, Wimbledon. The way it is planned and grouped is the outcome of two chief factors. The site is small, for land in Wimbledon is costly, while the road and the best view are on the south side. The practice in suburban building estates is to lay down a building-line a fixed number of feet from the road, and to forbid the placing of houses in front of that line, which is generally determined to allow of gardens front and back. Nearly all speculative builders, and not a few architects, accept the building-line as though it were bound up with the Law and the Prophets, and never build behind it, with the result that all the houses in the road conspire to create a dreary uniformity of frontage. Had Mr. Baillie Scott kept to the line, the back garden would have been sunless, and the south windows, while commanding no view of it, would instead have been subjected to the dust of the road. He therefore put the house towards the back of the site, a course which has produced a front garden unusually ample, with room for a lawn tennis court, and a small kitchen garden behind, instead of two equal gardens, both trivial. All this is obviously to the good, but there were risks to be guarded against. At present there are no houses on the plots immediately adjoining, but they will doubtless come, and it was needful to remember that, if they kept to the building-line, they might be an eyesore to the dwellers in Rosewall. In order to avoid such a possibility, the plan of the house has been most judiciously contrived. The middle part of the south front is recessed, and the two wings brought forward with a double break, so that they act as screens. Another danger, viz., a lack of privacy in the front garden, has been skilfully avoided by setting the drive at the side and dividing it from the garden by a tall treillage. A hedge will protect the garden where it fronts the road. Reference to the picture of the south front will show how completely and successfully Mr. Baillie Scott has broken away from all the miserable conventions which have too long held suburban architecture in thrall. Unhappily, black and white can give no idea of the quiet warmth of the admirable bricks which came from Cranleigh, Surrey. They tone in the mass to a rich plum

197.—TERRACE AND PAVED WALKS.

colour, but seen close at hand are a medley of purple, red and gold. Their varied colour is due to their being burnt in clamps in a primitive way. A touch of variety is given by the bright panels of white plaster, which are formed by the half-timber of the recessed front, while the whole composition is balanced by the chimney-stacks that flank the main gables. Their diagonal placing with respect to the lower parts of the stack and the herring-bone arrangement of the brickwork in the main gables give distinction and interest without any increase of cost or creation of unstructural ornament. The picture of the terrace shows with how just a judgment the house has been brought into relation with the garden. Privacy has been given to the terrace by the extension of the south walls of the two verandahs which open out of study and drawing-room. The paving, which is of rough stone flags, overflows (as it were) by round steps on to the upper part of the garden, is continued as paths round the rose-beds and leads down to the tennis lawn by more semi-circular steps. The sundial and the trim little trees in tubs add a gracious touch of formality. The house is entered on its west side and we pass across the inner hall direct into the house-place or sitting hall. The hall is the key of the planning throughout. The pressure of the economic limitations of small houses is often applied equally to the plan as a whole, with the result that all the rooms become resolved into little rectangular boxes. The architect of Rosewall holds that such an arrangement is not the expression of normal needs and that the comfort of an average family is best secured by providing one room of ample size, the house-place, with one end reserved for meals, and by appending two small rooms for special purposes, the study and drawing-room. In order to save space, the end of the hall which is used for meals is fitted with permanent seats, so that the long dining-table projects the minimum amount. This dining recess is reached directly by a door from the kitchen quarters, and can be separated temporarily from the body of the hall by the curtains provided.

The chief objection that can be brought against this arrangement is that the smell of food cannot be excluded entirely from the sitting hall ; but one cannot have everything with a limited expenditure, and the pictures show how spacious and delightful a room is secured. It is wholly divided by doors from passages and stairs, and the long low window with its deep seat, the massive oak beams, the dado of oak boarding and the great open fireplace give

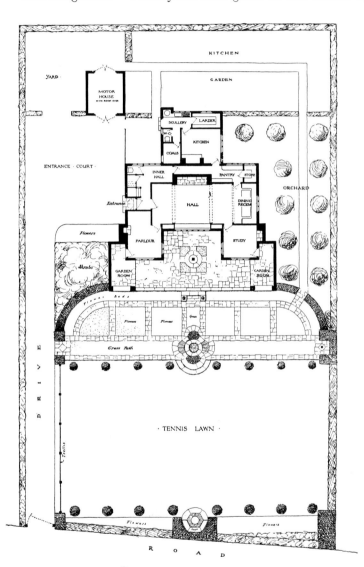

198.—PLAN OF ROSEWALL.

a peculiar sense of comfort. The fireplace is the feature of the room, and it may be said without hypercriticism that its proportions are somewhat too ample for the size of the room. In this matter of open hearths, the French proverb, *il faut souffrir pour être belle*, is apt to force itself on the attention of the owner. Since the photographs were taken a large and, it must be confessed, an unsightly hood has been added in the attempt to minimise the smoke difficulty, which has proved highly disagreeable, but without complete success. In the drawing-room, too, a small open hearth has also given trouble. Open types of fireplace almost invariably work badly until the flue gets seasoned. They present a most exasperating problem. Even if one that works perfectly be imitated exactly in every detail of construction, the copy, for some

199.—THE FIREPLACE AND DINING RECESS.

200.—THE HOUSE-PLACE.

reason wrapt in mystery, may smoke abominably. It seems, on the whole, wise to use modern slow-combustion grates in every room except that in which the architectural scheme (as in the hall at Rosewall) calls loudly for an open hearth, and, with the latter, to settle down in philosophic calm to a period of discomfort varied by experiment. The ideal arrangement is doubtless a system of heating by hot air or radiators coupled with wood fires on the open hearth. It must be confessed that coal does not take kindly to basket grates and wide chimneys. The fact that for generations it has been burnt in grates of a more enclosed form is an indication of its wishes, which can be ignored only at some peril.

When we leave the ground floor we find the bedrooms approached by an oak staircase of charming design, with a hint of Jacobean feeling in its newels. The bedrooms are six in number, with a bath-room, and on the second floor is a large attic, admirably lighted. It would, perhaps, be indiscreet to describe in any detail the troubles bred by the building bye-laws, which at Wimbledon are singularly strict. Suffice it to say that the plans were submitted to the local council, duly approved and signed, though they did not comply with the regulations in certain quite unreasonable particulars. The authorities did not, until the work was well advanced, realise their own reasonableness, but, having done so, demanded that the plans they had themselves approved should be altered to comply with the bye-laws. This course would have meant practically the demolition and re-building of Rosewall ; but happily the trouble was dissipated by the blessed spirit of compromise. That any new demands should have been made after the formal approval of the plans is, however, a circumstance sufficiently extraordinary, and the story is a useful warning as to the treatment sometimes meted out by local authorities to those who build.

One feels that the simplicity of Rosewall is real and not mannered, for, with all its solid oak construction, the price of the house represents only eightpence per cubic foot. It is such a building which makes true the phrase of Ruskin : " No architecture is so haughty as that which is simple ; which refuses to address the eye, except in a few clear and forceful lines ; . . . and disdains either by the complexity or the attractiveness of its features, to embarrass our investigation, or betray us into delight."

HARPSDEN WOOD HOUSE, HENLEY.

DESIGNED BY MR. M. MABERLEY SMITH.

The Balance Between Science and Art in Building—The Problem of Trees Near a House—
The Hall—Varying Levels—The Electric-light Plant.

AT Harpsden Wood House, Mr. Maberley Smith has had a free hand, for the house was built for his own occupation, and as regards plan, design and material he was free to carry out his own ideas and aims. As regards cost, while checking any tendency to extravagance, he was ready to incur all that was necessary for the adequate building and appointing of a house where simplicity was to be a ruling principle, and charm to depend on form rather than on ornament. There is much, both within and without, on which the eye dwells with pleasure. But there are also clever planning and thorough engineering. The most is made of the accommodation both in respect of quantity and of disposition. The offices and water services leave nothing to be desired, and the electric lighting is not only adequate, but easy and inexpensive to work. Much of the spirit which we admire in the architecture of the past has been

201.—THE HALL AND GALLERY.

202.—THE GARDEN FRONT.

caught and is brought into amicable partnership with all those comfortable contrivances and mechanical conveniences which pass under the name of " the needs of the day." It is a product of a practical brain that has nevertheless forbidden the science of construction and sanitation to usurp a territory which it should share with the art of architecture and of living.

Harpsden Village lies south of Henley, and after leaving the low-lying church and Court the road rises and passes through a wood. That wood, and a large tract of land lying west and south of it, have been laid out as an estate of which the fringes are to be built on and the middle occupied by golf links. A well-considered and definite lay-out for the building portion, with a proper oversight as to the design of the houses, would have added value to the estate and amenity to the locality. Signs that its omission is unfortunate are already not wanting. Mr. Maberley Smith's house will add to the agreeableness of outlook from the other residences, but it is to be feared that some of the latter will not be improvements to the landscape. The site of Harpsden Wood House consisted partly of wood and partly of open field; and it is in the latter part, and at some distance from any tree, that he has placed it. There is something to be said for and against this position. It gives a site open to the south, with wide views to the west and sheltered by a belt of trees to north and east. But the house and garden are, and must long remain, rather bare and shadeless, while there is no linking or cohesion between the two portions of the ground, no merging of terrace and lawn into woodland, no gradual passage from full sun to deep shade. As the wood not only forms an eastern belt, but stretches westward at the northern boundary, a more agreeable grouping, a more matured composition, might have been obtained by cutting away sufficient of the wood for the house to have stood partly within its area, and to have had a few single trees and small groups near it to afford shade and to give foreground and value to the distant outlook. This would have meant the sacrifice of a large number of trees and some limitation of the westward view. The more heroic plan was adopted of setting the house in the open field and awaiting the growth of new plantings for the full realisation of the amenities of the environment. The drive leads through the east section of the wood and then runs parallel with the

203.—THE GUEST PARLOUR.

north belt, which forms one side of the forecourt. The house and its offices lie on the opposite side, while to the west a line of low roof juts out, of which the centre is an open loggia with the porch to the left, and to the right is a bicycle shed intended in the future to be expanded into a studio, which will appear as a pavilion, and will greatly assist the grouping and sky-line of the buildings. The walls of the house are mainly of a red brick of very pleasant colour and open texture made at Nettlebed, near by. They show an agreeable variety of tone from the kilning, and seem to have a power of attracting natural growths, for a yellow hue that can only come from a microscopic lichen is already making its appearance here and there, especially on a high wall with a central archway through it which separates the dress from the untidy garden. In some portions of the upper part of the house the brick is varied by the introduction of solid oak framing with a filling-in of plaster. This occurs between the windows at the north-east corner of the house and on the south side above the great bay of the hall, where it fills in the gable and stretches out on either side until it reaches steadying masses of brickwork in two chimneys. Beyond the stack on the left this work breaks out again, as the excrescence of the sitting-room and of the bedroom above it is so framed, much of the filling being of glass forming long lines of casements. All the window frames and mullions are of oak pegged and unmoulded, giving the whole house an aspect of seriousness and solidity, which the simple and little-broken lines of the tiled roof accentuate. Yet there is nothing dull or heavy about the appearance. The change of material where lightness was desirable, the detail of the hall bay and gable, the elegance of the shafting and moulding of the chimney-stacks, the right placing and proportions of the windows, the sufficient but not obtrusive projections, all join to make up a picture of a satisfying kind. To the south, the ground rises slightly, and scope is thus given for a certain amount of terracing and stairways which, when yew hedges are fully formed and new-planted trees and shrubs are grown, will give the house a dignified garden setting.

As to the arrangement of the rooms, the annexed plan speaks for itself, or if the language occasionally seems foreign to those who are little accustomed to drawings, it is easily intelligible with a little translation. A lofty central hall is the dominant feature ; around that the rest of the rooms cluster like chickens about the mother hen. But this is not the central hall of mediæval planning. It is its length and not its width that runs through the house, and therefore its gallery is a connecting link to the two portions of the upper floor, which the mediæval arrangement absolutely severed. With our present ideas of service the strict revival of the old is extremely inconvenient, and only an antiquary bent on giving an exact reproduction of the past, both in his house and in his mode of dwelling therein, should indulge in it. At Harpsden we get merely a savour, not an imitation, of old times. The house is entered at the north-west corner and past

a lavatory and a staircase ; the broad way leads to the guest parlour, known as "the afternoon room" from its aspect. Thus the hall, which is the principal sitting-room of the family, is private as regards outside callers. It has a floor space of some 18ft. by 28ft., and it has this to the full, as the fireplace is slightly recessed from the side wall. It is framed in by pilasters and by the cornice which runs round at gallery height, and its various projections and shelves are all faced with tiles. The plain ones are of the mottled surface and soft tone known as "antique white," while the subject

204.—THROUGH THE HALL INTO THE DINING-ROOM.

pieces are mostly Dutch and blue ; but the three of large size, one of which represents a duel, are brightly coloured, and are therefore rightly placed as the central objects above the open hearth. The hall is lit to the north by low windows both above and below the gallery, while to the south the great double-transomed bay admits floods of sunshine. On each side of it are the double doors opening into guest parlour and dining-room respectively, and when they are open a vista 53ft. long is obtained, with the recessed chimney-piece of the dining-room at one end and the west window of the guest parlour at the other. It forms an extensive but quite homely composition.

Though the hall is lofty, it is not of the height of the two storeys of rooms on each side of it. There is no more than enough headroom both below and above the gallery to walk along without feeling that the rafters are oppressively near. This needs about 16ft. from floor to ceiling of the hall, and no more pleasing height in relation to the general proportions of the room could have been chosen. On the other hand, the sitting-rooms and the bedrooms above have an altitude of over 9ft., and thus the two staircases have needed careful planning to arrange the various upstairs levels without awkwardness. The accommodation at the west end consists of a bedroom over the low entrance, and therefore level with the gallery, and of a bedroom and bathroom over the guest parlour reached by four additional steps. It is the same with the three bedrooms at the east end, while their bathroom is on a slightly higher level, for it has two storeys below it, a larder and some other offices in the half-cellar and the servants' sitting-room on the half-landing. The attic arrangement consists of a fine lofty bedroom and of a roomy gallery passage over the hall, while on the higher levels at each end are airy servants' quarters. Changes of level and heights in rooms are always rather an engaging feature, but are difficult to combine with that complete convenience and economic use of space which we expect in small-sized modern houses. The quite satisfactory solution of this problem at Harpsden is one of its successes. The conjunction of the agreeable and of the practical is everywhere present. The arrangement of the gallery gives an idea of the quite entertaining glimpses which the house affords. It also shows the very acceptable character of the woodwork—solid and simple, but good in form and grouping. The

205.—A BEDROOM FIREPLACE.

same attributes apply to the bedroom fireplaces. The general form, the placing of the mouldings and the spacing of the white glazed earthenware blocks in the example illustrated are just right, and the little oak entablature above is neat. On the left, part of a wash-table shows. Mr. Maberley Smith has used the form and detail of one of the small shut-up washstands of the eighteenth century, but has, as it were, pulled it out to make apt dressing and wash tables. The change has been made thoughtfully and without destroying the balance and sufficiency of the design, and very satisfactory pieces of furniture are the result.

As much of this architect's work lies in the domain of hospitals, it is needless to say that the sanitary side of the house has received full attention. The glass shelves of the larder, the fittings of the pantry, scullery and bathrooms all show the scientific advance, joined to good taste, which now rules over this very important department of the building craft. The electric installation is typical of the handy, efficient and economic manner in which small country houses can now be lit. It is a 25-volt plant using metal filament lamps. The dynamo is driven by a 2 b.h.p. engine. The cost was as follows :

	£	s.	d.
Wiring sixty points	65	0	0
Battery, engine, dynamo, etc.	105	0	0
Fittings and lamps	40	0	0
	£210	0	0

It is interesting to know that, including this item, the total outlay on this very well finished and completely appointed house has been under £3,000, and the cubic foot price works out at ninepence halfpenny. The whole thing is a praiseworthy piece of work.

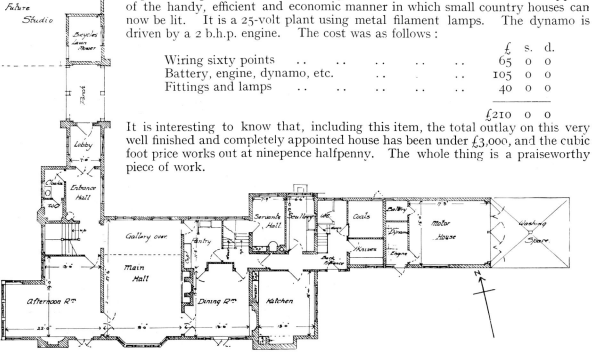

206.—THE PLAN.

FIVES COURT, PINNER.

DESIGNED BY MR. DUNBAR SMITH AND MR. CECIL BREWER.

Ingenious Planning for a Sloping Site—A Fine Marble Fireplace—A Children's Gate on a Landing—
Space-saving Furniture.

PINNER is only thirteen miles from London, but when we pass from the station into its wide street we find ourselves in an old-fashioned English village, and not in a mushroom suburb. Fine chimney-stacks of early seventeenth century type rise through ample tiled roofs, and the general appearance of the houses and shops is that of a well-to-do late Georgian agricultural community, for a wide-spreading farm, with its great barn, breaks the line of the street near the church. Houses of the type which London citizens built for their summer residence when they still mostly lived at their places of business are still to be found on the outskirts of the village, nestling amid the tall elms and surrounded by the rich meadow lands. Thoroughly in unison with its environment is the house which has been built for Mr. Ambrose Heal. It is a place which anyone who only enjoys the elaborate

and the ornamental in architecture will pass by with a sniff. The simplest forms, the plainest materials have been chosen. Its rough-cast walls are pierced with wooden casement windows. Rough-cast chimneys, devoid of detail, break its stretch of red-tiled roof. A gable or two, a lead-roofed bay window, an oak-posted loggia are the only incidents except the little arrangement of outhouses that makes the fives court which gives the cottage home its name. Nothing more than this was needed to give it, in a modest but undeniable way, the qualities of distinction and agreeableness. Of course, it needs its setting. That is part of the considered composition. The shady grove of tall trees which called for the covering of the chimney tops as a preventive to down-draught; the clever trimming of two young hedgerow elms into a dignified archway over the entrance gate; the little gravelled terrace in front of the loggia; the broad grass way between herbaceous borders leading the eye to the box hedges, the rose arches, the orchard and the distant trees and meadows—these, and other garden incidents, are integral parts of the picture. The deft touch is even more apparent in the interior than in the exterior of the Fives Court. It is all done in simple fashion, but to the appreciative appears at once as the result of very considerable thought. Much has been done to use all available space not only to the utmost convenience of the body, but also to the largest satisfaction of the eye. The architects had to deal with a site which slightly sloped from north to south. Here was a little gift of Nature not to be

207.—THE WAY IN.

208.—THE GARDEN FRONT.

209.—THE LOGGIA.

missed. Small as the house was to be and normal the accommodation, a note of individuality might be struck by following the lie of the ground and introducing two levels. But how should this be done without awkwardness and inconvenience? The answer was given by a clever bit of planning. The house is entered through a lobby which opens on to the side of the passage. Corresponding to the lobby at the other end of this passage is the spring of the enclosed staircase, and the space between them is the opening into the hall, which is fitted with three steps. This opening is about seven feet wide and four feet deep, and there is a slight cove in its ceiling which allows segmental panelling on each side. The hall on the lower level is a pleasant spot, with a large window to the east; while its south

side is occupied by a chimney-piece and the wide door into the drawing-room. The result of the arrangement is that this hall is screened from both the entrance and the stair, although the passage these are in is made part of the hall by the seven-foot opening. The two levels, the steps between and the breaking of the ceiling into three sections, give size, dignity and variety to a very small space, and cause a pleasurable surprise to the visitor. The effect is so far unusual as not to be expected and yet so unstrained as to be accepted at once as fitting. The illustration is taken from the lower level looking north, and the open door reveals the dining-room occupying the north end of the house on the higher level. It has a curved bay to the east, while the northern portion is arranged as an ingle with a lower ceiling than the main part of the room, round which runs a plaster frieze of rope pattern. Behind the dining-room are the offices, and the kitchen is remarkably well fitted and arranged. It will be seen that it is approached through the pantry. In a small house where there are only maid-servants this is a very good disposition. The pantry is only used for the washing and storing of glass and silver. There is, therefore, no objection to its use as a passage which shuts off the sounds and smells of the kitchen without wasting an inch of space.

The south end of the house is devoted to the drawing-room and loggia. The dining-room, offices and staircase are all on the same level as the front door, and the level of the garden door and terrace is the same as that of hall, drawing-room and loggia, so that the three steps into the hall are the only

210.—THE ENTRANCE.

ones needed, and being broad, and in the full light, they can occasion no stumbling. Until recently the drawing-room was small and had a corner fireplace. It has been much added to, and now is a room of size and presence. The new fireplace, being of marble, is rather more sumptuous than anything else about the house; yet it produces no dissonance because it is perfectly plain. A great semi-circle of marble forms a raised hearth; the grate itself is of iron, but it is framed in marbles of two kinds, the projection of which, without any cornice, forms the mantel-shelf. The panelling of the upper part of the chimney-breast completes an excellent composition, full of character and reserve. The loggia, which is much used for sitting, eating and even for open-air sleeping, is formed by bringing down the roof in a sweep.

211.—THE ROSE ARCHES.

212.—THE PARLOUR.

that also covers the projecting part of the parlour and the garden entrance into the lavatory. It is rather a pity that the exigency of light on the upper floor has needed the breaking of this fine stretch of tiling by two rather spotty little dormer windows. Windows set in the wall at either end would have been preferable.

Ascending the staircase, the first landing leads to a very complete set of rooms over the parlour, loggia, etc., dedicated to the use of the children. The suite is shut off by a gate of the simplest pattern of the Chippendale Chinese fret period, copied from an old one at the village butcher's shop. A short second flight of stairs leads to the ample landing and rooms over the dining-room and offices. At the Fives Court there is complete harmony in the furnishing, though much that dates from to-day is associated with examples

213.—THE HALL AND DINING-ROOM.

214.—GROUND FLOOR PLAN.

of the seventeenth and eighteenth centuries. There are some very ingenious new pieces in a dressing-room where space is limited. The semi-circular washstand, into which an old copper basin is fitted, is convenient and pleasant-looking. The looking-glass on the dressing-table slides forward so as to allow the casement to open, which it does inwards, as the window is fitted with outside sun shutters. The attic floor should be visited.

The southern end of the house, which, as we have seen, is lower than the other portion, is left open on this top floor and forms a long gallery with sloping ceiling, as was often the case in Jacobean houses ; in fact, the famous galleries at Little Moreton and at Hever are finely wrought adaptations of such a space on a large scale. On the higher level are the servants' quarters—remarkably bright, picturesque and comfortable roof-rooms, not to be included under the rather opprobrious term of garret. The architects have, in this case, been fortunate in working for a client who, in his manner of furnishing and living in the house, fulfils their conception. That is why a dwelling which in idea and in substance is modest and unpretending yet produces a sense of satisfaction and aptness. It needs no soaring ambition to dwell in such a habitation. But it needs something which is almost as rare—an educated taste that sees wherein lies the essence of quiet beauty and informed mode of living and infuses that essence into the substance of the dwelling and the spirit of domestic habits.

ACREMEAD, CROCKHAM HILL, KENT.

DESIGNED BY MR. DUNBAR SMITH AND MR. CECIL BREWER.

Sir Henry Wotton on Sites—Walls in Random Rubble—An Unbuilt Billiard-room—A Study in Terraces—Hot-air Heating.

ON the side of Crockham Hill is a site that was known in the old tithe-books as Acremead, and had been for unrecorded years a hopfield. It faced a trifle east of south, the ideal aspect. On this side of the lower greensand range the slopes are often so sharp that it is difficult to perch a house on their sides, and impossible to form a garden. At the point chosen by Dr. Philpot, however, there seems to have been a landslip at some time remote, for the slope is flatter, and by dint of laborious terracing, which needed the removal of some thousands of loads of soil, a delightful and unusual garden has been made. As one stands on the upper terrace the fertile Weald of Kent stretches out like a map due south to Crowborough, while Leith Hill rears itself to the west, and the poplars in the middle distance give an individual touch to a landscape of a beauty unusual even in Kent.

A site so precipitous indicated a house long and narrow, a form which allows of dignified elevations, but demands that skill in planning which is evident here at all points. In order to ensure an easy approach, there is but a small forecourt of pleasant shape between the road and the north front. By this means has been met the delightfully worded warning of Sir Henry Wotton regarding the "scituation" of a house, viz., "That it bee not of too steepie and incommodious Accesse to the trouble both of friends and familie." There is nothing too "steepie" at Acremead, for both car-

215.—THE ENTRANCE, NORTH FRONT.

riage and motor-car can readily reach their homes from the road, without any quaking in the breasts of their occupants. The entrance door is an outstanding feature, with its massive projecting wings of masonry topped by an arched hood, the under-side of which is made gracious by decoration of modelled plaster. Above, the triple overhanging weather-boarded gables give a happy sense of relief without taking away from the sobriety of the general effect. The soil of Acremead is kindly to the gardener's zeal. By the porch trails the Tropæolum speciosum, a capricious growth which does best in a north aspect and demands that its roots be cool. Here its brilliant red flowers look delightful against the local sandstone, whose gold weathers in patches to a warm grey.

It had been intended to use brick for the house, and this was done for the stables, which were built first. The preparation of the site, however, yielded such a store of stone that the house was

216.—THE GARDEN FRONT.

217.—EAST FRONT AND PERGOLA.

built of it, and the architects have followed a custom which may be noted often in the district, of building in random rubble, using stones roughly squared only for the quoins. This and the making of all the windows of teak give an altogether valuable feeling of mass and of contempt for the gales which blow against the house from the unsheltered south. The change from brick is justified, not only in a lower cost of building, but in honour being done to local materials and methods. A greater repose in the texture of the walling would have been won if the masonry had been of

218.—THE PERGOLA FROM THE WEST.

squared stones throughout; but the cost of the house, £4,300, would have been much increased thereby. The cube foot price of slightly over ninepence tells little, for owing to the slope of the ground it is difficult to arrive at a fair cube measurement. As we enter, the old millstone which paves the porch attracts notice. A small lobby leads into the vestibule containing the staircase, and the hall is wholly a sitting-room, save for a northern arm which serves as passage to the morning-room and the drawing-room door. The dining and drawing rooms both possess bay windows, and the simple decorations and mouldings have the air of refinement and scholarship which is characteristic of the work of Messrs. Smith and Brewer. Particularly are these qualities to be seen in the attractive lead gutter which forms a parapet to the top of the drawing-room bay. Of the kitchen quarters no more need be said than that they are compactly arranged. A serving hatch between the kitchen and the servants' hall is a useful contrivance, which enables the maids to take their meals away from the disorder of the kitchen, with a minimum of extra labour. This, indeed, seems a more justifiable use of a hatch than between kitchen or pantry and dining-room. The desire to save work is laudable, as is any device that will prevent

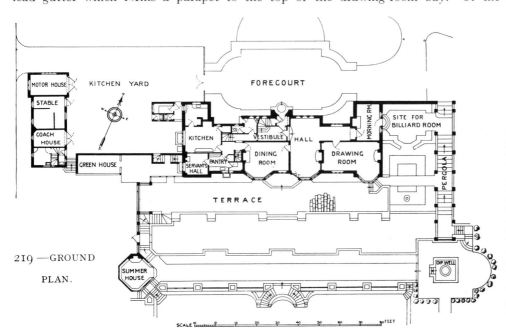

219 —GROUND PLAN.

the cooling of hot dishes; but it should also be borne in mind that a dining-room hatch is in the nature of a megaphone to the servants' quarters, and that with it the privacy of after-dinner discussion is endangered, if not destroyed. Perhaps the most interesting feature of the house-plan is that which has not yet been built, the billiard-room. Its site has been put to delightful use in relation to the pergola and to the garden generally. The north wall of the room is there, and serves to screen the entrance gate from the stepped pergola. The latter would well serve as the text for a sermon on the right use of garden architecture. The solid masonry piers bring it into relation with the construction of the house, with which it directly connects. The stepping of its open timber roof emphasises the drop in the ground, while the whole composition flanks the upper terrace, separates it from the simpler stretch of garden to the east, and leads one to the bastion at that side of the lower terrace. Here we find a dip well, which serves the garden, and is a charming decorative expression not only of that practical purpose, but also of the need to find an outlet for the rain-water from the house roofs.

The illustration of the lower terrace shows the dip well in its more ornamental function of a lily tank, to which one goes down by steps to find it pleasant with pigmy water-lilies, Japanese iris and ferns. This same picture also shows well the rampart-like boldness of the compacted masonry which holds up the upper terrace and seems to buttress the very foundations of Acremead. By a wise economy, which also brings its reward in heightened effect, the upper and lower retaining walls

220.—THE LOWER TERRACE.

of the lower terrace are built of dry stone, *i.e.*, without mortar, and rock plants are beginning to make their home in the crannies. The upper terrace has been wisely made of generous width, and the great flagstones, not too evenly laid, with their joints hospitable to stray tufts of weed, are eminently satisfactory in carrying on the idea of solid well-being. The making and maturing of such a garden as this is a matter of time, and the interest here is enhanced by the co-operation of architects and client. The work on the lower terracing and garden has been carried out not only under the constant direction of Dr. Philpot, but often with his own hand. There is a keen pleasure for the man whose larger life is spent in the solution of problems which play round the issues of life and death, in attacking the small but for the time engrossing problem of how best to split a flagstone and to lay it well and truly. In the outcome of such labour there must always be for the self-appointed mason a peculiar charm, a feeling that his home is essentially his own. It is the same direct personal interest which has made its mark on the house itself. It was originally designed without dormer windows, but the desire for useful attic rooms caused a modification, and these windows were added. It is often that dormers spoil a roof, but here they are unobtrusive and by their existence make possible much extra accommodation, without any æsthetic disadvantage. A word must here be said of a charming internal effect produced by the north slope of the roof. The ceiling of the first-floor corridor is for this obvious constructional reason sloped on one side. This gives, in conjunction with plain, cream-coloured walls and green carpet, an air of cloistral freshness that is most attractive. In all practical devices the house is rich. It is lit by electricity. The well is in the stable-yard and all ancient methods of raising water have abdicated in favour of a pump driven by a small motor which is run off the cells. Within the house every room has its fireplace for cheerfulness, but there is a highly successful installation of hot-air heating, which keeps all the passages at an even temperature. People are apt to think that central heating is a modern arrangement. It is nothing of the sort. Sir Henry Wotton, already quoted, reminds us (he wrote in 1624) that Palladio "observeth that the Ancients did warme their Roomes, with certaine secret Pipes that came through the walles, transporting heate (as I conceive it) to sundry parts of the House, from one common Furnace ; . . . which whether it were a custome or a delicacie, was surely both for thrift and for use, far beyond the German stoves ; And I should preferre it likewise before our owne fashion, if the very sight of a fire did not adde to the Roome a kinde of Reputation." By the combination of open fires with central heating, one gets the best of both worlds. Perhaps one more quotation from the same enchanting author may be pardoned. He began his "Elements of Architecture" with a maxim about the aim of the Mistress Art. "The end is to build well. Well building hath three conditions,—Commoditie, Firmeness and Delight." It can be truly said that Acremead abundantly fulfils these demands. "Commoditie," its fitness for its use as a home, is written over all its arrange-

221.—THE UPPER TERRACE.

ments. "Firmeness" is expressed in the simple massiveness of its masonry, and "Delight" in the charm which comes to us on its ample terraces from the view which lies open across Kent to the hills of Surrey and Sussex. Wotton lays down a number of rules (based on Vitruvius) which deal with the design and comfort of buildings, but, when he has said all, he falls back on the wise generalisation : "The rest must be committed to the sagacitie of the Architect, who will bee often put to divers ingenious shifts, when hee is to wrestle with scarsitie of Ground." The designers of Acremead had no "scarsitie" to face as far as concerns actual area ; but there was no flat surface to suggest any inevitable plan, and the "sagacitie" with which they have schemed a wholly attractive house on a difficult site is evident at every turn.

BELCOOMBE, SAXLINGHAM

DESIGNED BY MR. F. W. TROUP.

A Doctor's House—The Surgery and Its Approaches—A Curved Garden Wall—Architects and Craftsmanship—The Avoidance of Cleverness.

THE planning of a doctor's house presents all sorts of problems which are absent from an ordinary country home. The surgery and its approaches are obviously features of great importance, but the success of the architect will appear chiefly in the skill with which he works them into the general plan without taking away the precious element of privacy from the residential quarters. That Mr. Troup has at once fulfilled this condition and devised a house unobtrusive and entirely characteristic of Norfolk traditions, this chapter and its illustrations will show. That he has done it at an unusually small cost is clear from the total expenditure of £1,420, which works out at the very low figure of 5½d. per cubic foot.

Dr. Hugh Webb-Ware, for whom the house has been built, was fortunate in obtaining an attractive

222.—WALL OF PIERCED BRICKWORK AROUND THE FORECOURT.

site, an orchard of four acres, with some oaks and a great walnut as well as fruit trees. There was a small old house near the road, now demolished. The new house is set well back. It is the advantage of such a site that the old trees give a feeling of maturity, but the number of them affects the light and consequently the design of the house. A casual glance at the illustrations suggests that the windows are unusually many and large. Actually they are needed to counteract the over-shadowing of the trees, and the interior gives the sense of right lighting. The house is approached by a long avenue which branches to the left for the forecourt and main entrance, and to the right for the surgery court with its door to the waiting-room, and for the kitchen court. The latter is divided from the surgery court by a wall that veils the domestic concerns of the household from the visiting patients. The forecourt is enclosed by a low wall of pierced brickwork, as effective in appearance as it is inexpensive. The entrance door has a flat hood with a valance of sheet-lead wrought lace-fashion, a little mark of Mr. Troup's keen interest in the art of the plumber. After crossing the forecourt we turn round to the south front of the house. Here is found a delightful loggia which runs up the height of two storeys, but is divided at first-floor level by an

223.—BELCOOMBE.

224.—THE SOUTH FRONT.

open timber framing, well seen in the picture of the loggia. Climbing round the brick piers and laced through the oak joists is a wealth of purple vine, wistaria and clematis. The plan shows a pergola bay added to this verandah. It will increase the vista which is now seen framed by the round brick arch. The pergola has not yet been built, but when it comes it will greatly add to the effect of this side of the house and of the lawn it faces. Already there is a valuable sense of privacy, for the verandah is altogether invisible from the avenue or forecourt ; but the pergola will shut in the picture and emphasise the feeling of enclosure.

In garden-planning, as in much else, there is merit in a touch of mystery. A reasonable amount of division gives the onlooker the feeling that there is a beyond where are fresh fields for the conquest of pleasure. The west front looks out over a large croquet lawn with the fine old walnut tree in the foreground. This has been made the happy excuse for a seat with a circle of paving. We follow the path round the kitchen premises to the well which heads a long walk fragrant with lavender on one side and gay with herbaceous plants on the other. The boundary wall is curved on plan, a device valuable for many reasons. It looks attractive, it provides for wall fruit concave bays that serve as sun-traps, and it can be built one brick thick, which is impossible with a straight wall of such a height. Although the linear measurement is obviously greater, the cubic measurement is only about five-eighths as compared with the content of a straight wall two bricks thick. If this were generally recognised, curved walls would doubtless be more often used. There is a similar wall, but planned in small semi-circles with short straight connecting pieces, at Wroxall Abbey, Warwick. It is not built on the economical lines described above, being 18in. thick for the first 2ft. and 12in. above but nevertheless has a special interest. The Abbey was bought by Sir Christopher Wren,

225.—THE LAVENDER WALK.

and it is alleged (with what truth deponent knoweth not) that the great architect was himself the designer of the wall.

But to return to Belcoombe. The building itself has an entirely local character. The bricks were made in the village and the pantiles three miles away. The tile-hanging was done with the spoils of the old house which was pulled down. But, no—" pulled down " is not wholly true, for the walls were left to such a height as is befitting for a small walled garden, and, stripped of their plaster, now form the home of fruit trees— an economy none the less highly ingenious for seeming obvious. Of the brick summer-house thatched in Norfolk fashion and other charming features of the garden there is no room to write ; but the birds deserve a word. It is not often that one is driven to complain of nightingales, but at Saxlingham they are a grave cause of insomnia. Mrs. Webb-Ware is a lover of birds, and the trees are well supplied with bird-boxes. Wrens, nuthatches, owls and four kinds of tits return her affection and are almost as friendly as the doves which flutter round the loggia tea-table for crumbs.

The plan of the house within is simple, yet with a simplicity that meant skill and thought. The surgery and its offices are in direct communication both with the entrance hall and with the kitchen quarters, yet entirely separable from both. Happy the doctor so ideally housed ! The hall is reminiscent of the timber treatment which was customary in the neighbourhood. The beams here and elsewhere in the house are relics of the older building, the floor-boards from which were used to line the hall walls for lack of better panelling. They are fixed with hand-made hurdle nails, a pleasant variant from the odious machine-made nail of commerce.

The hall ceiling takes an arched form, but was not made in that shape merely out of fancy. There were many old oak joists left over, but no beams. Mr. Troup therefore used the short lengths as bracket-pieces for the joists of the floor above and filled with laths and plaster between the joists. The doors are ledged and braced, fitted with wooden latches and leather thongs instead of the more sophisticated lock and handles. On the first floor are six bedrooms and a dressing-room. A fragment of the upstairs plan is reproduced to emphasise an ingenious arrangement whereby the two chief bedrooms secure large cupboards. These are available either as wardrobes or as tiny dressing-rooms to take a washstand. The latter use is particularly satisfactory in a room which has no dressing-room opening out of it. The attics are fine rooms, at present unused, but one is destined to become a billiard-room. Until recently the house was lit by oil-lamps, but an air-gas system is now at work, to the great saving of time and temper.

The impressions to be taken from Belcoombe are wholly satisfactory ; but some might find it difficult to give a reason for this, since there are no outstanding features that seize the eye. This is entirely characteristic of its designer's art, which is none the less real for being modest. Mr. Troup is

226.—THE LOGGIA.

one of a small band who would, and they could. revolutionise the training of the budding architect. He calls for a course of education which shall have an element of the severely practical, while it does not neglect, of course, due instruction in the theory of this most exacting art of architecture. He would send the student to the bench to work for a time at the crafts with his own hands. He is scornful of mere paper designers who have had no experience of actual craftsmanship and are consequently apt to design without reference to the qualities and capabilities of the materials to be employed. His æsthetic gospel is of that restraint which shall destroy the

227.—THE CURVED WALL.

element of the self-conscious. There is no demand that the student shall acquire a smattering of all, or even half, the arts that go to house-building, but that he shall at least learn the rudiments of one or two. By this means he will win a kind of instinctive knowledge of the rest, and, by learning the limitations both of handicraft and material, may escape many pitfalls into which the ignorant too often fall. Mr. Troup has insisted long and emphatically on these aspects of his art, and the following quotation from a lecture delivered at Carpenters' Hall is characteristic :

" In designing, above all things avoid being merely clever for the sake of effect. Cleverness is not art —more often it is mere licence and a want of restraint. Be certain of this, that your best work is not that part of it which you most admire yourself, and you will be safe ruthlessly to cut out that part from your design. The clever features are like the smart sayings of an author. The latter often ruin a book as the former may ruin a design—they distract and disturb, even if they tickle the fancy. Although they may be admired for the moment, it is more than likely they will live to be laughed at."

All this seems to be the outcome of a massive common-sense. Perhaps some will bring the railing accusation that it leads to the apotheosis of the commonplace. Even so, Mr. Troup's withers would be unwrung, for he would wisely reply of smartness, *voila l'ennemi*. A joke is a good thing, but when frozen into a feature of a building, unhappy is that man who has to live with it.

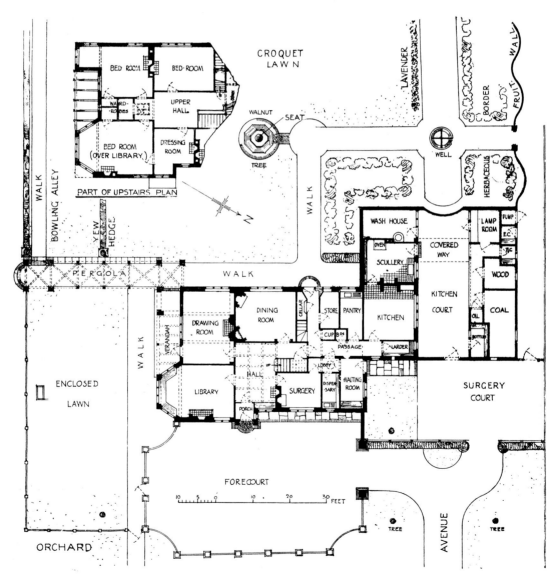

228.—GROUND AND UPSTAIRS PLANS.

THE PLATTS, NEAR PETERSFIELD

DESIGNED BY MR. W. F. UNSWORTH AND MR. GERALD UNSWORTH.

A Satisfactory Grouping—Open Fireplaces—Sir Joshua Reynolds on the Composition of Buildings—An Admirable Garden.

THE counties of Sussex and Hants meet in a very picturesque embrace, and their borderland is full of both landscape and architectural charm. It is a country of hill and dale ; of breezy uplands and well-watered hollows ; of shady lanes prudently circumventing or boldly breasting steep hillsides, and serving scattered homesteads or secluded villages that preserve many of the pleasant dwellings of the yeomen of Stewart days. No wonder, then, that Mr. W. F. Unsworth should have chosen this locality for his home. He was one of the first of our architects to appreciate fully, to feel inwardly, the principles and practice which made the modest local architecture of humble men of old so excellent and so sympathetic. Before moving to the neighbourhood of Petersfield he had built himself a house near Woking, amid the pine woods that line the Thames and Basingstoke Canal. The district was even twenty years ago a jerry-builder's promised land, and Mr. Unsworth's home stood out like a little jewel in an immense setting of pinchbeck. Since then much has been done to drag our native architecture, as applied to modest domestic work, out of the Slough of Despond in which Mr. Unsworth, as a lad, found it wallowing ; and the fifty houses illustrated in this book will convince readers that it will not be the fault of the younger race of architects if Englishmen remain ill-housed But our gratitude

229.—THE RECESSED CENTRE OF THE SOUTH FRONT.

is due to the veterans who began the good fight. Among these Mr. W. F. Unsworth takes high rank, yet he is still very much on the active list in conjunction with his son and Mr. Inigo Triggs, and it is with their work of to-day that this chapter is concerned.

So recently has The Platts been built that its garden has as yet scarcely taken shape, let alone reached the stage of maturity. The growth of plant and of shrub, the weathering of wall and of roof, are needed before the designer's conception of the finished product is realised. Yet the composition is so good, the materials so well chosen, the features, simple as they are, so rightly ordered, that even now it is the permanent and inherent merit of the work rather than the present rawness of its immediate environment that strikes the eye. It is just an unambitious home, neither large nor costly. It contains a hall and three parlours

230.—THE FORECOURT AND NORTH FRONT.

231.—FROM THE SOUTH-EAST.

downstairs, nine chambers upstairs and fully sufficient offices. It works out at about eightpence farthing per cubic foot, bringing the full cost to two thousand five hundred pounds, with some two hundred and fifty pounds to be added for extras. It is thoroughly well built and well finished, but without any elaboration or ornament. It is an L-shaped house, the office wing running out at right angles to the main block, which itself is long and narrow. Two sides of the fore-court are thus obtained, and a breast-wall completes the enclo-sure, which is entered at the corner between two round piers constructed out of the same local rubble stone that forms the walling of the house. Much of it comes in small pieces, though due selection gives the right air of solidity to the quoins, while variety of size, tone and surface produces a very agreeable sense of texture in the walling. The chimney-stacks are of red brick, and exceedingly

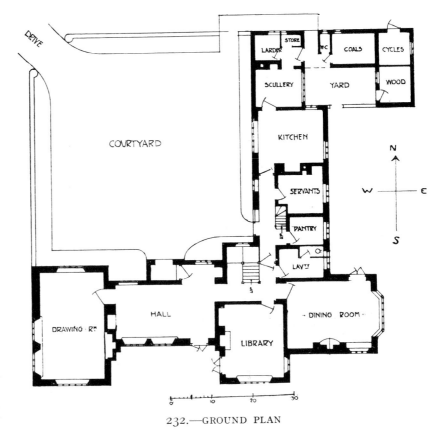

232.—GROUND PLAN

233.—THE FORMAL GARDEN.

well shaped and grouped. The bricks are narrow, hand-made, open grained, yet hard and weather resist-ing, and they har-monise well with the red tiles which cover the roof and the upper storey of the wing. On the garden side, between the two projecting gables, oak framing, mas-sively used and pegged together, projects beyond the facial line of the hall wall and rests at the ends on stone piers and centrally on the great beams of the hall ceiling, which are projected through the wall for this purpose.

The scheme of windows has been well thought out. It is extremely restrained on the entrance side. The house does not unbosom itself, does not shower indiscriminate friendship alike on stranger and on intimate. He who gets no further than the forecourt will have the impression that he is being treated with ample courtesy, with finished manners, but with some distance and a total absence of effusiveness. He may be cold and inimical like the north wind which blows on to this elevation, and the windows, studiously small in number and size, betoken a severity of deportment called forth by the circumstances. But he who, like the south wind, is a friend of the house, will go round to the garden side, where all is smiling and open, where windows, frequent and large, greet you warmly, and where glazed doors open their two arms towards you and invite you in. You find yourself in a hall twenty-four feet long, lit on both sides, and with an agreeably designed open hearth and chimney-piece of Ham Hill stone at its western end. Next to it is the door into the drawing-room, an apartment of rather large size and with abundant outlook. The northern window is high-silled, but those to west and south enable the sitter to see into the garden. Here again the hearth and its framing are of an engaging design, but the too generous opening is a temptation to the smoke to take to evil and undisciplined ways, which it showed a readiness to adopt, and the copper hood that has been introduced may be curative, but, like many a medicine, it has unpleasant ingredients.

234.—THE STAIRCASE AND UPPER CORRIDOR.

In this case the hood takes on something of the outward forms loved by the *art nouveau* school, and jars sadly with the rest of the work. The entrance into the hall from the forecourt is well managed. The porch, with its round-headed archway and its coped gable, is a marked and charming exterior feature. Between it and the staircase projection a pent roof carries an annexe to the hall, which forms an entry from the porch and adds much to the feeling of privacy in the " sitting " hall. Beyond this lies the staircase hall, from which doors open into the library, the dining-room and the office wing. The staircase is of oak, solid and simple, yet perfectly apt and pleasing. We may rightly praise both design and workmanship, and, as to the latter, it is interesting to note that the influence of Mr. Ernest Gimson has spread from the Stroud Valley to Hampshire. It is a craftsman trained in his workshops who, having set up for himself in the Petersfield district, wrought the staircase at The Platts. The offices are well ordered. The lighting of the kitchen from both sides is a comfort to the cook at both her stove and table operations. The water service and drainage of the house, on both the ground and the upper floors, are at once convenient and concentrated. The yard arrangement is effective not merely from the utilitarian, but also from the æsthetic, point of view. It is an important part of the general composition. It proves that the same fundamental architectural principles apply equally to a huge pile like Blenheim and to the smallest country house, so that one may say of Mr. Unsworth as Sir Joshua Reynolds did of Sir John Vanbrugh, that he took care that his work

" did not abruptly start out of the ground without expectation and preparation." Now that so few out-buildings are essential to a moderate-sized house, and that clients are not often prepared to incur the cost of raising unessential " supports " to the main block, architects are apt to find the problem of avoiding a packing-case appearance difficult of solution. But it is evident that at The Platts some moderate outlay was allowed, beyond that needful to wall and roof of the necessary lodging, and the architect, while respecting the client's purse, has taken good advantage of the permission. Thus, the little yard and its encircling buildings are the modest link between the ground and the main building. Even the dwarf forecourt walls play their part in this scheme, while on the south side the different levels and simple terracing of the formal garden afford just the right connection between the work of man and that of Nature. The house stands on ground sloping slightly to the south, and full use is made of this circumstance. The centre of the house is recessed about eight feet, and thus a very sheltered paved nook is obtained, which a low wall divides from the main terrace. An awning has been found convenient here, but, unfortunately, was not provided for in the original design, so that the wood posts that help to fix it have but a makeshift appearance. There is a single step down from this nook to the terrace, which is itself raised five steps above the parterre—a square of about a hundred feet. It is kept up at its southern edge by a dry wall, in the centre of which a low arch carries little stairways down to the lower level and creates a play of both shadow and reflection on the water of the semi-circular lily pool which lies before and under it. The middle portion of the parterre is arranged in beds divided by narrow paved ways, the circular centre having a nine-inch drop and a round pool in the middle. As the disposition shows very well in the illustration, a plan of it is not given. Its design reveals a nicely ordered judgment. Without elaboration or expense it gives interest and distinction to the garden, and in size and character it fits in perfectly with the house with which it is associated. It is part of the composition. It is here pictured in its raw state. With double arabis and aubrietias, Alpine pinks and rock roses succeeding each other in its dry walls ; with sizable but well-selected herbaceous stuff in its broader borders ; with tall clipped yews marking its points and giving vertical lines ; with close and disciplined growths filling its smaller and more elaborately shaped central beds without unduly obscuring the geometrical lines by too wild a trespass over the flagging—with such sympathetic culture it will prove a thing of beauty and a lasting pleasure.

THE HOMESTEAD, FRINTON-ON-SEA.

DESIGNED BY MR. C. F. A. VOYSEY.

Sincerity in Building---Sham Half-Timber Work—Foolish Bye-Laws—Unity of Design.—Fitted Furniture—
Saint Francis and the Birds.

FEW will be found to cavil at Mr. Voysey's dictum that "true originality is the outcome of sincerity." It amounts almost to a truism when applied to architecture, but is none the less valuable or worthy to be repeated on that account. One could wish that the makers of Frinton had adopted it as a working principle. It is not that the buildings there are inferior to the usual equipment of an English seaside place; they are perhaps rather above the average. The town has been laid out on broad lines, its roads and avenues have a certain dignity, and the landowners, by their building covenants, have obviously laboured to secure a satisfactory type of house. When all is said, however, the results cannot extort much admiration. It is true that original features of a sort are present in some of the houses, but sincerity of artistic motive is hard to find. It seems to have been the prevailing idea that half-timber work is the be-all and end-all of domestic architecture. In the early days of Essex, when Waltham Forest covered a great part of the country, timber took a large place in the making of its homes, and the more so as no building stone is quarried within its borders. Brick and timber were therefore the chief materials, and what stone we see was imported. To-day all that is changed. Epping Forest, though still spacious, is of trifling size when compared with the great wooded tracts which it has survived, and, needless to say, its trees are jealously preserved. Probably ninety-nine per cent. of the timber used in the modern buildings of Essex comes from abroad, and a form of construction which makes pretence of a richness long departed seems as futile as it is insincere.

235.—THE ENTRANCE FRONT.

To speak of the black and white confectionery which adorns so many of these houses as a form of construction is to do it an honour it does not deserve. Most of them which ape in this way the building manners of a bygone day have simple brick walls on which boards an inch thick have been nailed, and, behold! half-timber work. Sometimes their authors have not even troubled to remember that at

236.—FROM THE WEST

237.—THE SOUTH-EAST CORNER.

corners this pleasant method demands two boards if the similitude of a post is to be indicated credibly. A single board showing its inch-thick edge is a piece of incompetence e v e n as a fraud. This elegant insincerity does not, however, always make so large a concession to architectural decency as is involved in a board clapped on the wall. No little of the " half-timber " is no timber at all, but broad, raised bands of plaster duly painted black. It is almost pitiful to record the brilliant achievement of

238.—FROM THE GARDEN.

one plasterer who was observed by this writer laboriously scratching the grain of oak timbers on the wet plaster. Can ingenuity go further? After this it is a small thing that the struts and braces are indicated in shapes that no earthly tree ever produced, and that the mazes of lines and the wealth of quatrefoils profess to indicate a construction that the old-time carpenters never attempted in their most luxuriant moods. There is another point by no means deserving of neglect. Year by year the nation spends increasing sums in building and staffing technical schools, whereat craftsmen are to be taught not only the mechanical but also the artistic sides of their trades. No sooner have competent and sympathetic instructors turned them out imbued with some idea of truth and beauty in their handiwork than their masters, impelled thereto by a tradition of insincerity, set them to scratching the grain of oak on wet plaster. How satisfactory it is to be quite sure that we are a practical nation!

It is therefore with a sense of refreshment that one turns from pretentious futilities in sham half-timber to the quiet sincerity of The Homestead. The walls are of brick, covered with white rough-cast, with dressings of

239.—THE PARLOUR.

Bath stone, and the roof is covered with green Westmorland slates. The whole effect is cool and pleasant, and the slight patches of red in the tile arches at the entrance and on the little roofs of the chimney offsets give a grateful touch of warmth to the colour scheme. The site, which runs up to an acute angle at the junction of two roads, dictated the plan of the house. The building covenants of the estate demanded that the frontages should be set twenty-five feet from both roads, and the north elevation breaks back at the porch to follow the road-line. The entrance hall is small, and we find the dining-room on the left. It is of an interesting shape, suggested by the fact that no one sits in the corners of a room. One of the angles is cut off and thrown into the hall, two more are fitted with big store cupboards and the fourth with a sideboard. The more usual square is thus turned into an octagon, and the room adequately furnished without any loss of practical floor space. Adjoining the dining-room is the big parlour, which not only serves as the general living-room, but houses the billiard-table. It is a fine apartment, floored with black Dutch tiles, and the fireplace, with its lintel in black-leaded oak, is set in a splayed ingle. The whole of the timber used in the house, whether for construction or furniture, is English oak, which gives a valuable air of solidity and architectural well-being, but is inevitably costly It is not often that an architect has the opportunity, as Mr. Voysey had at The Homestead, of designing not only the building but everything that equips it, from the billiard-table to the dinner service, and the house and its furnishings thereby have a unity which is the outcome of a single aim. As the south front faces a plot of land which will be filled with another house, it is but slightly windowed, but in the parlour it has a circular light, which, as becomes a seaside house, suggests a porthole. The colour scheme is pleasant —white walls and black floor, grey oak, green carpet and upholstery, their coolness brightened by the scarlet of the curtains. A feature of the bedrooms is the use of fixed furniture built into its place. In a bachelor's room is a fitment which comprises wardrobe, chest of drawers and washstand, an arrangement which economises space and gives a certain dignity to the room despite its smallness. In an exposed situation like that of The Homestead the treatment of chimneys demands great care, if the trouble of smokiness is to be avoided. Mr. Voysey has gone about it in a thorough fashion. Under each grate is an inlet from the outer air, and in the chimney-breast an outlet leads to a separate shaft in the chimney-stack, a device efficient but costly. On the west front a big verandah opens from the parlour, and from it one goes through a massive pergola down the steps to the garden. The wind is an enemy here, but euonymus hedges are growing up to protect the pergola, which now is stripped by the blustering north-west gales. Roses have proved impossible in this gusty spot, though they flourish exceedingly in more sheltered Frinton gardens, and berberis flowering shrubs have taken their place.

240.—HALL AND STAIRCASE.

The character of The Homestead is most apparent when one sees it from the golf links, and compares its quiet, grey roof, dropping in four steps as the site falls, with the rather clamant red roofs of its neighbours. The very inconspicuous nature of the house makes it stand out as a thing of character, and marks it as truly a country home. On the links Nature drives away the ideas of suburban trimness which much of the architecture of Frinton bids us remember. Efficient driving and putting is seriously imperilled by the singing of larks. One needs the deafness of the Philistine or of the wholly inspired golfer to disregard the full-throated song, which seems the rather to increase while the lark mounts and, still mounting, disappears.

It may be that East Anglia is no richer in feathered life than the rest of England, but, for this writer at least, its birds have conspired to make an urgent impress on the mind. Not many miles from Frinton is a village church where at vespers one summer evening the birds seemed to have won a peculiar dominion. Two swallows flew in and out through the open porch, while the lesson told of the ravens' ministry to Elijah, and the psalm was of the young ravens which cry. On the bench-end was carved a pelican in her piety, and on a hatchment there gleamed the tarnished gold of a phœnix. The church was dedicated to St. Lawrence; but it seemed a mistake, and that in some sort the Poverello had been defrauded of his own, for St. Bonaventura's story of St. Francis came insistently to the memory: " When by reason of the twittering of the birds, they could not hear each other reciting the hours, the holy man turned unto them, saying : ' My sisters the birds, cease from singing, while that we render our due praises unto the Lord.' Then the birds forthwith held their peace, and remained silent until, having said his hours at leisure and rendered his praises, Francis again gave them leave to sing. And, as the man of God gave them leave, they at once took up their song again after their wonted fashion "

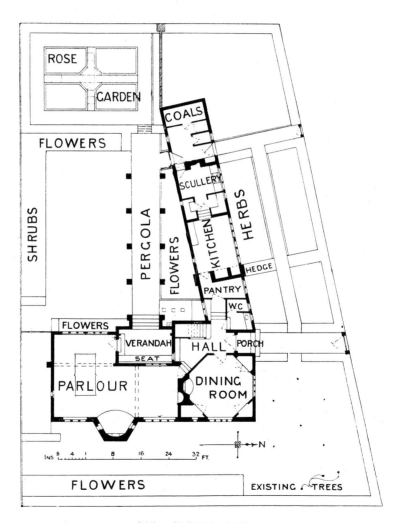

241.—GROUND PLAN.

BREACH HOUSE, CHOLSEY.

DESIGNED BY MR. EDWARD P. WARREN.

*Vanishing Roads—Reasons for Using Old Tiles—Proportion and Symmetry—Concerning
Dormers—A Point in Kitchen Planning.*

Hinchcliffe had given the car a generous throttle and she was well set to work, when without warning
the road—there are two or three in Sussex like it—turned down and ceased. " Holy Muckins," he cried, and
stood on both brakes.

AGAINST the time when Mr. Kipling shall rejoice us with another " Steam Tactics," a road near Cholsey
may be commended to him, for it plays the same engaging trick. When the writer of this chapter
reached the village by way of Wallingford, he was informed, and with childlike faith believed, that
Breach House was a mile or two up the hill that leads to the Downs. The turning was missed.
A mile or two more, and the road turned down and ceased on a broad and grassy down. While
many will sympathise with Mr. Kipling's passion for Sussex, he should know that Berkshire is not behind in
this matter of vanishing roads. There was no need to call loudly on a patron Saint, as did Hinchcliffe,

242.—THE ENTRANCE.

for no unwelcome
passenger was
aboard. Indeed,
the great wood
to the right, the
level springy turf,
the keen air and
the splendid soli-
tude of the great
ridge wooed rather
to adventure. For
miles the car sped
down the long
slope, but no
Breach House
appeared till it
had returned the
same way again.
The wood was
Kingstanding Hill,
where King Alfred
camped before the
great fight with
the Danes, and
the ridge of turf
the Fair Mile which
passes through the
Roman Camp and
so on to Ilsley.

The Berkshire Downs have a character wholly their own, and as the turf of the Fair Mile rolled up behind
the car like a green ribbon, the sense of open distance brought back the flavour of another of Mr. Kipling's
creations, the Thirty Mile Ride in " The Brushwood Boy."

The house which Mr. Edward P. Warren has built for himself stands in a lane which owns the charming
name of Halfpenny Lane, perhaps from some forgotten toll. It stands out graciously yet vigorously on its
wind-swept site. On the east side a plantation has been begun, which in time will temper the present sense
of bareness and give shelter to the garden. The garden front looks to the south-east down the Thames Valley.
Westwards and southwards are the Downs. So happily placed is the house that the views on all sides can
only be described as magnificent. The walls, of Basildon brick, have been coated with sand-faced cement

(a wise provision for so exposed a site) and colour-washed. The roof is of old red tiles. One has heard people talk of such an use of old tiles as though it grew from some faddish liking for old materials. It may be admitted that, æsthetically, they are eminently desirable, for they give an air of mellowness which a new tile will take many years to achieve. But they have two great practical advantages. The beautiful tones that variegate the colour of an old tile are due partly

243.—THE LOGGIA.

to the tiny lichens, to which (as Ruskin splendidly wrote) " slow-fingered, constant-hearted is entrusted the weaving of the dark, eternal tapestries of the hills." Partly, too, are they the result of dimly understood chemical changes in the fabric of the tile, to which, even in the clean airs of a Berkshire down, the chimneys contribute something. In any case, time has the effect of weather-proofing their surface, which is one practical gain. New tiles, if hard surfaced, will never take on those tender shades which crown the beauty of old farmsteads. If they are soft surfaced, their resistance to the weather is at first so much the less. A flat tile should have, both in length and breadth, slight curves, for they prevent rain from being held between the joints. If there is a little space, the rain will run down at a lull in the wind. Tiles which are truly flat and slates are both apt to

244.—THE SOUTH-EAST FRONT.

hold the water once it has been blown between them. Modern tiles are mostly made by machine, which gives them a deadly accuracy and flatness and enables them to pack more easily and travel more safely. Thus the risk of breakage is decreased and their popularity

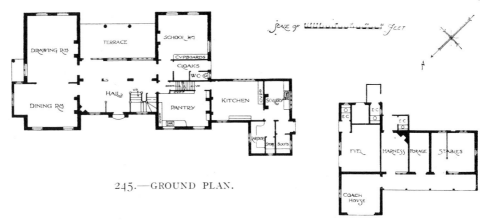

245.—GROUND PLAN.

with builders proportionately enlarged. For all that, the old tiles and the old hand-making of them are better. So much by way of *apologia* for the use of old tiles, if such were needed. The elevations of Breach House, and notably that of the south-east front, give the spectator considerable pleasure. It is worth while to consider whence the pleasure comes. The theories about architectural design are innumerable, and the words used to express them legion. Most of them darken counsel and make the way of the student of architecture devious and weary. It is doubtful how much of definite value people have taken even from " The Seven Lamps of Architecture." From Ruskin may be acquired a general tendency of thought in the direction of architectural righteousness ; but, as Mr. John Belcher, R.A., has said, Ruskin had a difficulty in preventing the " Seven Lamps " from becoming " eight or nine or even a whole vulgar row of footlights." Ruskin divided his illumination between Sacrifice, Truth, Power, Beauty, Life, Memory and Obedience, but did not raise to the dignity of capital letters the principles, qualities and factors which are also of the essence of good architecture. Among the many factors which go to create the happy impression made on our minds by a good building, two at least are notably present in Breach House—proportion and symmetry. The nature of proportion need not here be discussed, for it is a very baffling study. People are more apt to talk about its harmonies than to discover what produces them. Robert Morris set up a magnificent theory based on parallelopipeds (whatever they may be), but it now

reposes peacefully on the everlasting dustheap. Suffice it to say that at Breach House the relations of the two wings to the centre and of the walls of the building to the roof leave one satisfied that the proportion is right and the theories can be left alone. Then as to symmetry—it is more important that this factor be observed in public buildings, where it serves the purposes of a large dignity proper to civic life ; but it is of great value in domestic architecture if it can be achieved

246— THE HALL.

247.—FROM HALL TO DINING-ROOM.

248.—DRAWING-ROOM.

without pomposity. This is clearly the case at Breach House, where wings, dormers, chimneys and windows preserve a perfect and unaffected balance without straining the natural arrangement of the plan. Particular attention may be drawn to the unobtrusive way that Mr. Warren has managed his dormer windows. Their little roofs harmonise admirably with the hipping of the main roof (there is not a gable anywhere). Too often a roof, otherwise excellent, is ruined by dormers that over-emphasise both themselves and the attics they light.

As we reach the entrance doorway we note it as a very refined feature of the north-west front. The curved head with cartouche beneath and the pendant strings of fruit give an air of scholarly richness in happy contrast with the rectangular sobriety of the windows and moulded panels. The hall is a dignified composition. An ample staircase ascends to the right after the front door is entered, while to the left a corner fireplace forms the *raison d'etre* of a sitting-place. It is well lit both from the entrance front and by the long high row of casements which give on to the pillared terrace. To the left are the two chief reception-rooms.

As the present uses of the ground-floor rooms are to be regarded as temporary, one piece of rather obvious criticism falls to the ground, for the position of the present dining-room in relation to the kitchen seems faulty. From door to door they are 42ft. apart, and the pantry has to be threaded and the hall crossed when dishes are carried for meals. Mr. Warren's desire, however, was to treat the dining and drawing rooms decoratively as one, dividing them by wide folding doors, so that for occasional purposes they could be used actually as one room. That in a relatively small house a large room can be improvised by opening a pair of doors is obviously a great measure of convenience. The more natural arrangement will be to use the present schoolroom as the dining-room, and *vice versa*, and this is contemplated for days when the schoolroom will no longer be used as such.

The loggia, with its two simple columns, is a pleasant and useful feature of the house, and serves as an open-air sitting-room and for meals in fine weather. Unhappily, the day on which the photographs were taken was dark and lowering. They consequently lack those strong shadows which would have emphasised the projecting eaves and told of the sunny atmosphere so usual at Cholsey. On the north-east front is another little loggia, which is reached from the drawing-room by casement doors. The picture of the latter room shows the restrained and delicate ornament and mouldings of the chimney breast which are characteristic of their designer's art, while the pictures there and over the hall fireplace are reminiscent of early eighteenth century overmantels at their best.

The kitchen and offices are in a western wing of one storey, and adjoining, but not connected, is a stable, with coach-house, etc., which groups pleasantly with the main building. The first floor of the house provides not only seven bedrooms, but a study. This Mr. Warren has made his own, a refuge for quiet work, an ideal retreat for the busy architect delivered from the bondage of the telephone-bell. It is in such a country home that one realises, even more sensitively than Claudian when he wrote in the fourth century, the longing for " freer air, a grander, broader sky."

On the second floor are four bedrooms and the indispensable lumber-room. In so exposed a place some heating system was clearly indicated, and Mr. Warren has installed low-pressure radiators. All other practical things are well devised. For bathing and cooking the rain-water is filtered and stored in a large underground tank, while drinking water comes from a deep well. Altogether, Breach House is a very interesting example of the family home costing £3,000. The cubic foot price of the house itself was tenpence halfpenny, and of the stables and offices sixpence. The last memory is of the garden, not yet matured—the house dates only from 1905—but brilliant with masses of great daisies.

THE RED HOUSE, UPTON, KENT.

DESIGNED BY MR. PHILIP WEBB.

A Landmark in the History of Housebuilding—The House of William Morris—The Great Settle—A Clothes Press painted by Rossetti—Defective Planning—The Roofed Well—Three Main Factors in Design.

THE RED HOUSE was built as long ago as 1859, and is illustrated here not as a typical work by Mr. Philip Webb, but as a fresh starting-point for domestic architecture, of which the importance cannot be exaggerated. It stands for a new epoch of new ideals and practices. Though the French strain which touched so much of the work of the Gothic revivalists is not absent, and the Gothic flavour itself is rather marked, every brick of it is a word in the history of modern architecture. The circumstances of its building must first be set out, for they are intimately bound up with the revival of the decorative arts. This is now regarded as part of the established order of things, but in 1859 it was a stumbling-block to many and foolishness to the rest. At Oxford in 1857 William Morris became engaged to Jane Burden, and in the following summer he and two of his friends (and later partners), Mr. Faulkner and Mr. Philip Webb, the latter then senior clerk to G. E. Street, rowed down the Seine in an Oxford boat. Jaunts of this kind are usual enough in these days, but represented almost unheard-of adventures in 1858. For the present story, however, the feature of the voyage was that they discussed the building of a home to which Morris should take his bride. As Mr. Mackail has eloquently written in his " Life of Morris " " a new kind of life opened out before him, in which that ' small Palace of Art of my own,' long ago recognised by him as one of his besetting dreams, was now peopled with the forms of wife and children, and contracted to the limits of some actual home." The dream materialised in The Red House, for which, after many journeyings, a site was found at Upton, then a little village three miles from a railway station. Fifty years of development have brought the railway closer and have crowded Bexley Heath with many unbeautiful little houses ; but there remains the orchard in which

249.—WEST FRONT.

the house was built, and the garden is an oasis in a district not conspicuous for either natural or ordered beauty. Here, then, near the Roman Watling Street, the great Dover Road, trod by the feet of countless Canterbury pilgrims in mediæval days, Morris and Philip Webb devised the house which was the first fruits of a notable reaction from the dreary futilities of Early Victorian building. Mr. Aymer Vallance in his " William Morris " (another valuable book) claimed that it was the first modern house in which red brick found its artistic use. Certainly it was one of the first, but absolute priority cannot be claimed for it. George Devey had already for some years been busy with the creation of worthy houses, and in 1856, or earlier, reintroduced the curved Dutch gables in red brick which form so charming a feature of some of the small Kentish houses of the seventeenth century. In these days, when red brick is the commonplace of house-building, it is difficult to remember that in 1859 the world still gave its devotion to what Morris loved to stigmatise as square stucco boxes with slate lids. A red house was then The Red House, and no more distinctive name could be found for it. Before describing the house we may jump forward and consider one of the results of its building. The actual construction presented no particular difficulty. It needs no great imagination to suppose that some trouble must have arisen in getting workmen to carry out the ideas of Morris and Mr. Webb in anything like the traditional way at that time so long forgotten. Be that as it may, the designs were there, and no difficulty could have presented itself so insurmountable as to prevent the shell of the house being built to the architect's drawings. The question of decoration and furnishing was another story. Practically nothing modern that Morris could have tolerated was to be had for love

250.—SOUTH-EAST CORNER AND WELL.

or money. A few things existed, it is true. In 1856 the rooms at 17, Red Lion Square, once occupied by Rossetti, were taken unfurnished by Burne-Jones and Morris. The Victorian stuff then purchasable could not be thought of, and Morris hastily designed tables and chairs of a massiveness that suggested the Dark Ages, and in particular a settle of Brobdingnagian proportions. These things were made by a local carpenter, and rather a scene was created by the home-coming of the settle (the dimensions seem to have got increased by a blunder), for it filled a third of the studio. Rossetti came in, "laughed but approved," and designed some paintings for the panels, which, however, do not now adorn the settle, which was removed to the drawing-room of The Red House, and forms the subject of an accompanying picture. For the hall there was made a big combined bench and clothes-press, which was begun to be painted, probably also by Rossetti, with scenes from the Nibelungenlied, but never finished, as can be seen from the illustration. Much of the rest of the furniture was designed by Mr. Philip Webb, and built under his supervision, and he concerned himself as well with table glass, copper candlesticks and the like. The great dresser in the dining-room was (this writer believes) designed by Morris. In common with the other two great pieces already mentioned, it was too bulky to move when Morris sold The Red House in 1865 to return to life in London, and the three remain there to this day, and are duly treasured by the present owner, Mrs. Maufe. Some stress has been laid on this furniture, because it was symbolic of much that was to follow. The Red House was ready for occupation in the early autumn of 1860, and in April of 1861 the firm of Morris, Marshall. Faulkner and Co. was founded, an undertaking destined to affect the decorative ideas not only of England, but of the civilised world. Of this firm Mr. Philip Webb was one of the seven original members, and the actual work he did in the designing of furniture was considerable. The Red House was the outcome of Morris's growing passion to be up and doing things to change the domestic art of England. It is also true that its building and furnishing served to clarify his ideas and bring to the point of definite enterprise the manufacture on a reasonable and artistic basis of " every article for domestic use," as the firm's first circular put it. But we must close this brief *résumé* of the place the house takes in the wider history of its time, and attempt some detailed description. It was notable in 1860 not only for an exterior of red brick, with its red roof of lofty pitch, but for its then unusual plan— L-shaped instead of box-form. One enters through a wide porch with a painted arch and carved over the door is the text :

251.—CHIMNEY AND ORIEL.

DOMINUS CUSTODIET EXITUM
TUUM ET INTROITUM TUUM.

The hall is wide, and the dining-room parallel with it on the right. The fireplace here must have astonished the people of 1860, for it lacks any mantel-shelf, and is built in simple red brick. That of the drawing-room is even more ambitious, for it slopes upwards and backwards almost to the ceiling. The dining-room ceiling was originally patterned in distemper, the outlines being pricked out on the plaster so that the colouring could be renewed easily. To the left of the hall are two sitting-rooms, in one of which, the library, is a simple painted corner cupboard, a relic of Morris's occupation. The L of the plan is marked by the corridor, which is at right angles to the hall and runs to the garden door and loggia. Here, again, in the leaded lights that fill the windows there is evidence of Morris's passionate return to reasonable craftsmanship. There are not only figures of Love and Fate in stained glass, but pretty devices in simple outline. The staircase is markedly Gothic, and is built in the internal angle of the L with, over it, a tall pyramidal roof, left open on the inside and patterned in blue and green, a little Persian in feeling.

The drawing-room is on the first floor with an oriel window, which is carried from the ground by a stout buttress. It has an open roof, and its chief piece of furniture is the great settle of which the early history has already been given. It has been called the minstrels' gallery, for a wooden ladder stood at one side leading up to its top, from which a small door communicates with a loft beyond. How these facilities could ever have been used in practice can only dimly be imagined. Right and left of the settle are pictures in tempera by Burne-Jones, from the story of Sir Degravaunt, a romance in which Morris delighted to the end of his life. The other large room on this floor, at the east end of the north front, was his workroom. Connecting the two, the corridor has round windows with leaded lights that bear the motto, " Si je puis." Of the bedrooms, it need be said only that the fireplaces are of heavy masculine design and built in red brick.

A word now as to the plan in general. It must be confessed that it has many faults, a statement in which Mr. Philip Webb would be the first to concur, for though his plans are often unusual, his later work follows all the ordinary laws as to aspect. The south faces of the house are altogether wasted, one on corridors, the other on a kitchen court. The kitchen looks to the west, and is insufferably hot in the evening, when the preparation of dinner ought to find it at its coolest. The two chief fronts are to the north and east, both unpleasant. The only good feature to be espied is that both dining and drawing rooms catch some rays of the setting sun. One must assume that Morris had some odd predisposition in favour of cold and sunless rooms, though that idea seems foreign to his large and generous nature. The site does not suggest any reason, and though it is on record that the building was planned with a view to causing the least destruction of orchard trees, that can hardly be the explanation, which perhaps may be sought in the fact that the north faces the open country. When we come to regard the outside of the house, the voice of criticism is stilled. Looking northwards from the garden, the well with its conical red-tiled roof is a delightful feature.

The stair-space, with its loftier roof finished in a leaded lantern, almost takes on the quality of a tower. The bullseyes of the upper corridor are simply charming. The use of sliding sash windows gives food for thought. The gift of architectural common-sense, which has always been Mr. Philip Webb's, showed itself thus early. Few men would have dared at that date to mix sliding sashes with pointed door-heads — the useful with the ecclesiastical; but here it is, and how reasonable it looks! This corner in its orchard setting would be an achievement if devised to-day. Remembering that it is a work of fifty years ago, we may well admire. The west front is of a graver sort, but the flat, dormer-like projections and the fine gaunt chimney, with its cleverly diminished top, give it a character all its own. The stable is an attractive little building with its high-pitched roof, neat dormer and herring-bone brickwork in the gable

252.—DINING-ROOM FIREPLACE.

253.—THE SETTLE.

end. When it is remembered how the spirit of the Icelandic sagas clutched at the heart of Morris, there is a pleasant sense of fitness (albeit inadvertent) in the knowledge that an Iceland pony lives in this stable to-day. Of the garden there is no space to write more than a few words. The orchard gives the note of a rich domesticity, and the long bowling green of a return to gracious homely sports. In such surroundings Morris dispensed hospitality to a wide circle of friends, whose

184

names are inseparably associated with his in those great days of artistic aspiration and achievement. The garden was his especial delight, and (once more to quote Mr. Mackail) " of flowers and vegetables and fruit trees he knew all the ways and capabilities. Red House garden, with its long grass walks, its midsummer lilies and autumn sunflowers, its wattled rose-trellises inclosing richly-flowered square garden plots, was then as unique as the house it surrounded apples fell in at the windows as they stood open on hot summer nights."

With this hint of open-air idylls we may well take leave of a building which has flung its influence afar on the making of English homes.

In the days when The Red House was built, Upton had no water supply from the public mains and the well

254.—THE STABLES.

was a need. How delightfully Mr. Philip Webb has made an artistic virtue of a necessity is abundantly evident. With a characteristically Northern touch he has emphasised the protecting roof rather than the well-head itself, though the latter is supplied with an encircling bench which reminds us of the immemorial usage of wells as resting-places. The lofty conical roof is reminiscent of the French feeling which was running through the work of many Gothic designers in those days. In Eden Nesfield the influence went so far that his earlier work can hardly be recognised as English, though he later shed the extravagances which marked the intrusion of an art beautiful on its own soil but alien on this. Nothing, however, is more notable in Mr. Webb's long career as an architect than his steady consistency. It is the mark of an unstable mind to be swayed by passing fashions, but there are few with the strength to be untouched by their environment. Among them is the architect whose first work is here illustrated.

Once more must be emphasised the unique character of the Red House. Not only was it the starting point of a renascence of English domestic work, but it stands for a

255.—DINING-ROOM SIDEBOARD.

256 —CLOTHES PRESS AND BENCH.

definite architectural policy. It crystallises the revolt against reproductions of byegone art, where that art was based on conditions which have gone, never to return. Mr. Webb always followed traditions of sound building with a reverence none the less deep for being regulated by a fine independence of thought, but the formulas by which historical design was ruled he rejected with vigour.

It has been well said that, apart from the imagination and inventive power of the artist and his technical skill, there are three main factors that contribute to a work of art—observation, selection and convention—and that the best results are got from a due harmony in the contributions of all three elements. This was applied to sculpture, but is equally true of architecture. It is the disadvantage of what is unpleasantly called " art criticism " that a cloud of words, mostly long, seems to be inevitable for the expression of very simple notions. Hence one may, perhaps, add a gloss. " Observation " shows an architect the capacities of the site in relation to his client's needs, " selection " enables him to draw out from the Pandora's box of varying forms and arrangements those which will precisely clothe them, and " convention " guides him to those traditional uses which make a building at once the expression and the satisfaction of those needs.

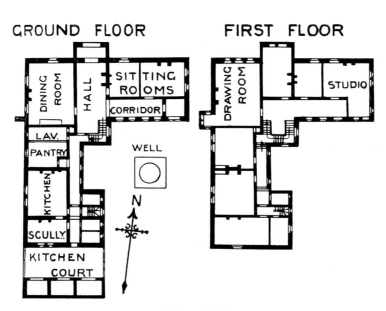

257.—PLANS.

UPMEADS, STAFFORD.

DESIGNED BY MR. EDGAR WOOD.

Architecture in Laputa—Flat Roofs, Their Advantages and Defects—Austerity v. Prettiness—The Placing of Windows—A Stimulating Conception.

THOUGH the merits of Upmeads are considerable, it will be generally agreed that the house is unusual to the point of oddness. It rather recalls the criticism which Mr. Norman Shaw made on a design submitted for the Soane medal by an architectural student—" rather boxy, isn't it ? " Despite the criticism, the boxy design won the coveted prize, and Upmeads cannot fail, by its logical qualities, and (one may safely add) by its originality, to rivet the attention of everyone and the admiration of not a few.

When Gulliver made his voyage to Laputa he found " a most ingenious architect, who had contrived a new method of building houses, by beginning at the roof and working downward to the foundation, which he justified to me by the like practice of those two prudent insects, the bee and the spider."

Perhaps Jonathan Swift was here satirising some architectural fad of his day, but there is nothing faddish about Upmeads, because Mr. Edgar Wood has pursued a perfectly logical purpose. He is convinced of the practical advantages of flat roofs, and for the following reasons. It is sometimes supposed, rather thoughtlessly, that a house can be planned simply with reference to the required disposition of its rooms, but that is not the case. If a pitched roof is contemplated, it has to be considered from the start, so that its gables or hips may be rightly contrived. A markedly irregular ground plan involves all sorts of difficulties with eaves gutters and other practical necessities, and the original scheme has often to be modified to ensure satisfactory roofing. In that sense the Laputan system of beginning at the roof and working downwards is a common-place of planning. The employment of flat roofs simplifies things immensely. The plan can have any sort of projection or recess without the creation of difficulties higher up. Mr. Edgar Wood is also insistent upon other advantages. Access to a pitched roof for the repair of slate or tile or for the change of a chimney-pot is often trouble-some, and not seldom involves the use of scaffolding. A flat roof can be made absolutely weather-proof, though the employment at Upmeads of concrete alone is unduly optimistic as to its wet-resisting powers. A layer of asphalte is a

258.—THE ENTRANCE.

wise addition, and gives the certainty of absolute and permanent resistance to the weather. Another practical advantage is the reduction in the number of down pipes necessary to carry off rain-water, and the immunity from the vagaries of wind and driven rain and snow, which are apt to try slate or tile beyond their endurance. From the point of view of habitability must be mentioned the avoidance of sloping ceilings in attic bedrooms, though they are no great harm, and the provision of an additional outdoor living-room in summer. From such an elevation there may perhaps be enjoyed fine distant views, invisible from the garden by reason of encircling trees, and in any case the garden itself lies open beneath one's eyes like an unrolled map.

The general aspect of Upmeads is fortress-like. It not only lacks anything approaching *prettiness*, which is all to the good, but presents an air of austerity, which shows the designer's devotion to extreme simplicity and restraint. There is, of course, nothing novel about flat roofs—they were common form in the last half of the eighteenth century, when a crown of red tiling was regarded as the mark of a taste not only vulgar, but depraved. Such houses in the classic manner had the relief of pilaster and cornice, while the windows were adorned with projecting architraves and pediments, which gave a rhythmic variety and balance to the composition, and the sky-line was perhaps lightened by an open balustrade. Mr. Wood, however, starts out on a fresh quest. His fronts are balanced only when symmetry is the natural outcome of the plan. Some of his window compositions are long and low, and he has realised to the full the large restfulness of great surfaces of unbroken brickwork. The whole scheme of design brings into play new ideas, both structural and æsthetic, and creates new problems which are capable of interesting and subtle development. The objections which may be put in array against such a new departure, or rather against a fresh presentment of an old idea,

259.—ENTRANCE COURT AND SOUTH-WEST FRONT.

are in part those which confront all development. The middling mind is always ready to revolt from the unusual, relying on the principle that what is new is not true. Criticism of Mr. Wood's standpoint must start, however, from something more than prejudice against change. The question that arises is whether any given departure from traditional methods carries with it the seed of enduring betterment. The case for the flat roof has already been stated, but the pleas of tradition must alike be heard. The pitched roof has many justifications. Its timber construction is markedly cheaper in first cost than the steel and concrete of the roof at Upmeads, and the useful space of rooms partly in the roof is secured at a lower cost per cubic foot than is possible in a flat-roofed house. Rain is thrown off readily, whether the eaves are fitted with gutters or not. The air space between tiles and ceilings serves as a non-conductor, and makes the upper rooms cool in summer and warm in winter. These are utilitarian points, but architecture is not merely a matter of accommodation and cost.

The roof is the crown of the house. Among imperial ornaments the Iron Crown of Lombardy has its own charm of austerity, but none will deny on that account the beauty of crowns of gold that, brilliant with jewels and blazing with colour, typify the rich variety of royal power. So it is with houses. We are not all or always in mood to hail with pleasure the presentment of a strength which has a thought of the forbidding. We are entitled to demand of the house we dwell in, as of the life we live, that it shall be crowned with graciousness as well as girt about with strength. The withers of our taste may well remain unwrung, if we look to our roofs to cut against the sky with outlines even playful, to intrigue our interest with unexpected gablets and with dormers slyly issuing from broad slopes of tiles. We are assured that there are nine-and-sixty ways of constructing tribal lays, and the same is true of home-building. It suffices now to welcome Upmeads, as illustrating one of the nine-and-sixty, and as a way which gives a pleasant stimulus to thought.

And now for some description of the house itself. It stands on the south-east slope of a hill which looks across to Cannock Chase. The entrance court is on the north-west front, and the front door is set in a porch of Bath stone, which is carried up to the parapet of the attic storey, and by its rigid verticality gives effect to the flat and outward reaching curves of the brick front. A similar tall stone panel is the central feature of the south-east front, where the hall door and window emphasise its upright lines. Very ingeniously contrived is the upper terrace, which appears in the accompanying picture, with its curved steps relieving the prevailing severity. From this point the ground falls away quietly to the road with appropriate terracing. We enter the house from the garden, to find a hall which

260.—ON THE GARDEN FRONT.

runs up two storeys, and is crowned with a simple vault. Opposite its lofty window is a balcony projecting a little from the first-floor corridor. Its balusters make a graceful feature and have an ingenious touch in their design, for the square members are slighter at the top than below. A hall like this adds greatly to the spacious, airy character of the house, but this very merit defeats its use as a sitting-room, and it absorbs a good deal of space,

261.—FROM THE SOUTH-EAST.

189

262.—HALL BALCONY FROM CORRIDOR.

263.—THE HALL.

the area, in fact, of an extra bedroom. The dining-room is notable for the well-designed mantel-piece. It is of green marbles, Swedish green and Irish moss, while the lining above the shelf is Siena marble, like onyx. The drawing-room is large, and it suited the owner of Upmeads, Mr. Frederick Bostock, to have it thus, rather than to make two small rooms of it, a wise decision, which might be followed often with advantage. In both these rooms the windows are carried right up to the

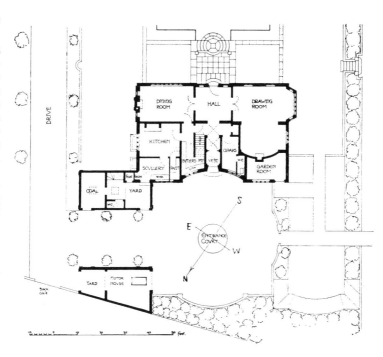

264.—GROUND PLAN.

ceiling and the transom-lights afford good ventilation and brilliant light.

Upstairs the windows are kept some way down from the ceiling, as too much top light is dazzling in sleeping-rooms. The first-floor passage is particularly light, an incidental advantage of the flat roof, which makes skylights simple. The working parts of the house are well arranged. All the water-pipes in the scullery are cased in cement, which is not only neat, but protective against frost.   At the west corner, with its door only to the garden, is a good room, where are stored garden chairs and tools and the equipment of the croquet lawn ; but it seems of doubtful wisdom to have provided no access to it from within the house.   In addition to the accommodation shown by the ground plan there are six bedrooms and one dressing-room.   The house cost under £3,000, and the price per cubic foot worked out at 8⅝d.   It will thus be seen that the flat-roof method does not greatly affect costs.   Even were it rather more expensive at the onset, the after cost of repairs is likely to be low, and it is, moreover, worth something to be relieved of the bother of them.   Mr. Edgar Wood has embarked on a way of building which is distinctive and interesting, and we can always be grateful for the thing that stimulates thought and makes us enquire a reason for the architectural faith that is in us, whatever it may be.

265.—DRAWING-ROOM FIREPLACE.

OF THE REPAIR AND ENLARGEMENT
OF OLD HOUSES.

WITH one exception, where an old cottage forms the core of a new house which entirely dominates the old work, the houses so far illustrated in this book have been new buildings. They represent original thought to which architectural form has been given to meet modern needs. The Red House, designed for William Morris, was included because it was felt that no survey of modern domestic architecture can be complete without some reference to that notable and epoch-making work of Mr. Philip Webb. By it and by his later work he has exercised an influence on the art of his day which is being understood all too slowly. Save for The Red House, then, the houses thus far described are essentially the work of the twentieth century. There is, however, a branch of architecture which links the builders of elder times with the designers of to-day—the repair and enlargement of old houses. Six examples of such treatment find a place in the following pages, and because it is of great importance, some prefatory words on the spirit in which it should be approached may be useful.

There is, perhaps, no more searching test of the general fitness and capacity of an architect for his task than his manner of dealing with additions and alterations. In the case of a dwelling the process calls for more inventive ingenuity and for no less conservative restraint than in the case of a church. How hopelessly architects have failed to appreciate how the latter work should be performed, the sad condition to which most of our churches have been brought loudly testifies. Yet in church "restoration" the architectural and historical side can receive large, nay, often exclusive, consideration, whereas in house alterations, the utilitarian requirements of the inhabitants are apt to dominate the position and render the most capable and sympathetic architect's labours equal to those of Hercules—even of Sisyphus. Many a rich man has expressed his admiration for an old house and bought it. Yet he has bidden his architect convert its moderate accommodation and primitive planning into a residence "fit for a family of distinction," as house agents phrase it. Too often the old house is smothered by the additions, overwhelmed by the greater size and ambitious showiness of the new work. Nor is this misfortune limited to places of some importance. England is peculiarly rich in its yeomen's homes. Picturesque dwellings of a native type, and varying with local materials and customs, form one of the great delights of rural life in many parts of England. They are often seized upon for inhabitance by those who demand very different accommodation from what was needed by the original builders, and the result of the consequent altera-tions is apt to be the disappearance of the old charm. This has probably depended not so much on any fineness of design or elaboration of workmanship, as upon complete adequacy of line and proportion to the size, character and purpose of the house and its outbuildings. It does not need the crushing juxtaposition of large additions to throw such a group out of harmony. The intrusion of differently proportioned windows, the breaking of a roof-line, the spoiling of the existing tone and texture, may all together or one alone be sufficient to produce this misfortune. Must, then, such buildings be left untouched? That were in many instances to doom them to destruction. Changes of habits and the development of the locality too often make them unpopular as the dwelling of a small agricultural holding, and they are either roughly patched into a semblance of unintelligent modernity or left derelict. On the other hand, there is a growing pleasure taken in such little places by people of educated thought and taste, who understand the ethical as well as the æsthetic conditions which have been at work, and are willing to pay some homage to them and to submit themselves partially to their rule if only a measure of reform may be introduced. They will use what they find in its own manner and for all it is worth if some modifications following in the lines of amplitude and convenience are permitted. Seldom need a proper exercise of judgment and ingenuity fail in producing a satisfactory compromise, in transforming what already is, or threatens to become, a neglected wreck or a slovenly makeshift into a little homestead that will still impress by its pleasant old-time spirit, and yet amply fulfil the needs of modern habit and hygiene if they are kept within virile and simple bounds. But before an *entente cordiale*, free from disruptive tendencies, can be established between the old and the new, careful preliminaries of peace should be drawn up. Anybody seeking one of the delightful little cottage homes of seventeenth century type which are still plentiful in the out-of-the-way parts of Kent, Surrey and Sussex, should be certain that the one he settles upon already satisfies him, in the matter of character and size, as the dominant partner in the future arrangement. If the old has merit and is worth preserving it should be given its full value, and any additions made should be its humble supporters, not its domineering masters. It is a pity and a waste to lose the scale and quality of a distinctive piece of seventeenth century architecture, however humble, by making it the dwarf annexe of a modern house. The modern house would probably be better, as a piece of design and of planning, without it, while the old work is bereft of its purpose and lies like an uprooted specimen on a museum shelf. This may be laid down as a general principle. Lesser points and details can only be considered rightly in the light of concrete examples, for which the reader is referred to the stories of the six houses that follow.

In some cases, of course, the amount of the new work is comparatively trifling, and the labour of the architect is chiefly directed to the wise repair of tottering walls and decaying floors and roofs. For such an enterprise two qualifications are peculiarly necessary—reverence for the old work and a large knowledge of the materials and workmanship which made it what it is. Often the first and most important point to consider is as to how far the accretions of later years are to be swept away and how far they are to be regarded as an integral part of the structure, and deserving, therefore, of jealous preservation. Too often domestic work of the sixteenth to the eighteenth centuries has been ravaged by ignorant " restoration " in the nineteenth. It is impossible to lay down rules as to what should be kept and what may be removed ; but this general advice seems to be safe—that nothing be held common or unclean which was done while a definite tradition still governed England's building. In the nineteenth century no such tradition survived, and only now is it being slowly, laboriously and, it must be confessed, fitfully renewed. The old idea that an Elizabethan house is defiled by an eighteenth century addition is, happily, dying, but it is by no means dead. The passion for uniformity of style at any cost of destruction was, perhaps, the most deadly vice of nineteenth century restoration. The men who were devoted wholly to Gothic would sweep away the fifteenth century porch of a thirteenth century church, and substitute a sham erection in the latter style because, forsooth, they chose to regard Perpendicular work as debased. Debased is a fatuous word to apply to the work of any period which is in the normal line of architectural development.

When it comes to the detailed consideration of how particular damages are to be repaired and how additions can be made so that they harmonise with the old work, no better advice can be given than that an architect with experience in such matters shall be consulted. The following pages show how diverse are the problems involved when an old house has to be dealt with, and more is to be learnt from the treatment of definite examples than from vague information unrelated to actual facts. Practical points as to the treatment of masonry, timber, ironwork, etc., are treated at length in a little book published by the Society for the Protection of Ancient Buildings and in a pamphlet which bears the imprimatur of the Royal Institute of British Architects. Both these publications, however, deal rather with churches and with other public buildings than with houses ; but few people are aware of their existence, and they should be studied by all who are serving on committees charged with the restoration of churches and other national monuments. They establish for the layman the attitude of mind in which such serious matters should be approached; but he would be ill-advised indeed who regarded them as sanctioning any amateur attempts at reparation or new building. The plea addressed to the public throughout this book to take a keen interest in building of all kinds, whether new or old, will have grievously failed of its purpose if it leads to amateur experiments in the art which more than any other is broad based on wide technical knowledge and large experience. One has only to look to St. Alban's Abbey to see what terrible havoc has been wrought there within and without by the itch for amateur restoration which has made the name of the late Lord Grimthorpe a reproach and a hissing wherever the lovers of our national heritage of building are gathered together.

It should be borne in mind, however, that the owner of even a little cottage which garners within its weathered walls and lowly roof the traditions of English craftsmanship possesses in fact a national monument, even though the strong light of history may not beat upon it and the romance of some strong name may not lend it an aroma of greatness. He is morally, though not actually, the trustee for a fragment of the architectural story of England, and should not feel that the mere fact of possession entitles him to destroy the character of a home of our forefathers.

WHIXLEY HALL, NEAR YORK.

AND ITS REPARATION BY MR. WALTER H. BRIERLEY.

The Early History of Whixley—The Will of Christopher Tancred—And His Body—Unruly Pensioners—
The Maltreated Hall—The Renewal of the Windows.

THE later history of Whixley Hall is in the main the outcome of the will of Christopher Tancred. Not content with the testamentary method of spiting his relations, the instructions he left as to the care of his body caused trouble for over one hundred and fifty years, as will presently appear. The earlier history of the house must first be given, and then the odd proceedings of old Christopher, which led in the long last to Whixley Hall being restored by Mr. Walter Brierley. Charles Tancred was its owner at the beginning of the seventeenth century. He married Barbara Wyvill of Osgerly, and died in 1644, leaving six children, of whom Richard was the eldest. Ten years later Richard greatly altered the east side of the house, as a dated stone attests, but a stone-mullioned window of the original house was left in the kitchen. Doubtless this was part of the house built by his father when he acquired the manor shortly before 1600. Richard was knighted in 1665 and died in 1668. His eldest son, Charles, married Dorothy Wyvill. She bore him three sons, of whom the eldest, born in 1659, brought the name of Christopher into the Tancred family. He took his part in the public work of his day, for in 1684-85 we find Captain Christopher Tancred of Whixley High Sheriff of Yorkshire and Member of Parliament, in which offices he served through James II.'s reign into William and Mary's. It was to him that Whixley Hall owes its next reconstruction. In 1680 was added a fine suite of reception-rooms, which form the west wing. The hall and south front were evidently remodelled, and the main staircase built at the same time. To the elder Christopher, therefore, must be attributed this characteristic and delightful example of the architecture of Charles II.'s reign ; but it is with his second son, the younger Christopher, the last of his race, that the Hall will always be most associated. He had quarrelled with his five sisters, whom he describes in his will, executed in 1721, as "inhuman creatures." One may assume they were sensible people, bored by the eccentricity which is clear enough from the will, but they evidently did not know how to handle him, for they got "one shilling apiece."

The pursuit of learning at Cambridge and Lincoln's Inn benefited by the misdemeanours of the sisters. Of his benefactions, vested in an imposing

266.—THE 1680 STAIRCASE.

body of trustees, perhaps the best known to-day are the Tancred Studentships at Lincoln's Inn. His interests were not limited to the legal reforms with which his name is also associated, but were flavoured by a pretty taste in racing and the devious joys of horse-dealing.

The residue of his estate, after payment of the studentships, went to endow Whixley Hall as a hospital for twelve pensioners, indigent and decayed gentlemen, clergymen, commissioned land or sea officers of over fifty years of age.

267.—MOUNT AND GARDEN-HOUSE.

Which is all very proper, but in his will he added the inconvenient provision that his body should remain at the Hall and not be put underground. This was met by putting Old Tancred (as his neighbours

268.—THE ENTRANCE FRONT.

called him) in a brick vault in the cellar. where he remained some seventy years. An odd flavour in the drinking water led to some researches into cause and effect so the coffin was raised and, if tradition is to be believed, slung in chains in the hall to cheer the old men as they dined. Some of them seem to have taken a not unreason-able objection to

269.—FROM THE TENNIS LAWN.

this near presence of their benefactor, and, indeed, it seems a rather drastic form of the *memento mori*. A short sojourn in the cellar followed, and then a marble sarcophagus was placed in a room prepared as a chapel, which sheltered the uneasy remains until 1905. The pensioners lived at the Hall from 1754 until 1867, when their general conduct became the subject of enquiry by the Inspector of Charities. It was decided, and con-firmed by special Act of Parliament, that the Hall should be let and the pensions paid to the old men, who were granted freedom to live where they pleased. The original foundation had provided that they should pay for their own meals. Each month a caterer was elected by the pensioners, and all paid him their contribution towards the common board. This led to quarrels, for the caterer not infre-quently took a holiday with the proceeds. Though the vicar of Whixley was Warden of the Hall and read prayers there twice a day, there was no regular supervision. One of the decayed gentlemen obtained a big drum and varied his performance on it with dancing in the corridor. A group of them on the roof would enliven the reverent demeanour of the villagers by throwing empty bottles at them as they went by to church. An old sea captain seems to have taken to heart Swift's benediction on those who make two blades of grass to grow where but one grew before. He planted tobacco in the park, put up a shanty with the legend "At the Sign of the Blue Boar," and therein comforted his friends with liquor and tobacco, both home-made. The provision which limited the charity

270.—QUEEN MARY'S BEDROOM.

to "necessitated gentlemen" was honoured greatly in the breach. In 1811 a barber got a pension, and cheered his days and swelled his purse by shaving his brethren for a fee. Further, there are iron staples still fixed to the old staircase which tell of needful aid to legs not wholly steady. The wisdom of scattering this necessitated dozen cannot therefore be impeached, but the Hall suffered. It was let, but afterwards becoming empty fell into swift decay, and

271.—THE HOUSE AND THE CHURCH.

was a poor shadow of its seventeenth century self when Mr. A. Taylor took a long lease of it from the governors of the charity in 1905 and jointly with them restored it. The work fell into the able hands of Mr. Walter S. Brierley. The gardens were a wilderness and the house a wreck. A faculty was obtained to transfer the sarcophagus containing the much-moved remains of Old Tancred to a resting-place in the church

272.—THE HALL.

not fifty yards away. The chapel whence it came (never consecrated as such) became the billiard-room. Unhappily, one serious outrage on the fabric was committed some twenty years ago. The hall originally ran up two storeys, and with its fluted pilasters must have been an imposing apartment. Some vandal tenant, wanting more bedroom accommodation, inserted a floor, and Mr. Brierley's efforts to remove it and to reinstate the hall in its original condition unfortunately proved fruitless. It is some small consolation that the fireplace was not destroyed; but the whole aspect of the hall, with its grievous proportions, is a commentary sufficiently damning on the wanton stupidity of making such organic alterations in an ancient house.

Other villainies of bygone years have, happily, been corrected. The shape and size of the window openings on the entrance front had been altered and mean sliding sashes inserted. By careful examination the size of the original openings was determined, and casements proper to the period were fitted to them. Both staircases had, happily, escaped mutilation; the earlier is of oak, and that of 1680, with its massive balusters, is of deal painted. Upstairs one bedroom, and that a small one, has been treated with especial care. The accompanying picture shows the delightful tall panelling. Close to the ceiling are carved gilt masks of considerable merit, and so markedly Italian in feeling as to suggest that they came from abroad. At the cornice there is some painted decoration. On a pane of the old kitchen window was found scratched with a diamond " Orinda Katherine Tancred " and the date " March 4, 1600." The lady with these romantic names was not a daughter of the first Charles of Whixley, and no such name as Orinda can be traced to a Tancred. Probably it was not baptismal, but a fanciful assumption. The writing is of interest, as fixing a date when the Tancreds were in occupation.

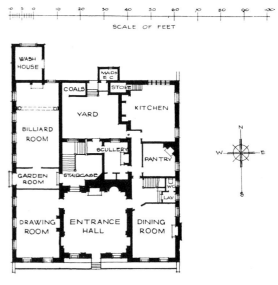

SCALE OF FEET

273.—GROUND FLOOR PLAN.

Externally the house is delightful. Of red brick and stone slates, its grave, simple fronts to the south and west are altogether pleasant. The recessing of the middle of the south elevation, the slight projection of the brickwork in broad, vertical bands that take the windows, the exquisite detail of the brick string above the ground-floor windows, all go to build up a composition none the less subtle for being so sober. The gardens have been admirably treated. Behind the house and running east and west is the original mound. At its west end there are some old stable buildings, part of which has been converted into an arcaded summer-house, a very happy idea. For the rest, the pictures adequately show the simple terracing and the handsome steps which have taken the place of wild disorder.

Altogether, but for the maltreated hall, for which Mr. Brierley was not responsible, Whixley is a peculiarly satisfactory example of the reverent and adequate repair of a seventeenth century house. Standing as it does almost in the shadow of the parish church, where old Christopher's body lies at last, it remains a notable memorial of that distinguished, if eccentric, benefactor of law and learning

274.—THE EAST STAIRCASE.

THE POULTRY COURT, PAINSWICK,

AS ENLARGED BY MR. CURTIS GREEN.

Additions to an Old Cottage—Cotswold Masonry—A Varied Sky-line.

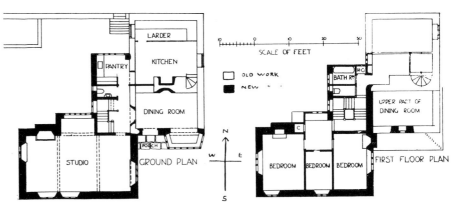

275.—THE PLANS.

P AINSWICK is a little out-of-the-way town, high up amid the Cotswold Hills, that has a very good architectural past. Both our Earlier Renaissance style and the full Palladian of the eighteenth century are well represented in its streets and its outlying habitations. Of the latter the most important is Painswick House, which is situated a little out of the town and environed by a small but picturesque park. The house, a vigorous sample of Palladianism, with its range of lofty windows flanked by rusticated columns and topped with pediments, stands very high and dominates an extensive distant view, while rising knolls and leafy glens occupy the foreground and middle distance. In the very centre of the latter, less than a quarter of a mile from the house, and still in the park, was an old Cotswold cottage which, for some reason, was not swept away when the great house was built and the land laid out. Architectural objects seem to have appealed to the "landscapist" who was employed. Thus a great octagonal building of stone with a lead cupola—a columbarium above, a look-out room below—occupies the apex of the most prominent knoll, with trees grouped around. The cottage was brought into this scheme. On its northern gable, conspicuous from the house, was erected what has the appearance of a Palladian belfry, with two little arched apertures for bells, only the bells were left out. Extension was given to the end of the cottage by adding sloping walls, pierced by arched doorways and ending with pilasters that

276.—FROM THE SOUTH-EAST.

carry classic urns. Westwards, this wall is continued to hide the cottage yard and garden—or was it a place for poultry and hence the name of the little dwelling? Then beeches and elms were planted to afford a screen and a grouping to this point in the general outlook from the squire's house. Thus it remained till three years ago, when the amenity of the spot and the potentiality of the building led to its extension as an artist's home. Mr. Curtis Green has effected the transformation in a very engaging manner. He has left untouched the main

277.—THE PORCH AND DINING-ROOM.

block of the old cottage and its northern adornment, but by a rearrangement of the low building to the south he has obtained a delightful porch and a hall which serves as a dining-room. To the west he has added a new building, containing a studio below and three bedrooms above and having a staircase and offices behind it. The materials and the forms given to them are of Cotswold type—rubble walls, ashlar for quoins and mullions, the roof stone-tiled; and as old tiles were obtainable for the new work, it was brought into immediate colour harmony with that which previously existed. The scheme of the additions leaves the old cottage almost as a separate entity, the new block is merely juxtaposed: so that, although we have but a small dwelling we have a group of buildings with most varied sky-line Although it is the smaller and the simpler half, the old cottage retains its form and value, a result greatly to the credit of Mr. Curtis Green The new block projects forward to the south-west, and is on the edge of a rapid

278—THE STUDIO.

descent which, beyond a little grass terrace, forms a steeply sloping kitchen garden and then takes shape as a timbered glen falling to a vale.

The photographs of the entrance or south-east side show the happy relationship between the old and new portions. The low part of the former has had a pent roof brought forward from its gable, which covers the dining-room bay and affords an ample porch. The mullioning of the bay, which has nothing but the roof to support, is of wood, not of stone like the windows in the walling. The framing is flat and unmoulded, and flush with it are casements of flat bar iron, one and a-half inches wide. The entrance door is of oak and constructed in a manner known to mediæval carpenters. It consists of two sets of planks laid back to back, the inner set placed horizontally, but the outer set vertically, so that the rain may not lodge in the joints. The two sets are clamped together with wrought-iron nails, which are arranged over the surface of the door in patterns of fives at the edges and of sixes in the middle. Bold strap hinges stretch across the door

on the outside, thus connecting and stiffening the vertical set of planks. It is a thoroughly satisfying model, where the ancient spirit of country building, straightforward and severe, is to be retained.

The room thus entered must have been a shed added to the old cottage, of which the outer wall has been left unplastered and shows the stonework. A fireplace, with a cleverly devised hood of old Dutch tiles supported on stone brackets, has been inserted, and the bay window is, of course, an addition. The window-sill is composed of dull red tile quarries, a foot across and two inches thick, and the floor is laid in the same material. The room has not been ceiled, but shows the roof construction. A reference to the plan will make clear the disposition of the rooms. The staircase is of oak, very pleasantly designed and conveniently arranged to reach the two levels of the upper floor. The new part, besides an ample well-lit lobby, has three bed-rooms, two of which have chimneys. Height is given to them by leaving them open to the roof, of which the boards and rafters are painted white, while the walls are finished in tough granular plaster, which has dried out a pleasant cream colour and, having no wash laid on, shows its texture. Below these rooms the studio occupies the whole space, being thirty feet long and lit on all four sides. The north window, occupying the outer wall of the excrescence which forms the lobby above, is the largest and loftiest—as

279.—THE DINING-ROOM.

lofty, that is, as the nine-foot height of the room permits. It is, after all, primarily intended as a comfortable sitting-room, and not for large work needing top light. The ceiling is of beam and rafter type, the beams, which are not of considerable depth for their length, being well supported by curved braces springing from the walls. These, being composed of the local rubble stone, are amply thick and afford arched recesses to the windows, which, with the constructional ceiling and the stone mantel-piece, give the thoroughly architectural character to the room which the sketch reveals.

Returning outside to look at the back of the house, we note that the little gables of the lobby and stair-case projections are carried up in elm weather-boarding—stone would have looked rather cyclopean for these lesser features. The apex of one of them is slightly bracketed forward, and fitted up as a dovecote. The multiplication of roof-lines and incidents thus created might have appeared slightly confused and frivolous but for the mass and severity of the chimney-stacks, which brace and discipline the whole composition and render it perfectly agreeable. Here, certainly, is a case of a cottage conversion and extension carried out on right lines. Nothing that previously possessed the slightest merit is lost, and a most enjoyable general effect is produced which could not well have been obtained—which, indeed, it would have been blamably eccentric to attempt—in an entirely new construction. The Poultry Court has strong individuality reached without strain, and arising naturally and obviously out of its past circumstances and present purposes. That is a simple statement of the facts ; but to those who know about this sort of thing it will be recognised as strong praise none too frequently deserved. The cost of the work was one thousand and sixty-five pounds.

A HOUSE AT TIDEBROOK, SUSSEX

ALTERED AND ENLARGED BY MR. G. H. KITCHIN.

A Difficult Piece of Restoration—An Undue Variety of Material—Interesting Doors.

THE little old Sussex homestead at Tidebrook is a complex instance of the class of renewed houses, because it has twice been through the mill. It was added to in deplorable manner some time ago, and has lately been again altered with a view to giving back to it more of the spirit of its early time and to cloaking in part the improprieties of its middle period. At the same time it has been necessary to increase the accommodation and introduce a water service, a heating apparatus and adequate offices.

Tidebrook is part of Wadhurst parish, and lies in that tumbled section of Sussex where hill and dale have been close packed in picturesque confusion and where ancient homesteads peep out at every turn. The one now illustrated is set on a bank that declines rapidly northward to the little deep-channelled and leafy hollow where runs the brook—a mere rill except in floodtime. The house is placed near the foot of the declivity and occupies a central position, with the farm buildings on each side and on rather higher ground. To the east are an ample barn and stabling, while to the west are an oasthouse and other shedding. These buildings are wholly of ancient character, toned and mossed with age, and group

280 —THE NORTH SIDE.

281.—THE SOUTH FRONT IN 1909.

282.—THE SITTING-ROOM.

delightfully with the house, which was, in its original state, typical of its district. It may be described as a chimney with a few rooms round it. The block of masonry forming the chimney-breast is 7ft. square, even on the upper storey, and on the ground floor is still wider. Round it the house clustered. Its tall shaft is admirable in design, for neither the breaks nor the mouldings are elaborate, yet it has an air of dignity and distinction. It was the one prominent and shapely feature of the simple dwelling, rising high above the great unbroken tile roof. The hipped gables and the long low windows, one of which is preserved in the attic, strengthened the general feeling of horizontal humility that would not venture to compete with the vertical dominance o the chimney-stack. It was a charming little composition, and it is a pity it ever was touched. It, unfortunately, fell towards the end of the nineteenth century into hands wholly unsympathetic and uninformed, and an effort was made to turn it cheaply into a modern villa. A deplorable arrangement, composed of two bay windows of totally different size and projection, set one on the top of the other, and with their transoms wrongly placed, was made to protrude from the wall of the south gable, of which the original overhang, supported by oak brackets carved with flat strapwork, still remained as a protest against nineteenth century degradation of the art of building. Beyond this gable an uncompromising stuccoed annexe was run up, with a front door in the middle of its south side, approached by a pathway down the steep slope from the roadway above. The triumph of unintelligent commonplace was achieved, and the little yeoman's home was no more. It needed some courage to acquire the place after it had undergone such treatment. Yet the situation and grouping of the old homestead and the remaining features of the original dwelling were delightful. The place was still full of possibilities, and it was bought three years ago by the Dean of Durham. Even enlarged as it had been, it did not offer the accommodation he required, and so there could be no question of going back to the old size and appearance. The architect had to provide further rooms and give character both to the house and its environment. Moreover, it was essential that the outlay should be rigidly kept down. The architect must, therefore,

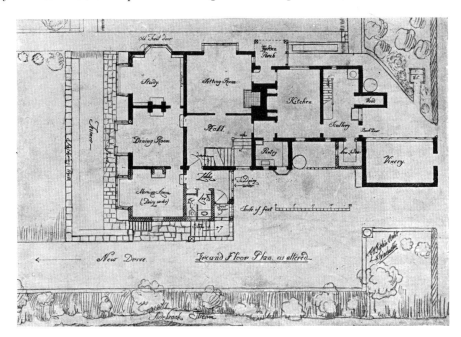

283.—GROUND PLAN, SHOWING ADDITIONS AND ALTERATIONS.

be judged from what he has done, and not from what he has left undone. As he had to extend the new east building towards the north and increase the size of the rooms it already possessed, he was given free scope here, and with excellent results. The east elevation, as he found it, and as an illustration shows, was a stucco flat pierced by ill-shaped windows. The long line of this front, rising from its rough stone terrace and broken by great and well-proportioned bays, is very satisfying. Oak of a cool grey-brown tone has been used. The upper part of the walling is hung with old tiles and the lower part is faced with a pleasantly-textured sandstone raised close by from the bed of the brook. Why, where all is so good and complete, the masonry which forms the base of the three bays should not have been built of this stone, but of some material which needed a coating of dull grey cement, is a puzzle. The saving of cost must have been infinitesimal, the blot on the composition is serious. It should always be borne prominently in mind that the better a thing is, the more disastrous is the least back-sliding, and the photographer showed judgment in giving this view from below the terrace and thus hiding the defect. As seen in the picture, the east elevation, in form and proportion, in colour and texture, deserves nothing but praise.

The south side is not at present so good, for the terrible excrescent windows are retained. This is merely a temporary fault, to be swept away when funds permit. Meanwhile they may be said to serve a purpose. They must wholesomely mortify the flesh of those who have to live with them, and they are a valuable object-lesson, showing how a thing should not be done. Remains of the original two-storeyed moulded oak bay were found at this place and gave the due indication for the new one to the right. When the same model replaces the Victorian intrusion, the south front will be pleasant and harmonious; but it is much to be hoped that the mechanically hard and distressingly restless fish-scale tiles will then be swept away. It is strange, indeed, how anyone could introduce such a jarring note when the original hand-made plain tiles were still hanging on the old gable above, and have been repeated on the upper part of the new gable next to it with admirable effect. At present the only elevation which is thoroughly in the spirit of the old work is the entirely new one to the east, for the fish-scale tiles on the north gables destroy the restfulness of that side. The weather-boarding of the old hipped gable consorts quite well with the plain tiling, and the stonework of the terrace and of the stairway to the new front door is an apt introduction. But there is too much variety of material at this point. Weathering of boards and of two sorts of tile, walling of brick, of stone, of stucco, woodwork of oak and of white painted deal—all this produces a spottiness of surface at a point where the structure is necessarily intricate in form. That is regrettable, as the design and arrangement are both decidedly clever. The south entrance has been abolished and a private and sheltered garden in rising terraces has been laid out on that side. A new drive has been run from a lower point of the road along the edge of the brook, and it widens out into a fore-court when the north side of the house is reached. The drop in the land brings the forecourt level some feet lower than the house, so that larders and dairies are contrived in a light basement, and a flight of steps leads to a simple and well-arranged porch and lobby. The old oak door of fifteen panels is worth notice. The inside of it has been new-lined with five planks very well moulded, and the wrought-iron hinges and other fittings are very creditable modern smith's work. Another form of door which has been much used here consists of old oak planks, probably from floors, tied by ledgers bolted on with square-headed wrought nails. An example appears in the illustration of the sitting-room, with its Adam mantel and extremely fine brass and iron basket grate. The open door reveals the stair, the least offensive product of the Victorian alterations, and now improved by the addition of oak

284.—THE EAST SIDE IN 1907.

285.—THE SOUTH FRONT IN 1907.

finials to its newels. The annexed plan shows the present disposition of the rooms. A thoroughly comfortable and roomy house has been arranged. To get the due accommodation some addition and alteration had to be made at the west end of the south front; that is, at the point where hitherto the old house had almost entirely escaped modification. The difficulty and danger of dealing with ancient fabrics are here well exemplified. It would have been better to have left the fine unbroken sweep of the old roof untouched; but a needed dressing-room required the throwing out of a little gable, and the servants' room imperatively called for a window that gave light and air higher than 3ft. from the floor. The new window and the new gable are admirable in design and execution—there is nothing about the house for which the architect deserves greater credit, and yet one regrets them, for without them, and with the proposed renewal of the old bay and the old tiling, the south front would have still retained all the old lines, would still have shown us how Sussex yeomen housed themselves when Elizabeth ruled England.   But a house is a place to be lived in after the manner in which each succeeding age understands life, and some amount of compromise is necessary in all adaptations from old ways to new.   It is not often that the task has been approached and performed in a more thoroughly appreciative and discerning manner than at Tidebrook House. Mr. G. H. Kitchin has satisfied his clients' requirements and respected their purse.   At the same time he has —or soon will have—obliterated the vandalisms of twenty years ago, and has given us delightful new work which has transformed an ancient dwelling into a house of to-day without losing the spirit, the form or the craftsmanship of the older time

286.—THE EAST SIDE IN 1909.

208

GUISELEY RECTORY, NEAR LEEDS.

AND ITS REPARATION BY SIR CHARLES NICHOLSON AND MR. H. C. CORLETTE.

An Elizabethan Rector—The Anabaptist Well—Internal Alterations—The Oratory—Details of Repair.

THE Rectory at Guiseley has a double interest to-day. Not only does it represent in delightful fashion the masculine, if rather dour, art of Yorkshire builders in Elizabethan days, but it is a peculiarly satisfactory example of a sound and conservative policy of repair, on which the architects are to be congratulated without reserve. Its history seems to have been peaceful until some fifty years ago, when it was allowed to fall into hideous disrepair, and alterations in details, such as fireplaces, were carried out as stupidly and badly as could be.

About its building we are left in no doubt, for on a tablet above the porch is the following inscription :

ANNO DOMINI 1601.

FIDELIS PASTORIS NON CAECIDUCIS NON LATRONIS DOMUS. ROBERTUS MORUS, RECTOR

ECCLESIAE DOMUS FUNDATOR. VAE SACRILEGO, VAE INIMICIS LEVI. R.M.

which, being interpreted, may be read, " This is the home not of a blind guide or of a robber, but of a faithful pastor. Robert Moore, the Rector of the church, is its builder. Woe to the sacrilegious ! Woe to the foes of the priesthood ! " This is conceived in a robust strain, and suggests that Robert Moore lacked nothing of the vigour belonging to the Church militant here on earth. Though he is careful to disclaim the title of robber, he seems, in Antient Pistol's phrase, to have " conveyed " materials for his rectory from the old Guiseley Hall, which had become derelict owing to the Wardes, lords of Guiseley Manor, having died out after the Wars of the Roses. Of the old house not a wrack remains, and it is not even definitely known

287.—THE GARDEN FRONT.

whether it stood on the present site of the rectory or near by. As, however, there was round the rectory a moat, of which part remains as a fish-pond, it is likely that the old site was used, and the fact that old people still call the place The Rectory Hall seems further evidence. Guiseley has had other distinguished rectors than Robert Moore, and one in particular, William Brearey, was active architecturally, for the sundial which we see below the hour-glass finial on the gable above the main porch bears the initials " W. B., 1685." He was a Churchman of note, for he served also as Arch-deacon of the East Riding of Yorkshire, and entertained the Archbishop at the rectory for some days, as the parish registers duly attest. Hitch, sometime Dean of York, and James Willoughby, one of the Middleton family, who built the old tithe-barn, now a parish hall,

288.—THE EAST FRONT.

were other incumbents of Guiseley. The rectory did not escape unhappy incidents during the Great Rebellion. There is a tradition—it can hardly be called history—that a Royalist spy was killed there just before the battle of Marston Moor. Fairfax and Cromwell were in the neighbourhood, and when the spy's pursuit of information as to their movements was discovered he met a spy's fate.

An odd feature of the garden is, perhaps, to be traced in its origin to the religious chaos of the same days. There are three stone wells, one of which was filled up and had to be excavated. It is oblong, with dressed stone steps and flagged bottom, sides and platform. It is filled with water by a spring. Mr. J. F. Howson, the present Rector, thinks that it may have been used by Anabaptists during the Commonwealth for baptism by immersion. It seems, by the way, not to be known generally that the rubric of the Church of England provides that " if the child may well endure it, the priest *shall dip it* in the water discreetly and warily," and this use is said to continue in a very few parishes even to this day. The well at Guiseley was, however, evidently designed for adult baptism, if for baptism at all. Indeed, one finds a difficulty in suggesting another use for it, for it is unlikely that any long-dead rector was an outdoor morning tubber born out of due time.

We come now to the work of reparation. Some alterations were needful to meet the requirements

289.—THE PORCH

of modern life. The staircase originally
stood, very inconveniently, in the hall
just inside the porch. It was taken down
and rebuilt against the north wall. The
kitchen and lavatory accommodation
was hopelessly inadequate, so extensions were made at the north-east
corner and on the north side to fill
the need. In the plans of the ground
and first floors the old walls are shown
in black, and the new work by hatched
lines. The arrangement of the north
bedrooms and corridor was altered, to
the great improvement of the house.
Three of the original fireplaces had
been bricked up and fitted with dreary
grates of Early Victorian pattern. The
latter were swept away, and the fine
masonry recesses opened out, as will be
seen in the picture of the study. The

290.—THE ANABAPTISTS' WELL.

GROUND

FLOOR.

FIRST

FLOOR.

291.—PLANS.

292.—FROM THE NORTH-WEST.

floors were rotten,
and had to be
renewed, but some
of the old beams
remained intact.
The room at the
north-west corner
was remodelled to
serve as an
oratory, and very
gracious it looks
with its well-
designed *prie-dieu*
and painted
reredos. In
the house there
was some original
panelling, which
has been gathered
together and used
for the oratory
walls. The out-
side of the Rectory
was, if anything,
in more lamentable

case than the interior. The gables were tottering, and the fine mullioned windows, though almost perfect in each stone, threatened collapse. Every stone was taken down to the level of the first-floor ceiling, numbered and rebuilt in its old place. The pictures show the extent of this work, for the mortar, though it will darken with time, now stands out white against the old joints. It is the delightful feature of Guiseley Rectory that, save by such normal signs as this, one cannot tell the old work from the new, yet there

293.—THE STUDY.

has been no desire to make the new masquerade as old, and the rights of the craftsmen who worked for Robert Moore have been respected. The view "From the North-west" shows the front which has been most altered, yet how naturally the new gabled projection groups with the old work. The positions of some of the original windows were changed and the walls pierced for new ones, yet the warm grey Guiseley stone and the Yorkshire stone slates of the roof have happily conspired, under able directing hands, to continue the Elizabethan story. And what a masculine air there is about the building. The big, simple corbels under the chimney-stack on the east front, the stout stone gargoyles at the angles, the massive stones which go to make the walls, all make up a picture free indeed from prettinesses but instinct

294.—THE STAIRCASE.

with strength. Elizabethan craftsmen were glad enough in gentler parts of England to spend their fancy in quips and conceits in stone; but, except for the finials above the north porch and elsewhere, Guiseley Rectory is finely typical of the restraint which is the note of Yorkshire building traditions. Fortunate, indeed, that in its evil hour it fell into such capable hands, and that it has now entered a new lease of life with an occupant so sympathetic as the Rev. J. F. Howson, whose taste and judgment in its furnishing have aptly crowned the architects' labours.

295.—THE ORATORY.

MARTIN'S, BURY, SUSSEX.

AND ITS GRADUAL ENLARGEMENT BY MR. CHARLES SPOONER.

The Enemy of Thatch—Growth of the Plan—A Roof of Reeds—A Story of Fire—
Du Bellay on Vernacular Art.

UNHAPPILY the subject of this chapter no longer stands as the illustrations show it, for last year the relentless enemy of thatched houses left it a mass of smouldering ruins, with nothing standing but the big chimney-stack and some small parts of the thicker walls. Though, as Villon would sing, it has gone with the snow of yester-year, the story of its growth under the skilful hand of Mr. Spooner, and the charm of the pictures which remain, make it worthy of record here.

At the top of Bury Hill in Sussex is an entrance to Arundel Park, a residence of the Duke of Norfolk. From there the eye can range over the Downs, southwards to where the sea marks the distance with a glittering line, and westwards to the spire of Chichester Cathedral, remote and only just discernible amid a group of trees. At the foot of the hill, straggling down to the river Arun, and rather more than a mile from Amberley, is the charming village of Bury. At its upper end a small half-timbered farmhouse called Martin's, which had been sadly altered and spoiled in the nineteenth century, stood in its yard surrounded by barns, cowsheds and stable. The horse-pond washed the walls of the house at the back, a pleasant circumstance which will indicate what needed to be done when Mr. H. W. Carr bought it in 1899 as a holiday home. From this point the plans should be examined with care, so that the succeeding alterations caused by growing requirements may be followed. The farmhouse originally consisted on the ground floor of kitchen, back kitchen, dairy, a small sitting-room, larder and store, with a stable twenty-six feet away to the east. The first work was to replace the decayed timbers of the half-timber framing with new English oak. The back kitchen and dairy were thrown together to form the parlour. The old kitchen became the hall, and a timber porch was added on its north side. A new dining-room was built partly on the site of the old larder and partly on new ground, with a new kitchen and scullery adjoining it eastwards. The old stable became a gardener's cottage. Though all the windows had to be made new, and the roof reconstructed, some fine

296.—SOUTH SIDE AFTER SECOND RECONSTRUCTION.

297.—EAST FRONT AND CONSERVATORY.

oak from one of the demolished barns was used again. The horse-pond on the south was drained and made to serve the more hygienic and more attractive purposes of a rock garden, while the general farmyard also surrendered to the dominion of flowers. Strict honour was done to the use of local materials by building the new work of Amberley stone dug from a nigh field, and Doulting stone was used where free-stone was needed. The banks of the Arun furnished the reeds with which the house was re-thatched. An intermediate stage of reconstruction, not shown on the plans, was the turning of the barn adjoining the old stable (by then a gardener's cottage) into a kitchen and a children's playroom. This enabled the kitchen and scullery o the main block to be turned into servants' bedrooms. When Mr. Spooner's client decided later to make Martin's his permanent home, still more serious additions became necessary, and were provided in a new eastern wing The parlour of the last stage became the library of the new, but a piece was robbed from it on the north to form a corridor to the fine new drawing-room, out of which opened an octagonal conservatory. Above, space was found for three further bedrooms and two dressing-rooms. The materials were the same as employed at the first reconstruction, and great care was taken by Mr. Spooner in devising the warming arrangements. A heating chamber was provided under the conservatory, from which hot water served radiators throughout the house. Coal was used

298.—SOUTH SIDE AND LOGGIA AFTER FIRST RECONSTRUCTION.

nowhere but in the kitchen, for when the radiators needed to be supplemented wood fires were elsewhere the rule. Some little stress has been laid on the heating arrangements, because they contributed in no way to the catastrophe of 1909, which came about in a mysterious fashion. A small patch of thatch was seen to be alight out of reach. The fire spread with such rapidity that it was impossible to do more than get all the household and a little of the furniture out through the drawing-room and conservatory. The particular danger of thatch lies not only in its liability to catch fire, but in its behaviour when alight. The front porch could not be used as an exit in this case, as wads of burning thatch rained all round the house; but the outlet from the drawing-room was safe, because its octagonal ingle was roofed, not with thatch, but tiles. Conditions inside the house soon became impossible, because the thatch fell in burning masses on to the ceilings and so through them, and the house caught alight all over at the same time; remedial measures were well-nigh hopeless, and the destruction was soon complete. For this, as for many another thatch fire, no cause could be discovered; but it may be that a lighted match was thrown from an open window. For this reason, there is a special fire-risk attaching to dormer windows in a thatched roof, though they are, perhaps, its chiefest charm. The increasing fireproof conditions of town buildings make people far less careful than they used to be, and devotion to My Lady Nicotine tends to pile up the risk, when those made careless by town immunities forget the risks of thatch and timber. It is curious how many fires arise in roofs, even when they are of materials not so ready to flame up as thatch. In the greatest of all English fires, the Fire of London, St. Paul's Cathedral first caught alight on the end of a board that was laid upon the roof instead of lead, the latter having been broken away. As a defect in a lead roof was the immediate cause of involving the old cathedral in the common ruin, it is worth noting from Rugge's "Diurnal" that "the first brick laid after the fire was in Fleet Street, at the house of a plumber, to cast his lead in, only one room." The illustrations of Martin's at two of the stages it

299.—PORCH AND NORTH FRONT.

300.—DRAWING-ROOM.

reached before it fell to the flames show how well Mr. Spooner kept the character of a farmhouse, while modifying the plan a far as needful to make it a comfortable home without archaic affectations. The drawing-room, added at the last reconstruction, was a fine apartment, with its octagonal ingle well lighted on both sides. This room, being part of an altogether new wing, did not need to follow the other smaller rooms in having an equally low ceiling, and the bold mouldings of the beams and the pleasant cushion capitals of the columns that flanked the ingle were carved by Mr. Palliser with simple birds and beasts. Outside, the length and simplicity of the roof-lines and the delightful modelling of the dormer thatching show a keen grasp of the conditions of Sussex architecture. Though the materials and their treatment are all simple, there is a marked air of refinement which comes from architecture using the natural speech of the country-side. Happily the days are past when nothing was regarded as worthy of an educated taste except buildings in a particular style to be read about in books. It was the same obsession by dead languages which needed the genius of the poet Du Bellay before the renaissance of French poetry could overcome the reliance on Greek and Latin for polite literature. "Those who speak thus," said Du Bellay, " make me think of those relics, which one may see only through a little pane of glass, and must not touch with one's hands. That is what these people do with all branches of culture which they keep shut up. . . ." It is partly by the attention which architects have given to what may be called the local dialects of architecture, that it has come to be understood of people generally, instead of being a technical mystery seen darkly through a glass obscured by rules and styles, like the relic of Du Bellay's fancy, which one might not touch with one's hands.

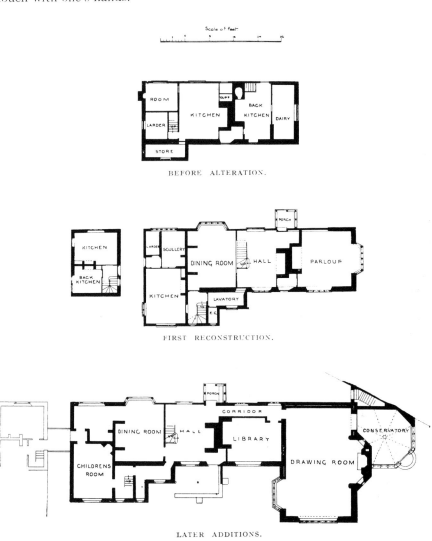

Scale of feet

BEFORE ALTERATION.

FIRST RECONSTRUCTION.

LATER ADDITIONS.

301.—GROUND PLANS.

BY THE CHURCH, STEEP.

AND ITS REPARATION BY MR. W. E. UNSWORTH

Smuggler's Cave and Public-house—From Ruined Tenement to Pleasant Home—The Retaining of Ancient Character—An Enticing Garden.

IN an earlier chapter Mr. Unsworth was considered in his character of a designer of new houses. Now is described the manner in which he has treated an old and much-decayed building. The little home he has made for himself in the village of Steep is now known by no particular title, but its neighbourhood to the church serves to identify it. This absence of a name is refreshing in days when a semi-detached erection on a clay flat is apt to be called after an Alpine summit, and when a royal palace often has to stand godfather to a host of jerry-built villas. But the little house we are now going to visit might easily have an appropriate name arising out of its own history. Indeed, it might have several, for it is a house with a rather shady past, and such (like human beings in the same position) are apt to have

302.—LOOKING UP FROM THE BANK.

aliases. Surely the old house at Steep was known as "Restalis" in the seventeenth century, for the Restalls were a local family that long appeared in the parish register, and the words "John Restall" with the date 1677 are incised on the back of some Jacobean oak panelling which forms a cupboard door. One hundred years later the house had changed its function and served as a public-house, very appropriately known as "The Castle in the Air." Its situation is certainly one of its charms. Steep is an extensive parish close to Petersfield, and contains within its limits some of the most picturesque bits of the beautiful district that forms the boundary between the counties of Sussex and Hants, in both of which it is situated. Rolling downland and steep beech-clad hanger alternate with gushing spring, leafy dell and verdant meadow. The village church stands at a very considerable altitude on a small plateau, and beyond the eastern boundary of its churchyard there is a margin of easy slope before the precipitous bank of a dell is reached. It is on this strip that the old house is located, a long, low building, brick-built and tile-roofed, that runs narrowly along its strip of ground and projects one broad gable to the east as far as the ground will allow. Almost too far, indeed, for the steep bank is apt to slip, and when Mr. Unsworth bought the building he found the southern corner of the east gable in a parlous state. The whole place, indeed, was reaching a miserable termination to its checkered career when he came across it. Steep, of old, was an out-of-the-way place, and a rough lot lived there. Tradition terms the cellar of the old house "The Smugglers' Cave," and its direct access on to a hidden way through wild

303.—THE HOUSE AND ITS SITE.

304.—THE FORMAL GARDEN.

woodlands must certainly have rendered it a convenient *cache* for those once numerous and popular gentry. They, however, shared the house with another outlaw class — poachers — if local tradition is to be believed. These are the days of long ago. The tone has changed, and Steep is now the most respectable of parishes and the site of a large and successful school. But the evil reputation of the old house clung to it. It was split up into four wretched tenements, its windows stuffed with rags, its roof mended with oddments of worn-out oilcloth. A few years more and it would have been a derelict ruin, had not Mr. Unsworth's sympathetic hand arrested the decay.

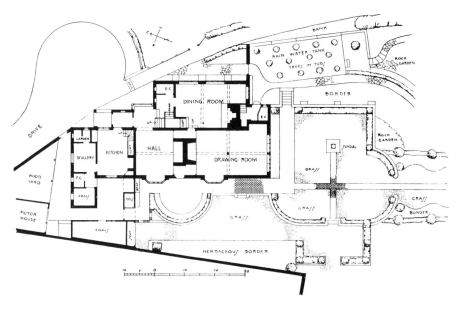

305.—GROUND PLAN.

It is now not only a beautiful but a very comfortable home, and yet it has been singularly little altered in its fabric. Mr. Unsworth has not been of those whose so-called love of a little old house shows itself in swallowing it up with great modern additions. His home, except that it is in perfect repair and surrounded by delightful gardens, has much the same general form and disposition that it possessed when it was "The Castle in the Air." The windows and their frames have nearly all of them been renewed, the upper one in the eastern gable being one of the exceptions. The old were rotten and small; but by means of long lines of casements and of transformed bays a flood of light has been shed into the house without in any way detracting from the charm and restful quiet of the exterior composition.

306.—THE DRAWING-ROOM.

The window framing is simple and unmoulded, the lead glazing correct in character, while the hinges, stays and fastenings remind us of the simple yet beautiful domestic wrought-iron work of our ancestors. It was a village smith who hammered these fastenings, but a village smith trained and supervised by Mr. Unsworth himself.

Even the rooms of the house retain most of the forms and characteristics which they possessed when John Restall carved his name on the cupboard door of what is now the dining-room. The house is approached from the north, where there is just enough level ground for a carriage turn. To the right as you enter the porch lies the kitchen, one of the old rooms, but with a new chimney. Beyond it are placed the scullery and other offices, which are the only considerable structural additions made. As these are all brought under the downward sweep of an extension of the old roof, the addition has made no appreciable change in the general composition, while convenient outbuildings, surrounding a yard cleverly contrived in a small corner of ground give ampleness and break to the sky-line and a pleasing support to the main structure. Passing from porch to lobby, the oak stairway fronts us, but we turn to the right into the hall. It is a typical old-fashioned cottage or farmhouse room of the district. There is a plain oak wainscoting

307.—THE DINING-ROOM.

on the walls, and overhead oak beams and rafters support the floor of the room above. The chimney-corner, built of long, narrow bricks, contains the hook and cooking pot which formed a large part of the culinary outfit of the Sussex yeoman of old. Only the excellent choice of the bits of ancient furniture, the careful tending of the apartment and the ampleness of the new bay window show us that the room, though old, belongs also to to-day. So ancient a domestic feature as the much-worn arch of the brick-oven door remains in the ample chimney-place. But the oven itself is gone, as it had to give way to a passage affording access to the parlours, so that the archway forms an amusing squint. To the left we enter what is called the dining-room. But meals are often served in the hall, which is more readily accessible from the kitchen, while the inspiring picturesqueness of the eastern parlour makes it an admirable retreat for work. It has much the same old features as the hall, and these are enhanced in value rather than effaced by such carefully chosen additions as the woodwork of its mantel-piece. The plan shows the great size of the chimney-breast; but the wide opening tempted smoke into the room and rendered necessary a drastic curtailment, which has been charmingly effected by large blocks of local ironstone supporting a tile arch. Unlike the chimney of the hall and drawing-room, the shaft here had to be rebuilt entirely; but as this was done on old lines and with old materials, it forms one of the most pleasing exterior features. It was ruined because it was near the spot where the slip of the bank threatened the collapse of the east gable. The ceiling beam sloped down a foot at least, and the brickwork, though buttressed, was falling out, so that Mr. Unsworth had to raise the heavy timbering with jacks and underpin and reinforce the foundations and walls.

The drawing-room shows rather greater alteration than the hall and dining-room. It is made out of two rooms, the square oak post marking the old division and supporting the ceiling beam. The south end is largely new, as a much-decayed chimney was removed and an ample window inserted. But much of the original brick of the walling remains, and the general form of the building is unchanged. At the north end is the fireplace, the best and least altered example in the house. Its sides of large chamfered stones support a very heavy oak beam, of which the lower side is also chamfered and slightly arched. Here, again, the smoke rendered some filling in necessary. Such alterations are unfortunate ; but the perfectly simple copper hood and the stone sides that have been inserted were, perhaps, the best way out of the difficulty. Mounting the stairs, we come upon bedrooms that have the same old-world spirit, wisely tempered, however, with a well-fitted bathroom. Except such a very acceptable bit of modernism as this, there is little new in the house. There are many specimens of seventeenth century English furniture at Steep. Some pieces, indeed, are decidedly older than this. One bed is possessed of a remarkably Gothic character. Good specimens, in original condition, of oak armchairs of the late sixteenth and early seventeenth century appear in various rooms. Those in the dining-room are most correctly portrayed in one of the careful drawings that Mr. Unsworth kindly furnished of this room and of the hall, as they were too small for the camera to do full justice to them. The longer drawing-room, however, is very well rendered by the photograph, and the cabinet which occupies the right of the picture is a very beautiful Italian piece, in admirably untouched state. Charming as is the interior of the house, there is much to entice outside. A good deal of incident has been introduced on the circumscribed and narrow level laid out in formal manner. The individual features are, therefore, very small ; but that is right, and they strike one at once as perfectly in scale with the site and with the building. Plan and pictures speak for themselves, and little description is needed. The low-roofed yard screen, of which the end forms a covered seat facing south towards the garden, is well managed. The garden door by the side of the hall chimney-piece opens on to a brick-paved semi-circle that gives an air of amplitude at this point. A low retaining wall of local stone sustains the grass plat and herbaceous border. A pathway is projected southwards far beyond the limits of the plan until it reaches the end

308.—THE HALL.

of the wedge-shaped level, and drops into a little woodland way through the finely timbered slope. Cut yews bound the narrowing formal plat, and there is just room at the end, on a lower level and before the wood is reached, for a little sunk rose garden enclosed in a framework of oak that carries the ramblers. The steep bank is set with shrubs, but part of it is used as a rockwork wherein aubrietia and arabis, sedums and saxifrages flourish exceedingly.

Here then is a *multum in parvo* indeed, concentrating in itself the most varied amenity, and yet so well managed that it gives no impression of over-crowding. A commodious habitation, perfectly linking the past and the present, time-worn and tradition-laden, yet never irksomely treading on the tender toes of the comfort-loving habits of to-day. A garden alive with interest, formal and natural, botanic and architectural, thriving excellently in a good climate and a clean air. A site that convinces one that our native land, with all its faults and limitations, is the sweetest and pleasantest place in all the world in which to dwell. It needed notable faculties and equipment to produce so excellent a combination. Mr. Unsworth rather prides himself that the gross outlay was only eight hundred pounds—four hundred pounds for the original purchase and four hundred pounds for the renovations and additions. Yes, but at what price are we to estimate his own judgment and experience? They are the qualities which make so small a creation stand out with distinction among its commonplace neighbours.

222

INDEX.